The Dragon and The Phoenix

Love, Sex and the Chinese

ERIC CHOU

London

MICHAEL JOSEPH

First published in Great Britain by
MICHAEL JOSEPH LTD
52 Bedford Square
London, W.C.1
1971

7181 0887 6

Printed in Great Britain by Northumber-
land Press Ltd., in 10 on 12 pt. Linotype
Plantin and bound by Dorstel Press, Har-
low. Paper supplied by P. F. Bingham.

The Dragon and The Phoenix

Love, Sex and the Chinese

Contents

Contents

Author's Note

For quite some time the idea of writing this book had been fermenting in my mind. But it was not without some hesitation that I eventually sat down to commence the work. Brought up in a society full of inhibitions and conventions, I could not but find it rather difficult to be the first Chinese to embark on a subject which my people have chosen to veil with discretion and reticence. On the other hand, years of poring over the Chinese classics and lesser works by ancient scholars and poets have convinced me that our ancestors actually treated sex and love with utmost candour—an attitude which the Sung School of Confucian scholars always strove to suppress. In short, it is due to the dual sex standards set by successive rulers that the ordinary people have been compelled to put up with taboos and hypocrisy. After weighing these points dispassionately, I suddenly felt no compunction in giving a frank account of this facet of Chinese life.

Naturally, it is not an easy task to tackle such an enormous subject singlehanded, especially in view of my personal limitations. But the fact that I have come into possession of some invaluable source material—hitherto unobtainable in the West—can be a redeeming factor. I do not have the temerity to claim that this book is an academic work, though all sources included herein can be authenticated.

Perhaps it is only appropriate for me to acknowledge here my indebtedness to three eminent Chinese scholars: the late Mr. Sung

Feng-nien; the late Professor Sun Shu-ch'en; and Professor Wu Mi, under whose guidance I spent my formative years.

As regards the private life of Chairman Mao and several Chinese leaders, the information has been supplied to me by some highly placed sources in the Peking hierarchy. Unfortunately, their names have to go unmentioned for understandable reasons.

Last but not least, I wish to express my gratitude to V.W., whose constant encouragement has inspired this little book to reach its present form.

Chelsea, London
May, 1970

CHAPTER ONE

From Legendary Times
to the T'ang Empire

To the outside world, China has always been a mystery, as vague as a flower enshrouded in fog, as intangible as an image reflected in water. But as a people, the Chinese have by no means intended to be mysterious. With a recorded history of 4000 years behind them, the Chinese people are proud of the continuity of their civilisation. Ancient traditions and early cultural achievements have taught them to follow their own moral codes and standards of value, disregarding what has been happening in other parts of the world. Language barriers and geographical self-containment made them unaware of the existence of other countries for many centuries until the arrival of Portuguese missionaries in the Ming Dynasty.

Perhaps it could have been the personal impressions of China brought back by Marco Polo that created the mysterious image of that huge country which has since become a commonplace.

Mysterious as China and her people may appear in occidental eyes, once one succeeds in overcoming the language barrier, in comprehending Chinese philosophy and in studying Chinese history thoroughly, the mystery will vanish into thin air.

Since China has become a mystery without her own doing, it is natural for the outside world to be eager to find out the nucleus of the mystery—the Chinese attitude towards sex and love.

But as far as the Chinese are concerned, sex and love are a natural part of their private lives, though subtlety and discretion, as well as convention, have made them veil these two essential elements of life in the utmost secrecy. Such an attitude does not mean that the Chinese cannot be as passionate as the Italians or the French. As early as some 2500 years ago, Confucius was already openly telling his disciples that 'food and sex are human nature', and in his *Analects* one can find these two points frequently reiterated.

Even Confucius cannot be regarded as the creator of the Chinese notion of sex. To trace the Chinese concepts and interpretations of sex, it is necessary to go further back to the Legendary Age, another 2500 years before Confucius.

In those days, the Chinese lived in caves and on the tops of trees, where they built nests big enough to shelter two or three people. Constantly threatened by floods, they had to move from place to place to hunt with stone weapons to feed themselves. They were nomadic tribes roaming the southern part of Shansi and the northern part of Honan. Their mode of life necessitated primitive promiscuity; jealousy led to fighting and killing among men and women alike, which caused the small population to dwindle.

THE WAYS OF YIN-YANG

It was at this point that Emperor Fu-hsi (2950 B.C.) began to realise the importance of sexual harmony for his subjects. The inventor of the trigrams, he racked his brains to study the theory of Yin-Yang (Female-Male; Moon-Sun; Earth-Heaven)—which had come into being before his time—for countless days and nights. All of a sudden it dawned on him that to regulate the hitherto unstable sexual relationships among his people would be the only sensible way to stop the frequent fighting and killings. Basing his ordinance on the principle of Yin-Yang (Female-Male) compatibility, he introduced the marriage system; for he recognised that 'Yin (female) without Yang (male) cannot give life while Yang without Yin cannot propagate'. He also realised that the possessive nature of human beings could only be satisfied by the 'one-man-and-one-woman' relationship. To his delight his marriage system worked. The nomadic tribes gradually settled down, moving southward to the basin of the Yellow River to form a more or less collective community.

As regards Fu-hsi himself, he seemed to have been the first confirmed bachelor in China; no extant sources mention anything about a wife or wives. His birth is surrounded with two conflicting legends. One legend says that he had the body of a dragon below the waist, for his maiden mother conceived him after having intercourse with a dragon in her dreams. This legend could have given rise to the Chinese use of the dragon to symbolise the emperor and might explain its association with sex.

The other legend claims that Fu-hsi was born after his mother stepped over the footprints of a giant, with the result that he possessed the wisdom and foresight of a supernatural being.

Both these legends build Fu-hsi up as a superman, though they differ in their approaches.

The sexual aspect of marriage seems to have been enriched by Fu-hsi's successor Emperor Shen-nung (the Divine Farmer, 2800 B.C.) quite unintentionally. He is reputed to have discovered the medicinal properties of one hundred kinds of herbs, thus laying the foundation of Chinese folk medicine. Of these herbs a number turned out to be aphrodisiacs, which have been in use ever since. The Chinese historians choose to remember Shen-nung as the first emperor who taught his people how to grow grain. Under his reign, China is believed to have formed the prototype of an agricultural society, though he was not sophisticated enough to offer his people proper clothing and dwelling places.

THE YELLOW EMPEROR AND HIS SEXUAL TECHNIQUES

In Shen-nung's old age, one historical source claims, he was assassinated by one of his court officials, who later became Emperor Huang Ti (the Yellow Emperor, 2968 B.C.). As wise as King Solomon, Huang Ti made the first compass and divided the year into four seasons and twelve months by creating the Chinese lunar calendar, which the Chinese generally call the Yellow Calendar. This calendar, apart from stipulating suitable times for sowing, ploughing and reaping the harvest, also clearly denoted the appropriate days for intercourse, bathing and travelling in each month. With the assistance of one of his court officials, Ch'ang Chi, the Yellow Emperor created the art of writing. He also ordered documentary material to be collected and filed.

His principal wife, Lo-chu, helped him by teaching the women to raise silkworms and weave. Thus the Chinese began to have clothes made of raw silk, and headgear as well.

To fight the Chih-yu Tribe, Huang Ti made chariots, to give his warriors the advantage over the foot-soldiers of Chih-yu. But apart from being a wise ruler and a good warrior, he appears also to have been a connoisseur of women. Chinese historians have so far failed to ascertain how many wives and concubines he had, but they all agree that he had so many children that practically all the rulers of the Hsia, Shang and Chou Dynasties were his descendants. (Even to this day the Chinese all claim to be 'the descendants of Huang Ti', though this is probably only a manner of speech.) It is alleged in Chinese history books that Huang Ti ruled his state for exactly 100 years. If this is true, he must have reached the great age of 120, if not more.

Many Chinese scholars have chosen to attribute his great age to his physical fitness and simple life. But according to some Taoist scholars in the Western Han Dynasty (106 B.C.), Huang Ti was able to live to such a great age and at the same time be so virile because he derived much benefit from his sexual techniques. To prove their point, these scholars claimed that Huang Ti was the author of *Su-Nu Ching* (*The Manual of Lady Purity*) which summarises the elementary principles of choosing virgins and of practising self-control during intercourse. Though Huang Ti did not do the actual writing, these Taoist scholars went on, he dictated the *Manual* to one of his court attendants, who then carved the whole manuscript on the shells of tortoises, thus enabling them to survive the burning of books by the First Emperor of the Ch'in Dynasty (221 B.C.) and eventually reach the hands of the Taoists. Another Taoist source says that Su-Nu is a Taoist goddess who lived in Huang Ti's time in her terrestrial incarnation. When Huang Ti in his old age became wary of love-making for fear that it might ruin his health, she convinced him that adequate sex techniques would prolong his period of virility and life-span. Huang Ti then took instructions from her and that was why he called the *Manual* after her name.

The *Manual* is written in classic Chinese, as concise and lapidary as Latin. On how to tell if a woman is a virgin it asserts: 'She never looks you straight in your face. When she smiles, her teeth are not shown. Her face does not look shiny. Her voice is as clear as a new flute. While sitting, she does not keep her knees apart. Her breasts are firm, their nipples pink and tiny. Her belly and hips are both flat and firm. The inside of her private parts is pink, the maidenhair soft like down. When she stands there in the nude, you cannot see through between her closed thighs.'

On sexual intercourse the *Manual* says in part: 'The aim of intercourse is to achieve the harmony of Yin and Yang. But as the male symbolises Heaven and the female Earth, the male should take the initiative. For the same reason, the male should be above the female while intercourse takes place. Before the intercourse, the male should take a deep breath. When he starts to enter her, he must allow her sufficient time to become aroused. While thrusting, he must put his tongue against the back of his upper teeth. Meanwhile, breathe evenly. Do not talk. Talking during intercourse wastes the male's breath, and thus weakens his enduring power. He must rest the weight of his body on his elbows and knees. Otherwise, he will not be able to control the initiative. When he feels he is about to discharge, he must swallow down the saliva in his mouth so that the discharge can be gradual, and not in excess. In the course of discharging, he must breathe in and his upper and lower teeth must be held tightly together. After intercourse, he should wipe himself with a dry cloth; then cover himself with bedcloth from neck to toe and make sure that there is no draught from any direction. It is now that he can start talking tenderly to the female for a little while, but he should avoid caressing or kissing so that the flame of love will not be rekindled. Then he should turn on to his right side to sleep, with his left leg resting on the right, holding his genitals with his right palm to keep them warm.'

Understandably, as the *Manual* was written from the man's angle, it mentions nothing about how to satisfy the female or even how to arouse her desire. But in a way, it seems to coincide with the Taoist theory about how to benefit from sexual intercourse by 'absorbing the Yin to complement the Yang'. Therefore, a number of Sung and Ming scholars were of the opinion that the Taoists in the Han Dynasty deliberately forged the *Manual* as a work of Huang Ti, to strengthen their own theory about the harmony of Yin-Yang. However, it must be admitted that whether the *Manual* was written by Huang Ti or the Taoists in the Western Han Dynasty, the concept of male supremacy in Chinese sexual life must have stemmed from it.

THE 'PLAYBOY KING' WITH A VIXEN WIFE

Though Huang Ti violated Fu-hsi's concept of the Yin-Yang harmony by taking many wives and concubines and so becoming the forerunner of the Chinese polygamists, it was King Chou-hsin of the Shang Dynasty (1558-1302 B.C.) who turned out to be the first 'Playboy King' in Chinese history, seeking sexual pleasures in the most fantastic way.

When he ascended the throne, the Kingdom of Shang had successfully established feudal rule. Surrounded by loyal vassals, the central government was able to develop agriculture, fishing and hunting in a more organised way. The unprecedented prosperity and prolonged stability enabled King Chou-hsin to leave state affairs in the hands of a few ministers, while he himself went out of his way to enjoy life. He drank to excess and played the drums and gongs as well as any of his court musicians.

More than eight feet in height, he was the tallest man in his kingdom. A strong warrior, he was described by a Han historian as a man 'with a back as strong as that of a tiger and a waist comparable to that of a bear'. According to *Feng Sheng Pang* (an ancient Chinese novel), Chou-hsin killed tigers and leopards with his bare hands. To demonstrate his strength, he often knocked out some of his knights with one single punch.

But his most astonishing characteristic was his insatiable appetite for sex. Night after night, he would cope with 'ten healthy and strong women in a row' without the slightest sign of contentment. Resourceful in the ways of love-making, he would sometimes order a naked woman to entwine her legs around his waist while his erected member, having entered her, virtually carried the weight of her body. With a huge bronze vessel brimful of wine in one hand and a roast shoulder of lamb in the other, he walked about in his palace throughout the process of love-making, gobbling and drinking at the same time. Even in this way, he still found himself unable to reach a climax.

Frustrated and exasperated, he suddenly heard of the beauty of Ta Chi, the daughter of one of his vassals Su Fu. 'Delicate as a flower and beautiful like the Moon Girl,' Ta Chi enjoyed the renown of being a 'heavenly beauty' throughout the Kingdom of Shang. Chou-hsin immediately sent an imperial order to Su Fu, demanding that the latter should send his daughter to the capital at Yin without delay. Naturally, Su had known all along about the licentious life led by his king. But, loyal as he was, he obeyed the order dutifully. He hoped that, with her virtues and feminine charm, his daughter might be able to transform Chou-hsin into a better king after becoming his royal consort.

But something unforeseen happened. Escorted by a squadron of horse guards, Ta Chi set off for the imperial capital in a chariot. Travelling on the rugged roads exhausted both people and horses. Each sundown, they had to stop at a stage station to recover overnight from their fatigue. One night, when Ta Chi was staying in a stage station not far from the imperial capital, the spirit of a female fox killed her during her sleep and was reincarnated as her. Though heavily guarded, the whole episode remained undetected.

The moment Chou-hsin caught his first glimpse of Ta Chi, he was bewitched by the fox's spirit within her body. By this time, Ta Chi had changed from a chaste maiden into an extremely attractive and sexy charmer. When they had their first night, Chou-hsin was very tender and gentle in the process of deflowering her. He feared that his potency might kill the delicate maiden who, he believed, had never had sex before in her life. But when he came into her, he found out that there seemed to be some sort of thing within her, sucking his member while growing tighter and tighter. For the first time in his life, he felt contented. A little suspicious, he held an oil lamp to examine her. There was blood on the square of silk under her; she had certainly been a virgin. But what he did not realise was that Ta Chi was actually the personification of a female fox.

THE WINE LAKE AND THE MEAT FOREST

For once Chou-hsin gave up all other women and concentrated on Ta Chi. They made love night and day. But each time Chou-hsin had to leave the whole process of love-making to Ta Chi's control. Sometimes, she would prolong ecstasy, while at other times she would make him feel wholly helpless. Enjoying his sex life as he did, the Playboy King began to worry that he might become unable to satisfy his beloved consort. Meanwhile, his male ego was acutely hurt, for he had never been 'defeated' by any woman as far as love-making was concerned.

After many a sleepless night, he suddenly had a fantastic idea. At the beckoning of his hand, thousands and thousands of peasants were mobilised to build an artificial lake near his summer palace, the Deer Mansions, which was in the middle of a forest of leafy mulberry trees, firs and pines. As soon as the building of the lake was completed, he ordered that it be filled with wine and called it the Wine Lake. Meanwhile, huge hunks of roast meat were hung on the branches of every single tree in the forest, which he now named the Meat Forest. But his imperial pleasure certainly did not end with wining and picnicking. Out of the garrison forces he selected 3000 tough young warriors and ordered them to saunter around the Wine Lake and in the Meat

Forest without a stitch on their bodies. They were allowed to drink and eat to their hearts' content. Needless to say, these naked warriors were thrilled. When their thirst was quenched after drinking with their cupped hands from the Wine Lake, they staggered into the Meat Forest to feed themselves. The appetizing smell of the roast meat dangling on the boughs assailed their nostrils from all directions. Laughing and shouting, these warriors dashed for their meat. But before they had time to grab the meat, numerous naked women suddenly appeared from behind the trees—arranged by Chou-hsin and Ta Chi of course. Though dazzled by the spectacular sight for a few moments, the half-drunk warriors instinctively gave chase and caught the women, pushing them on to the ground and making love to them like crazy horses.

All these erotic scenes were observed by the Playboy King and Ta Chi who had been standing on the verandah of the three-storied Star-reaching Pavilion, eagerly waiting for the spectacle to happen. Intoxicated themselves, the two of them started to make love as well. To his immense delight, Chou-hsin for the first time found himself reaching a climax simultaneously with Ta Chi. In consequence, the lake was constantly filled up to the edge with fresh supplies of wine and the roast meat on the trees was constantly replaced. Day in and day out, the same scenes went on and on.

But it did not take long for the Wine Lake and the Meat Forest to lose their novelty and excitement. Just then, some of the court officials pleaded with the king to stop this 'unkingly act'. Angered, Chou-hsin consulted Ta Chi. She suggested to him that the mouths of 'these fools' must be silenced, which Chou-hsin agreed. She designed a set of hollow bronze pillars, one foot in diameter, inside which piles of firewood were kept burning. Those officials who had annoyed Chou-hsin were stripped and their naked bodies were tied to these hollow bronze pillars to be roasted to death. To King Chou-hsin this was more than a punishment. The whole process served to excite him sexually as well. While these officials were being roasted, he and Ta Chi drank, laughed and indulged in sex.

THE KINGDOM FALLS AT A BEAUTY'S SMILE

A few years later, when King Chou-hsin's sexual perversions and cruelty became a disgrace to the whole kingdom, his vassals under the leadership of King Wu of the Chou Dynasty (1050-256 B.C.)

staged a rebellion. At a battle near the imperial capital, King Chou-hsin died in action and the rebel forces set fire to the Star-reaching Pavilion and burned Ta Chi the 'Heavenly Beauty' alive.

After a long line of wise rulers, the Chou Dynasty produced its own type of 'playboy king'. Enthroned in his early twenties, King Yu (reigning from 781 to 771 B.C.) could not match Chou-hsin in physical fitness and cruelty, yet his sexual indulgences were by no means overshadowed by his predecessor. After getting tired of all the women he had in the palace, one of his special envoys found in the Borough of Pao (now in the Province of Shensi) a beautiful girl named Pao Shih and sped her back to the imperial court at Kao. King Yu almost fainted with excitement upon seeing her. Too impatient to listen until the end of the special envoy's report, he took Pao Shih straight away into his royal sleeping chamber.

But to his great disappointment, King Yu found this great beauty frigid in bed. She went through the whole process with him dutifully, passive and unresponsive. For months she even denied the King a faint smile. He tried every possible way to make her smile without success. As a final resort, he did something very foolish. At that time, the Chuan Jung Tribe from the north-west posed a threat to the security of the Kingdom of Chou. To summon his vassals to his rescue, King Yu had arranged to set smoke signals on the Mountain of Li three miles from his capital in the event of the Chuang Jung invasion. However, having failed to make Pao Shih smile in every other way, King Yu impulsively ordered the smoke signals lit as a false alarm. Without knowing the truth, his vassals rushed their troops to his rescue. It was only when Pao Shih saw these panting troops rush to the palace at break-neck speed for nothing that she smiled. King Yu was much pleased with his little trick. In addition, he now found Pao Shih a different woman in bed altogether. Not only was she no longer frigid, but she began to enjoy sex and to let herself go. Unfortunately, her frigidity would occur from time to time and the only way to make her sexually responsive was to set the smoke signals. King Yu had to do it far too often. Eventually, his vassals simply ignored these smoke signals. When the Chuan Jung Tribe really attacked, both King Yu and Pao Shih were beheaded.

'SHARING THE PEACH' AND 'CUTTING THE SLEEVE'
After the death of King Yu, some of his vassals repelled the Chuan

Jung Tribe and moved the capital eastwards from Kao to Loyang.
Soon after, the vassals fought among themselves for territorial expan-
sion and created their dukedoms and earldoms like separate states,
though nominally still supporting the Kingdom of Chou. Confucius
(Kung Ch'iu) was born in this period. According to a Han scholar,
on the eve of his birth his mother, Chen-tsai, saw two dragons
descending on their roof, while the gods of Five Stars ringed the
house. Amid the sound of heavenly music, she heard a voice telling
her that an 'uncrowned king' was to be born in this household and
that he would rule the Central Kingdom for centuries and centuries.
But another source said something far less dignified about the birth
of the Chinese Sage. It claimed that his mother Chen-tsai, while still
a young virgin, made love with a seventy-year-old warrior in the
thicket of mulberry trees where she had been picking leaves to feed
silkworms. Confucius was then conceived and his father was forced
to marry his mother. The same source also said that Confucius was
born on a small hill and that was why he was given the first name
'Ch'iu' which means 'small hill' in Chinese. But a third source offered
the interpretation that the name 'Ch'iu' had been given to the Sage
because of his broad and protruding forehead.

Though the Confucian philosophy has dominated Chinese political
and social thought for centuries after his death, the Sage, during his
lifetime, had to wander from state to state in the hope of getting an
official appointment. To all the feudal lords he was obliged to humble
himself as low as possible. Under such circumstances, he even had
to put up with the licentious and promiscuous life of the nobles, no
matter how strongly he felt about the significance of such moral
virtues as loyalty, filial piety, chastity and sexual fidelity.

In one instance, he even accepted an invitation from the most
notoriously promiscuous woman of his time for a session because of
her social status. The woman, Nan-tzu by name, was the Duchess of
Wei. An extremely beautiful woman, she committed adultery with
the Duke's cousins and nephews almost indiscriminately, and yet her
husband did not bat an eye. After Confucius had had a long session
with her, one of his disciples, suspecting that the master could have
been attracted to the notorious woman because of her sex appeal,
was so furious that he confronted the Sage with a lot of pointed questions. Embarrassed, Confucius gave a few evasive answers, which
infuriated the disciple even more.

It was no coincidence that the first recorded instance of sodomy in Chinese history—figuratively described by Chinese literati as 'sharing the peach'—should have occurred in this very State of Wei. Duke Ling, the descendant of the aforesaid duke, committed sodomy with a young court official, Mi Tzu-hsia, who had a face 'as pretty as that of a blooming maiden'. Their perversion became a public scandal quite accidentally. One day, when the two of them were sauntering hand in hand in the Duke's Eastern Garden, Mi playfully picked a ripe peach from a tree. After having a few bites himself, he unceremoniously pushed the remaining part of the peach into Duke Ling's mouth. In those days, such an act was considered one of great disrespect for the head of a state. And yet Duke Ling gladly munched the peach and said aloud: 'This peach tastes so good because it has been in your mouth first.' The other court officials could not help witnessing the whole episode and thus the scandal took wing.

But Duke Ling was by no means alone in this sort of perversion. In 6 B.C. Emperor Ai Ti of the Han Dynasty did not let himself be outshone by the romance of 'sharing the peach'. Like Duke Ling, he used one of his court officials, Tung Hsieng, to satisfy his homosexual desires. One day, when they were taking a nap together, the Emperor was suddenly requested to deal with some urgent state affairs. As Tung's head rested on one of his wide sleeves, Ai Ti simply could not bring himself to awaken his beloved. He drew out his ornamental sword and cut off the corner of his sleeve on which Tung's head lay. Since then, 'cutting the sleeve' has become a term with the same meaning as 'sharing the peach'.

THE QUEEN MOTHER'S 'WONDERFUL THING'

The promiscuity of the Duchess of Wei seemed to be nothing when eventually the queen mother of the First Emperor of Ch'in (Shih Huang Ti)—enthroned in 221 B.C.—came on the scene. She had been a concubine of Lu Pu-wei, a high official of the State of Chao, where the First Emperor's father, then a prince, had been kept as a hostage. The young prince of Ch'in, depressed and forlorn, sought comfort in wine and women. However, at Lu's residence, he came across one of the host's concubines who fascinated him with her hour-glass figure and sexy voice. When the young prince woke up in the guest room after midnight that night, he found a naked woman by his side. The flame of desire made him feel like bursting, and without a second thought he opened her dainty legs wide and entered her. After the love-making, he dropped into another sleep. It was only when the first rays of the sun shone on their faces that he realised that the woman was the very concubine of Lu's that he had fancied. Nervous and feeling guilty, he hopped off the bed, hastening to make himself look decent. But it was already too late. On a chair by the window sat Lu Pu-wei, full of smiles. He told the young prince not to worry, for this was a part of his hospitality. After that, the prince became Lu's regular guest, always staying overnight with the same concubine whenever Lu was kept busy by his wife or other concubines.

In addition, Lu even helped the young prince and this concubine to escape back to the State of Ch'in, once he had discovered her pregnancy. When the prince succeeded to the throne and became King Chuang-hsiang, the former concubine of Lu became the queen and gave birth to Prince Cheng, who later wiped out the other States and became the First Emperor of Ch'in.

By this time, Lu Pu-wei had already been made a prince by the late King Chuang-hsiang and his influence was second only to that of the First Emperor. Widowed, the queen mother frequently summoned him to her palace to satisfy her hunger for sex. Though pleased to resume the old association, Lu found himself unable to cope with his former concubine sexually.

One day, when he was driving through a street, he caught a glimpse of a young man urinating by the roadside—a sight in no way uncommon in those days. But what was uncommon in Lu's eyes was the size of this young man's member. Without hesitation he took him back to his official residence, where he found his name to be Lao Ai. While poor Lao Ai was trembling with fear, Lu appointed him his personal secretary. He brought his new secretary to pay tribute to the Queen Mother and then tactfully feigned a headache and asked to be excused. With Lao still confounded and ill at ease, the queen mother signalled to him to climb into the royal bed. After they had both stripped, she simply could not believe her own eyes. After overcoming his initial nervousness, Lao Ai pushed his huge weapon into Her Majesty, making her at once feel like a virgin again. His endurance was beyond her belief. He was still thrusting vigorously after she had reached many a climax. After that she took turns to sleep with

Lu Pu-wei and Lao Ai. She called Lao 'Miao-wu' (the wonderful thing) and often told Lu how she enjoyed having Lao with her. By then Lu knew that it was time for him to 'retire' from her service, for the First Emperor was reported to be ready to take action.

Before long, the First Emperor had Lao Ai, 'the wonderful thing', arrested. Before Lao's execution, his 'wonderful thing' was cut off. Still, the First Emperor was not satisfied. He gave another order to execute all of Lao Ai's relatives.

While Lu Pu-wei was secretly pleased with his opportune 'retirement', he was suddenly summoned by the First Emperor who demanded that he explain how he could hold the title of a prince without being a member of the royal family. Lu begged to be deprived of his title. But the First Emperor told him that this was not enough. He ordered him to be banished to Szechuan. Knowing that he would not be able to survive the hazardous trip, Lu hanged himself. Immediately after Lu's suicide, the First Emperor built a palace miles away from the then imperial capital, Hsienyang, and confined the queen mother there for the rest of her life.

The emperor was so anxious to get rid of Lu because he feared that Lu might be his father—after all before his mother became pregnant she had been sleeping with Lu and the late King Chuang-hsiang alternately. Some Chinese scholars believe that this unsolved riddle could have been one of the reasons for the First Emperor to order all books, records and documents burned to ashes.

After the construction of the Great Wall was completed, the First Emperor became anxious to prolong his life expectancy. A Taoist named Hsu Fu was recommended to him. He convinced the emperor that he would be able to sail to Fu Sang (ancient name of Japan) to get His Majesty the medicine to enable him to live forever. With the emperor's consent, Hsu Fu took with him 500 virgin boys and 500 virgin girls for the expedition. But one Ming scholar claimed that Hsu's other mission was to find some medicine to cure the First Emperor of Ch'in of his impotency. He would have liked to have another son, for his only son Hu Hai struck him as unsuitable to carry on his imperial power. Unfortunately, Hsu Fu never came back and the First Emperor died in his middle age.

A PRINCESS WITH THIRTY 'FACE-HEADS' (MALE
CONCUBINES)

The queen mother of the Ch'in Empire would have wished to have
been born a few hundred years later if she could have foreseen how
the women of the imperial families during the period of the Northern
and Southern Empires (A.D. 316-589) indulged in sexual excesses,
even to the extent of openly taking male concubines.

In the Former Sung Dynasty, when King Ts'ang Wu was enthroned
in 473 at the age of seventeen, his elder sister Princess Shan-yin com-
plained to him: 'Now that you have 3000 women at your disposal,
don't you think it unfair for me to share my bed with the same man
night after night? After all, we were both born of the same parents.'
'That is very easy to solve,' King Ts'ang Wu smiled.

The following day he found thirty healthy young men and sent
them to Princess Shan-yin. He called them 'Face-heads' for the sake
of discretion and never bothered to find out their names and identities.
He made them thirty in number for in the Chinese calendar each
month has thirty days and he could thus ensure that his sister did
not have to sleep with the same man 'night after night'. Overjoyed,
Princess Shan-yin accepted these thirty 'Face-heads' and housed them
all in her palace. At first, she only made love with each of them one
at a time. But as her appetite increased she ordered an enormous
bed to be made. All thirty young men would lie in the bed, while she
rolled over their naked bodies. She picked out one of them at random
to have intercourse with her, while the other twenty-nine watched.
It depended on her mood how many of these male concubines would
receive her 'favour' each night. When the story took wing, a saying
began to circulate: 'On the way to Shan-yin (the two characters also
mean the 'shade of the mountain') the candidates come one after
another.' But neither King Ts'ang Wu nor Princess Shan-yin was
worried about the scandal.

About the problem of male concubines, King Yu Lin (498) of the
Dynasty of Southern Chi was equally tolerant. To 'entertain' his
widowed mother, he presented her with thirty 'Face-heads' too. This
was by no means a coincidence, in view of the fact he married the
daughter of Princess Shan-yin. It must have been at his wife's suggestion that he decided on the number of thirty. As for his own sex-
life, he seemed to enjoy watching more than practising. Out of sudden
fancy he picked up more than twenty young rogues from the street

within a day and treated them like close friends. They shared his table as well as his bed. His wife selected the more handsome ones of this group and made love with them before the king's own eyes. The king regarded this kind of love-making as highly entertaining. He always timed each man's endurance and commented on his love-making technique. Afterwards, he discussed the performances at length with his wife and showed her the list of names he had carefully compiled. By the names of the most potent ones, he put three circles (equivalent to the Western method of star-rating). Others got two or one circle. Whenever any one of them failed to merit even one circle, the king would replace him with a new recruit. Sometimes, he would insist that his wife describe to him how she felt inside herself while having intercourse with each of these men. Then he would make love to her and ask her to comment on his performance.

THE MOST EROTIC EMPEROR

In ingenuity and inventiveness of sexual pleasures, Emperor Yang Ti of the Sui Dynasty (581-617) stood head and shoulders over any other monarch in Chinese history. When he first succeeded to the throne, military ambitions led him to invade Korea, Formosa and the Ryukyu Islands. Only later in his life did he begin to concentrate on amorous adventures. He even forced two of his late father's concubines to submit to his desire and included them in his own harem.

To satisfy his sexual needs, he had one queen, two deputy queens, six royal consorts and seventy-two royal madames. There were also 3,000 palace maidens, handpicked by his special envoys throughout the country, eagerly awaiting his favour. However, though satisfied with the enormous number of women at his disposal, he attached more importance to novel ways of love-making. He also emphasised the desirability of the right atmosphere.

After the Grand Canal had been built to facilitate communications between the North and the South, he turned it to even better use for himself. On the maiden voyage up the thirty-foot wide Canal, he ordered a couple of hundred palace maidens to tow his dragon junk against the current along both shores. In the glorious sunshine, the colourful silk robes worn by these palace maidens were reflected in the water like a rainbow. While towing, these girls chanted and hummed melodiously, very pleasing to the royal ears. Looking at the rhythmic movements of their slender waists and hips, Yang Ti caressed some of his favourite concubines, all in the nude, who shared his cabin. In the adjoining cabin, the royal musicians played soft music on an assortment of Chinese musical instruments—bamboo flutes, pi-pa (Chinese guitars) and moon-shaped lyres. To the tempo of the music, Yang Ti pushed his 'jade-stem' into the 'porte feminine' of the concubine nearest to him, while his hands were busily fondling the breasts or the 'flowery paths' of the other naked beauties surrounding him, eagerly awaiting their turn.

For travelling by road, Emperor Yang Ti placed equal stress on sexual pleasures. One of his court officials designed the Seven-Precious-Chariots for this special purpose. On the outside of a Seven-Precious-Chariot, three layers of curtains of jades, corals, pearls, rubies, moonstones, ambers and emeralds formed such a dazzlingly colourful screen that even pedestrian or horseman gasped with admiration. But the real usefulness of these curtains was to prevent the sounds of love-making from being overheard by passers-by when the chariots rolled along. The dangling precious stones on these curtains made their own music, changing Yang Ti into a tomcat in heat. Whenever he travelled by road, he took a caravan of ten Seven-Precious-Chariots with him. In each chariot a naked beauty lay on the heavily padded red satin cushion awaiting his favour. Starting from the first chariot he would let his ten travelling companions share his 'rains and dew' one after another.

THE MAZE PALACE, 'VIRGIN WHEELCHAIR' AND 'AS-YOU-WISH-CAR'

Having perfected the travelling side of his sexual pleasures, Emperor Yang Ti appointed Hsiang Sheng, the greatest architect of his time to design and build the Maze Palace in Loyang (now in Honan Province). It took more than 50,000 carpenters, masons and other workers, on three eight-hour shifts, about eighteen months to complete this gigantic work. A vivid description of this very special palace is given in the *Erotic Adventures of Sui Yang Ti* by an anonymous T'ang scholar as follows:

'The Maze Palace was built on a site of 100,000 Chinese acres. The main palace was surrounded by thirty-six smaller palaces, all hidden in the forest of flowers. But it was because of the most ingenious design and intricate interior of the main palace that Yang Ti himself named it "The Maze Palace".

'The magnificent main palace towered over the tree tops with its three storeys, glistening in the sunshine like a golden pagoda of enormous size. On the verandahs circling each storey, hundreds of palace maidens, clad in robes made of cicada-wing-lace, stood there smiling, whispering or playing musical instruments. Without anything underneath their transparent robes, their firm breasts, slender waists and shapely legs could be clearly seen at a distance—even more suggestive than in the nude.

'Inside the building, the chambers of various sizes were separated by doors of every shape and countless intricate passages. It was in the main chamber, that Yang Ti spent his erotic days and nights. In this chamber, big enough to lay 100 tables, the emperor had four enormous silk tents, respectively named *Intoxicating Passion, Sweet and Fragrant Night, Delight of Autumn Moon* and the *End of Spring Sorrows*. In each tent, thirty to forty enchanting girls, with nothing on, walked about, played games, joked with one another or reclined on couches covered with tiger-skins. Though sedate in appearance, they were all secretly longing for the arrival of His Majesty like a descending cloud.

'The walls of this chamber, lined with shining bronze mirrors from corner to corner and hollow inside, emitted the aroma of a constantly burning incense of musk, jasmine, peonies and orchids through their well-concealed slits, forming a thin cloud of fragrance to linger in the air. Overhead, numerous transparent silk lanterns, painted with naked beauties in different postures, gave a light as of a faint moon. With candles burning and glittering inside these lanterns, the naked beauties looked as if they were about to descend any second.

'The moment Yang Ti arrived from his imperial court, four to eight eunuchs knelt down to greet him, then helped him take off his embroidered-dragon-gown and surrounded his royal waist with a leopard-skin lined with yellow silk.

'Having rid himself of his worldly attire, the emperor, exhilarated and full of vigour, started to wander about, though he would always end his journey in the main chamber.

'The chanting of "Ten Thousand Years" (Long Live the Sovereign) by female voices rose from all directions. Downing a few gold vessels of ginseng wine, he felt slightly tipsy, while the fire of desire made his jade-stem stir up beneath his leopard-skin loincloth. He proceeded to grasp any woman in sight; but with all the reflections of beautiful bodies in the bronze mirrors, he found it almost impossible to tell the real women from their images.

'Only now would he enter one of the four silk tents. With his eyes closed, he let himself be guided by the female voices. In this way he found more fun in catching a woman, pushing her on to a bed, a couch or a tiger-skin mattress. Throwing away his leopard loincloth in haste, he pushed his jade-stem into her moist porte feminine, thrusting with a vigour that could easily have penetrated an animal hide. Meanwhile, the giggling and whispering of the other women went on. Even more excited than ever, he let the woman under him lie there frustrated and jumped up to chase some other. When another woman was caught, he would try some different approach or simply come into her in a standing position. After he was satisfied, he dozed off for a little while. Then the love game would start up again. Since the light was wholly artificial, he could not tell whether it was day or night—which in fact made no difference to him.'

Since Yang Ti's desire for novelty knew no end, a junior minister named Ho Ch'ou built a love-making wheelchair for him. The moment a woman was put in this special chair, clamps would automatically spring up to hold her arms and spread her legs apart while the mechanised cushion would place her body in the appropriate position to receive the royal favour. After trying the wheelchair with many women, Yang Ti found it especially effective with a virgin. So he named it the 'Virgin Wheelchair'. Ho also made the emperor an 'Up-and-down' car (the prototype of a lift), to be operated by four strong silk ropes on pulleys. Inside the 'car' a couch was installed, looked after by a naked palace maiden. When Yang Ti made love to her, the 'Up-and-down car' in motion gave him the feeling of 'riding a small boat at sea'. Extremely pleased, he called it the 'As-you-wish-car'.

However, when all these new inventions failed to maintain his virility, Yang Ti found his 'Dream Baby'. Her name was Han Chun-erh. At this point, the emperor was suffering from insomnia. But after he had made love to Chun-erh, he always slept like a log. Loving her more than any other concubine, he called her 'My Dream Baby' for she gave him sweet dreams. Actually, Chun-erh's secret was to imitate the gentle movements of a trotting mare when Yang Ti was making love to her. Then, when she realised that the Emperor had finished the process of love-making, she massaged him all over.

But Emperor Yang Ti was unable to enjoy his licentious life forever. When the T'ang troops led by Li Yuan overthrew the Sui Empire and captured Loyang, Li immediately ordered his men to set fire to the Maze Palace. It burned for more than three months, long after the dead body of Yang Ti had begun to rot.

EMPRESS WU, SEX-TASTER AND THE 'MULE'S'

Though not as ingenious as Emperor Yang Ti of Sui, Empress Wu Tse-tien of the T'ang Dynasty indulged no less fervently in sex. Politically, her ambition drove her to banish her own son and rule the T'ang Empire from 685 to 701.

But it is undeniable that the driving force behind her was sexual frustration. At the age of sixteen, she was selected to be a palace maiden during the reign of Emperor T'ai Tsung (reigning 627-649), and looked after one of the royal toilets. One day, T'ai Tsung happened to use this toilet. She kneeled down with her eyes lowered, her dainty hands holding a gold basin of water for him to wash his hands. When he asked her to raise her eyes, the emperor impulsively felt the urge to have her. Quite unceremoniously, he deflowered her on the couch in the toilet. This led Wu Tse-tien to believe that she would soon be promoted to the rank of royal madame (seventy-two in number) and eventually advance to the state of deputy queen of the Eastern or Western Palace. But unfortunately, T'ai Tsung, as the founder of the T'ang Empire, devoted his energies to political affairs and military conquests. The casual sex he had with Wu Tse-tien faded from his memory as soon as it was over.

Neglected and frustrated, Wu Tse-tien trapped the Crown Prince (who later became Emperor Kao Tsung) with her charms. With extreme discretion they managed to spend many a secret amorous night in the Prince's palace. After T'ai Tsung's death, Kao Tsung ascended the imperial throne and decided to take Wu Tse-tien as his queen. But as the palace record showed that she had once been favoured by his late father, she had to be sent to a Buddhist nunnery to spend the rest of her life as a nun—a common practice at that time. But under a secret order given by Emperor Kao Tsung (the former Crown Prince), she was spared having her head shaved. Three years later—after the mourning period observed by Emperor Kao Tsung was over—she was secretly conveyed to the imperial palace to become the queen, against the advice of many court officials.

When Kao Tsung was alive, Wu Tse-tien enjoyed the glorious life of a queen, but sexually she found the emperor not potent enough. She had a few occasional affairs with some commoners through the aid of some eunuchs who were loyal to her. But on these occasions she had to disguise her identity by wearing a black veil and only partly undressing. She dared not talk, nor could she keep the man for the whole night. She had to rush through the whole process in a matter of minutes to avoid being caught. Instead of contentment, she found further frustration.

After the death of her husband, her son Emperor Chung Tsung succeeded to the throne. One year later, she banished him to a remote province. Thus she became Empress Wu Tse-tien, ruling the whole empire. By this time she was in her late forties and her appetite for sex was even sharper. She picked the two most handsome young court officials—two brothers in fact—Chang Ch'ang-tsung and Chang I-chih to be her 'face-heads'. She went through the process in a very cautious way. First of all, she ordered her favourite lady-in-waiting, Shangkuan Wang-erh, to act as a 'sex-taster', sleeping with the two Chang brothers in turn. It was only after listening to Wang-erh's comprehensive report that she summoned them to receive her favour. At first, she found the two brothers tolerably good at love-making, but she still did not feel that contented. She said to Shangkuan Wang-erh once: 'Ch'ang-tsung has got a face as beautiful as a lotus flower, but what a pity he is so much better to be looked at than to be used.' Wang-erh understood exactly what the empress meant. She whispered: 'Your Majesty owns the whole empire and there must be a lot of especially healthy and "talented" males who can be your match in bed. As for me, each time after I have had Ch'ang-tsung or I-chih, my back aches and I can hardly keep my legs from shaking. Your humble maid just does not have the dragon's spirit and strength of Your Majesty.'

Immediately after this session, Wang-erh was instructed to see the empress's nephew Wu San-ssu and ask him to act as a discreet 'talent scout'. As the garrison commander of Changan (the imperial capital), Wu San-ssu went out incognito to carry out his mission. Without much success initially, he went to the 'prostitute shops'. Quite by chance he overheard one prostitute cursing the other: 'You black-hearted bitch, may you die bleeding through having intercourse with

Hsueh Ao-ts'ao!' Puzzled, Wu San-ssu asked the cursing prostitute what she meant by Hsueh Ao-ts'ao, a god or a spirit? The prostitute almost laughed her head off, then retorted: 'Hsueh is that gambling rascal who has the biggest and strongest weapon!' Extremely pleased, General Wu sent two secret emissaries to fetch Hsueh to his residence. After personal inspection, he bathed Hsueh with scented water and dressed him elegantly. Then he took Hsueh to the imperial palace. Empress Wu could hardly wait to take Hsueh to bed. He was so big and strong that the empress almost fainted after having several orgasms. While wiping her private parts she sighed: 'The whole empire is less valuable than that thing of yours.'

One day, Empress Wu asked Hsueh to strip in front of Shangkuan Wang-erh, asking her whether she would like to have a go. Covering her face with her hands, the lady-in-waiting exclaimed: 'It must be a mule's! I beg to be spared the ordeal.'

Amused, Empress Wu started to make love with Hsueh and demanded that Wang-erh remain there as an 'observer'. Afterwards, when Wang-erh made mention of Hsueh to the two Chang brothers, they became very jealous, though, in fact, they never really enjoyed having sex with the empress. However, the young brother, Chang I-chih, resourcefully hastened to find someone who could beat Hsueh Ao-ts'ao. He learned of a Buddhist monk by the name of Huai-yi who was renowned for his sexual virtuosity. The two brothers, through the complicity of Shangkuan Wang-erh, brought Huai-yi the monk to pay tribute to Empress Wu. As Wang-erh had already informed the empress of Huai-yi's reputation, Empress Wu did not hesitate to try him out. He proved to be even more satisfactory than Hsueh Ao-ts'ao. According to what she later described to Shangkuan Wang-erh, the difference between the two men was like this: 'Hsueh charges all the time like a bull, maintains the same vigour and exhausts me physically, though I am contented. With Huai-yi, love-making becomes a subtle art. He may not be as big as Hsueh, but he is equally strong. When he pushes his "little monk" into me, it is as active as a snake. Inside, I feel so fulfilled. His thrusts are full of variety, sometimes vigorous, sometimes gentle. Whatever he does, I feel as if his thing reaches my heart.'

Huai-yi was appointed the Imperial Buddhist Adviser and had free access to the imperial palace. Empress Wu at first kept her liaison with Huai-yi from Hsueh. But Hsueh was not in the least jealous. They took turns sleeping with Empress Wu, and frequently compared notes. Never really feeling settled in the palace, Hsueh now had the time and the money to frequent the 'prostitute shops'. One night, he was so drunk that he fell into a sound sleep in the street. The following day he was found dead. He was intact except for that thing of his which had been cut off. It was believed that a man, whose wife had had an affair with Hsueh, had committed the deed. The whole affair was hushed up.

The Imperial Buddhist Adviser was luckier. He carried on with Empress Wu until she was forced by a group of generals to abdicate in 701. On her deathbed, the empress was heard mumbling 'The mule's ... that little monk of his' until she breathed her last breath.

CHAPTER TWO

The 'Peaceful' Co-existence
of Wives and Concubines

Confucius's attitude to sex, as well as his political philosophy, exerted little or no influence on the rulers and aristocracy of his own time. His only written work is the *Spring and Autumn Annals*, a sketchy chronology of main political events and military campaigns he had witnessed or heard of. His *Analects*, the gist of his philosophy, were compiled by his seventy-two disciples after his death. It was Mencius (372-289 B.C.), the disciple of Confucius's grandson Tsu-ssu, who first expounded the Confucian philosophy during the period of the Warring States. Then Emperor Wu Ti (reigning 140-87 B.C.) of the Western Han Dynasty promoted Confucianism on a nationwide scale to consolidate his political control and lay down the foundation of hereditary monarchy. Still, he did nothing to define the Sage's philosophy of sex and love. However, the Confucian scholars of the Sung Dynasty (A.D. 960-1278) such as Chu Hsi, Cheng Yi and Cheng Hao made every possible effort to interpret this aspect of Confucius's thoughts like stoics and taint it with hypocrisy. Their efforts, doubtless, have influenced the Chinese to become very secretive about their sex lives, except among their close friends and social equals.

CONFUCIUS' DUAL STANDARD FOR SEX MORALS
When Confucius was alive, he never opposed concubinage. To him, sex was a means of propagating the Chinese race. He regarded the sexual relationship between man and woman as the way 'to constitute the great human relationship'. Since he also emphasised the significance of having a son, this gave those who could afford the money to take concubines a sound argument. Moreover, some other Confucian scholars even frankly proclaimed the desirability of 'marrying a wife for her virtues and taking a concubine for her beauty'. Therefore, it would not be dogmatic to deduce that Confucius and

his followers actually had two sets of sex morals: sexual indulgence for the noble and the rich; sexual normalcy for the ordinary people.

It was also because of Confucian influence that in Chinese society the family has always played a significant role, for he emphasised that families were the basic units of the country. At first, in the Feudal Period, the aristocratic familes were tightly organised in noble clans. Later on, the ordinary people began to model their family structure on the aristocracy. It also became obligatory for people to adopt surnames. Surnames were generally derived from the family's home region, or from an office held, or from a city or town. (Though China now has a population of 750 million, there are only 100 different surnames adopted by the Chinese, as distinct from the national minorities.) In China there used to be a law stipulating that a man and a woman bearing the same surname could not get married no matter how far apart their home towns might be. This law was based on a Confucian maxim: 'A man and his woman bear the same surname, their descendants will never prosper.' Understandably, Confucius said this to forestall marriage between first cousins and other blood relations because of the smallness of each state in his time. Though not necessarily having a scientific approach, he intended to keep the family system pure and sound, as well as to forbid abnormal sexual relationships. To uphold this law, another Chinese saying has made a contribution: 'When you have the same surname, you must have come from the same family 500 years ago.'

Therefore, it was no mere coincidence that in the Dynasty of Chou (1050-256 B.C.) a match-making official (Mei Shih) was posted in each town and village to see that marriages were properly arranged so that 'inside the houses there will be no moaning maidens while outside, no frustrated men'.

But unfortunately, the post of match-making official was abolished with the downfall of Chou. After then, match-making gradually developed into some sort of profession.

PROFESSIONAL MATCH-MAKING

Since the family heads had the absolute right to pick the son a wife or the daughter a husband, a marriage concerned the families far more than the man and wife. Whether in the city or the village, there were plenty of professional match-makers—a group of middle-aged women eloquent in speech and wide in contacts. Though mostly illiterate, they abided by one principle: the family background of both parties must be about the same—an official family would only allow its son to marry a girl from another official family, though a business man might like his daughter to marry into an official family by offering a handsome dowry. In the city, once the match-makers had on their hands a number of marriageable young men and young girls, they would set about discreetly investigating their family backgrounds and wealth.

With the noble and the rich, the match-makers had to approach the maidservants to discover what they wished—including precise information about the looks of the girls. They had to bait these maidservants with small gifts or 'tea money'; otherwise, the maidservants would never talk. Where the looks of the potential young men were concerned, there was far less trouble, for they, unlike the girls, generally appeared in public. When a match-maker, after all calculations, considered a certain young man and a certain girl a 'good match', she would first seek to see the girl's mother, in order to wag her tongue untiringly about the riches, talents and good looks of the 'suitable' young man—even recklessly predicting that he would pass the State Examinations and become an imperial official in no time at all. Meanwhile, she would try to catch a glimpse of the girl and, if possible, have a few words with her. Sometimes, the mother would be expressionless, casually asking the match-maker to leave her address with one of the maidservants. At this point, the match-maker would be secretly pleased with her initial success. She would know only too well that the mother would not have asked her to leave her address if she were not interested. After the match-maker was gone, the mother would seek an appropriate opportunity to discuss the matter with the father, who really had the final say. If he was agreeable, she would then send for the match-maker and ask her to go ahead.

Now the match-maker would rush to the potential bridegroom's house and obtain an interview with his mother in the same manner. The match-maker would deliberately exaggerate the virtue, beauty and needlework of the girl; for by this time she had already invested quite a lot of money in bribing the maidservants to see the mistresses of both houses. If the mother of the young man were interested, she would then mention it to the father. If the suggestion met with his approval, he would invite the girl's father to dinner and propose on behalf of his son. When the girl's father accepted, the marriage was fixed, without having to consult either the prospective bride or groom.

THE WEDDING PAGEANT

Prior to the wedding, it was customary to have an engagement ceremony (Wen Ting). On the day, the groom's family would hire a number of footmen to help their own servants carry loads and loads of engagement presents—jewellery, silver and gold wares, lengths of silk and satin, antiques, deeds of houses and properties—in procession along the street to the bride's house. A butler would ride a white horse decorated with red satin ribbons, carrying under his arm a gilded red lacquer box which contained the 'Eight Characters' (hour, date, month and year of birth) of the groom, written in golden ink on a piece of red silk. The bride's father would take this document out from the lacquer box and replace it with that of his daughter. The butler would then rush back after having been handsomely tipped.

Etiquette demanded the bride's family to display all these engagement presents and invite all friends and relatives for dinner to have a view. The whole occasion was marked by gasps of admiration, sighs of amazement and smiles of contentment, though the prospective bride would hide herself in her own room for the sake of modesty or out of shyness, no matter how happy she might feel.

In nine out of ten cases, before the engagement ceremony actually took place, both families would have asked for the 'Eight Characters' of the prospective bride and groom to be studied by some reputed astrologer, to establish once and for all the suitability of the match. If their stars were found to be incompatible—which was very rare, for most astrologers believed it would bring them ill luck if they broke up a potential marriage—the whole thing would be called off by mutual agreement of both families.

The wedding day, picked out by an astrologer, could take place any time after the engagement ceremony. It started with the parading of the dowry from the bride's house to the groom's, generally three days ahead of the actual wedding day. The wedding ceremony took place after dusk. The groom, dressed in an official gown appropriate to his status, rode in a blue sedan chair, carried by four chairmen, to fetch the bride. (In ancient days, he would bring with him a wild goose—the symbol of faithfulness and fidelity.) Upon arriving at her house amid the deafening sound of firecrackers, he paid respects to her great-grandparents, grandparents and parents, while the band was playing the tune of 'Congratulating the New Groom'.

The bride was in red satin from top to toe, her head and face covered with a red satin shawl as well. After weeping and hugging her mother and sisters, she was assisted by two to four professional bridal companions into a red satin sedan chair, which had been placed in the rear Principal Hall, where not a single male was in sight. The band would now be signalled to play 'Heavenly Happiness' and strings of firecrackers were set off. The four chairmen would come in to carry the sedan chair, while in the front Principal Hall the groom would get into his chair, after having paid another round of respects.

Preceded by four to eight menservants on horseback, the groom's sedan chair would lead that of the bride, to be followed by an even number of smaller sedan chairs carrying the professional bridal companions and the virgin maids who were a part of the dowry.

The moment the wedding procession reached the groom's house, countless firecrackers would be set off and another waiting band would commence to play a variety of gay tunes such as 'Spring Glory', 'A Sprig of Flower', 'Joys of the Wedding Chamber'.

Alighting from his sedan chair, the groom walked straight up to the Principal Hall, where members of his family, relatives and friends had been waiting on tiptoe. The bride's sedan chair was set down in the front court. She had to remain inside while the band played another three tunes. This was in order to make proof of her patience, one of the feminine virtues. The lack of haste also indicated her 'reluctance' to part with her maidenhood.

A red carpet would now be rolled down from the Principal Hall to the door of the bridal sedan chair. Two or four of the groom's women relatives would gracefully come down to the front court to greet the bride in whispers, uttering a few auspicious words. Then the professional bridal companions escorted and guided the practically blindfolded bride slowly along the red carpet into the ceremonial hall.

In the upper end of the brightly lit hall, on a long and high table made of mulberry wood, there stood the Ancestral Shrine, which looked like a miniature temple, engraved and gilded to artistic perfection. Further down, a slightly lower square table of equal elegance was covered in the front with a red satin cloth embroidered with a golden dragon and phoenix playing with pearls. On this table, incense sticks were burning in a shining bronze tripod, while two huge red candles with the design of the dragon and phoenix were glittering joyfully.

On the wall behind the Ancestral Shrine, a golden tablet inscribed with the words 'Heaven' and 'Earth' enhanced the solemnity and grandeur of the occasion. When the bride was led to stand on the left of the groom, facing the Heaven and Earth tablet and the Ancestral Shrine, the master-of-ceremonies solemnly announced the commencement of the wedding rites. Immediately a hushed silence reigned over the Principal Hall; not even a small boy would dare to shift his feet.

Directed by the master-of-ceremonies, the wedding couple knelt down three times and kowtowed nine times. They changed sides after each kneeling. After that, two chairs would be placed in front of the square table. Great-grandparents, grandparents and parents took their turn to sit there, receiving three kowtows from the wedding couple. The ceremony ended with the groom and the bride turning to face each other and kowtowing three times.

At this point, the wedding guests began to applaud and shout words of good wishes, while outside in the front court, the band once again played the gay tunes, only to be drowned in the thundering sound of the endless strings of firecrackers.

The wedding banquet would now be laid out and guests were ushered to their seats. The dishes must always be even in number, beginning with four cold plates, to be followed by four fried dishes, ten main dishes and eventually four desserts. (In China the number ten means 'perfection' while the number four symbolises 'happiness in four seasons'.)

By now, the bride and groom were allowed to retire to the wedding chamber. The professional bridal companions laid out a small round table for two, serving food and wine. The groom, after sipping the wine in his jade, gold or silver cup, exchanged the cup for the bride's and each had another sip. With anticipation and nervousness he lifted the red satin shawl from her face to catch his very first glimpse. If she was pretty or beautiful, he would secretly congratulate himself. But if this were not the case, his roving eyes would quickly turn to those dowry maids. More often than not, the bride's mother, if she realised that her daughter had got a handsome husband, would deliberately select pretty and attractive dowry maids, in the hope that her son-in-law did not have to sow wild oats outside.

TEASING THE BRIDE

The lighter side of the wedding night started with 'teasing the bride', which the Chinese discreetly referred to as 'warming up the wedding chamber'. To the guests this was the highlight and they could hardly wait for the banquet to be over to rush into the wedding chamber. Some more daring guest would start telling dirty jokes, and ask the bride to do likewise. Some others might ask the bride aloud how she would cope with the groom when they went to bed. All this time, the bride lowered her head, pretending not to hear anything, while the groom smiled awkwardly. Some grooms could be more tactful than others, and such would offer to do something themselves to amuse the guests. But none of the guests would hear of this. Instead, they would put their heads together and force the bride to do something that embarrassed her even more. One of these popular tricks was 'baiting'. The bride was made to stand on a chair; she had to hold between her teeth a string fastened at the far end with an apple (or any fruit). The groom would be pushed forward to stand on the spot near the chair. With his mouth wide open, he had to bite the dangling apple until he had finished it. Meanwhile, the bride must not fail to hold the string. A naughtier game was 'touching the fish'. The groom was forced to thrust his hand into the bride's garment and give a running commentary. Another trick was to make the groom sip a mouthful of wine and pass it into the bride's mouth. If a drop of wine overflowed, the groom would have to do it again. This was suggestively called 'drinking from a flesh cup'. Any refusal of the bride would only lead the guests to become more difficult and adamant. The more bashful the bride was, the more excited they became. With a pretty bride, the teasing could last for hours. When such an occasion arose, one of the bridal companions would slip out to ask the groom's parents to come to the rescue. But this seldom worked, for according to the old Chinese custom, the wedding guests were allowed to tease the bride for three successive days and nights if they wanted to.

If the bride were not that pretty, the guests would pursue the teasing game perfunctorily. The groom, after a whole day's ordeal, would wish the guests to evacuate the wedding chamber at the appropriate moment. But strangely enough, he would not wish them to leave too soon, for this would indicate that the bride did not appeal to their eyes.

THE FIRST NIGHT AND VIRGINITY

After the guests had eventually left the wedding chamber, the ever-cautious bridal companions would search under the bed and in every possible hiding place to make sure that no naughty guest had hidden there unnoticed, to spy on the love-making of the newly-wedded. Assured, they would suggest to the groom that he leave the chamber for a short while so that they could whisper to the bride her first lessons in sex while helping her to undress. They would then tell her about the unavoidable pain while she was being deflowered, advising her to accept it with forbearance. They would advise her not to show any signs of enjoying intercourse even if she did so after the first few painful seconds. Most important of all, they would add, she should remain passive all the time, letting the groom take the initiative. After tucking her in bed, they would put a piece of white silk under her and whisper into her ear how to wipe her private parts carefully after the groom had performed his duty as a husband. They would then go out to take the anxiously waiting groom into the room and push him behind the bed curtains where he could undress himself.

Next morning, one of the bridal companions would come in with two silver bowls of stewed swallow's nest, for the bride and groom to restore their energy after having sex. While making the bed, she would cautiously take up that piece of white silk, examining the stains of blood and offering the couple her congratulations. Then she would tiptoe all the way to the mother-in-law and present the piece of white silk to her.

If there were no blood on the piece of white silk to prove the bride's chastity, she would be returned to her own family in a small sedan chair from the back door. But this seldom happened, for in those days Chinese girls never took any form of physical exercises which might break their maidenhead. Incidentally, the absolute necessity of virginity was advocated by the Confucian scholars in the Sung Dynasty and has since become an obsession with Chinese males. Before then, it was not infrequent for men to marry widows or women of loose virtue.

As for the groom's sex education, there were several ways to 'enlighten' him. His uncles, elder brothers or even menservants could all be his instructors, but certainly not his father. In some cases, for the sake of practice, he would be brought to visit a prostitute, who would be thrilled to coach him in the facts of life. Another practice was for some of the groom's uncles or brothers to show him some pornographic pictures and explain them fully for his benefit.

A village wedding was roughly the same in procedure, though much less extravagant and pompous from beginning to end. As a whole, the village people were far more uninhibited about virginity and pre-marital sex. And yet, oddly enough, professional match-makers and astrologers were still indispensable, even if it was public knowledge that bride and groom had slept together before the wedding.

SOME PECULIAR WAYS OF CHOOSING A SON-IN-LAW

In the case of high officials and scholars, however, they were too sophisticated to bother about professional match-makers or astrologers, preferring to arrange the marriages of their children in their own ways. It was not unusual for two fathers to make a marriage contract even before their children were born. Nor was it strange for a boy and a girl to get engaged when they were both toddlers if their parents were relatives or close friends.

Towards the end of the Sui Dynasty, General Tou Yi succeeded in choosing a future emperor to be his son-in-law in a most incredible way. An amateur astrologer himself, he was confident that his only daughter would definitely become a queen. He had a screen, painted with a peacock, placed in his Principal Hall. Whenever he received young eligible bachelors, the general would casually ask them to shoot at the painted peacock with two arrows. Secretly, he had promised himself that the one who hit both eyes of the peacock would be the right man for his daughter. This went on for months and puzzled many of his colleagues, who attributed this practice to his eccentricity. Eventually, a young officer named Li Yuan came to perform the same act. To General Tou's great delight, his two arrows pierced the peacock's eyes exactly. The general married his daughter to Li, who later became the first emperor of the T'ang Dynasty.

Later, in the same Dynasty, Prime Minister Chang Chai-keng picked his son-in-law in an equally ingenious way. When Kuo Yuan-cheng, the young military governor of Chinchow, came to visit him in Changan, the then imperial capital, he was so impressed by the young general's appearance and eloquence that his mind was immediately made up. He told Kuo that he would like to marry one of his three daughters to him. But as an impartial father, he asked his daughters to stand behind a heavy silk curtain, each holding a piece of red string in her hand. The other ends of the strings were carefully pulled into the Principal Hall from under the curtain. Then he let Kuo take his pick. It must have been a stroke of luck for the young military governor. The string he picked happened to be held behind the curtain by the most beautiful of the three sisters.

But another prime minister of T'ang took an entirely different approach. Prime Minister Li Lin-fu was so open-minded that he decided to let his six daughters pick their own husbands. In his Principal Hall, he ordered some craftsmen to build a specially designed window in the richly embroidered partition. Whenever some eligible young officials came to pay respect to him, all of his six daughters would already have been alerted to peep through the window which was invisible from the outside. Though the daughters all found the men they wanted to marry in this novel way, it soon became a scandal which ruined his political image and led to his eventual downfall.

Apart from these extraordinary examples, most prime ministers or ministers of various dynasties liked to test the eligible young men's talent in writing and knowledge of the classics before they would marry their daughters to them. Interesting though these pre-wedding examinations may seem, they are nothing if compared with an anecdote of an event of a similar nature which occurred in the Sung Dynasty.

Ch'in Shao-yu, a well-known scholar and poet of the time, was selected by the great Sung poet Su Tung-po's scholarly father to be his son-in-law. After the wedding ceremony, Ch'in found himself shut out of the wedding chamber. While he stood there amazed and annoyed, the bride, Su Tung-po's younger sister, sent her maid, who handed him the topics for three poems. He was told that he must compose these poems up to the bride's poetic standard before he would be admitted. With his pride deeply hurt, Ch'in felt like walking out. But on second thought, he racked his brains to write three excellent poems, which the bride approved. It was only then that he was greeted into the wedding chamber with three gold cups of wine and then allowed to perform his conjugal duty.

CONCUBINES AND THEIR ROLE

Compared with wives, concubines played a much more important part in the man's sexual life. Though deferring to the wife in social status, a concubine could always 'monopolise the bedchamber' if she successfully pleased the husband in whatever way she chose.

The system of concubinage started in the Feudal Age (841-221 B.C.). In those days, their wealth and power enabled the aristocracy to enjoy the luxury of polygamy. To some extent, polygamy was connected with the women's attitude towards sex. For a wife, having sex with her husband was a duty, in order to conceive. In bed, she had to maintain her feminine virtue by remaining passive and not showing the slightest sign of interest. As Confucius even advised women not to talk in bed, this would certainly turn love-making into boredom for the husband, if nothing more. In the Sung Dynasty, some stoic Confucian scholars termed sexual intercourse with the wife 'consolidating the human relationship'. But they did not refrain from using the expression 'seeking pleasures and creating happiness' when it came to sleeping with concubines or prostitutes.

Apart from knowing how to satisfy the husband's whims in bed, a concubine could also enrich her social life by being a good singer, an excellent cook or having the gift of writing poetry and telling witty jokes. As ancient etiquette demanded that men were not to see one another's wives, this gave concubines the chance to meet and entertain the husband's friends as a hostess. But to be a hostess was not always an enviable job, especially when one happened to be a concubine of Shih Ch'ung, a reputed multi-millionaire of the Hsi Tsin Dynasty (A.D. 265-419). A generous host, Shih enjoyed giving dinner parties in the most elaborate manner. At these parties, he always summoned his beautiful concubines to drink with the guests. Whenever a guest refused to drink, Shih would immediately have the concubine who proposed the toast beheaded. It gave the multi-millionaire immense pleasure for, unwilling to see these beauties killed, all his guests got so drunk that they had to be carried home. However, Shih's trick misfired on one occasion. With Prime Minister Wang Tao and General Wang Tun as his guests of honour, he made his concubines urge them to drink. Though normally a teetotaller, the prime minister forced himself to drink for fear that these beauti-ful women would lose their lives. But General Wang couldn't care less. He simply refused to raise his jade wine cup to his lips. Upset and angered, Shih ordered his attendants to kill three concubines one after another. Feeling sorry for these innocent women, the prime minister hastily told the general to have a few sips at least. General Wang calmly said: 'I just want to see how many concubines of our honourable host would have to die for his stupidity.' After that, Shih Ch'ung never did the same thing again.

But there was another side to Shih Ch'ung. Of all his concubines, his favourite was Lu Chu (Green Pearl) for whom he built the Golden Vale Gardens and the Green Pearl Mansions. He also wrote poems dedicated to her. They spent most of their time together like a pair of love birds. Unfortunately, the renown of Lu Chu's beauty aroused the burning jealousy of General Sun Hsiu. He led his troops to besiege the Green Pearl Mansions, demanding Lu Chu. However, Lu Chu was not in the least daunted. She jumped from the third storey to her death. More angry than remorseful, the general killed Shih Ch'ung and confiscated his properties, including more than 800 servants and maids.

THE 'PEEPING TOM' EMPEROR

Nevertheless, as far as seeking sexual pleasures from a concubine is concerned, Shih Ch'ung was not even remotely comparable with Emperor Ch'eng Ti (reigning 32-7 B.C.) of the Western Han. The emperor's favourite concubine was Chao Ho-teh, whom he had dis-covered in a 'Song and Dance House'. The girls there were actually courtesans similar to the Japanese geishas of today. In her late teens, Ho-teh attracted royal attention not only with her beautiful face, but also with her voluptuous body, like 'creamy white jade'. No matter how tired Ch'eng Ti might be, he would never cease making love to her for a single night. Excelling in sexual techniques, she knew how to kindle the flame of desire in the ageing emperor. Against palace etiquette and traditional decency, she deliberately kept the light on whenever Ch'eng Ti favoured her, for she was well aware that the naked curves of her beauty would definitely work him up the moment he set his eyes on her. During the actual process of love-making, she hummed, sighed, smiled and knitted her eyebrows in such a bewildering way that the emperor imagined that she was getting tighter and tighter down below. Moving gently, she would let every inch of her silky skin give Ch'eng Ti some indescribable pleasure.

When the emperor became more and more obsessed with her body, he had a sudden fancy. He tipped a couple of palace maidens handsomely, ordering them to inform him immediately whenever Ho-teh was taking a bath. Hidden behind the marble screen in her bedchamber, he peeped through the crevice between the panels. He could hardly control himself when he saw her shapely pinkness reflected from the magnolia-scented water in the golden bathtub. Naturally, Ho-teh knew only too well who was standing behind the marble screen. She would slowly and gracefully stand up, turning around to let the emperor have a fuller view. This was too much for him. He dashed out from his hiding place and took her to bed, though she hardly had the time to dry herself.

But the consequences of over-indulgence caught up with him in no time. To restore his dragon energy, Ho-teh consulted a Taoist monk, who was a household name for his expert knowledge of aphrodisiacs. Obligingly the Taoist presented her with a bottle of 'Grand Pills', warning her that she should never give His Majesty more than one each time. Ho-teh lost no time in trying them out on Ch'eng Ti. They really worked and the emperor suddenly became as potent as a young man in his twenties. However, one night something unpredictable happened. After they had both got tipsy on a few drinks, she offered him ten 'Grand Pills', which he swallowed without a second thought. Their love-making went on for hours and hours and exhausted Ho-teh completely; yet the emperor was still charging like a bull. Then, all of a sudden, he collapsed and died instantly. When the incident was reported to the queen mother, she immediately sent two eunuchs to poison Ho-teh to death.

THE 'BEWITCHING PIG'

Having no heir, Emperor Ch'eng Ti was succeeded by the Prince of Ting-t'ao, who became Emperor Ai Ti. Perhaps it was due to Ch'eng Ti's scandalous death that Ai Ti became a homosexual and enjoyed his role in 'cutting the sleeve'.

But it could also have been for the same reason that one of Ch'eng Ti's descendants, Prince Liu Ch'ang, took a Persian girl to join his dozens of concubines. This, in a way, could be regarded as one of the earliest mixed marriages. According to *Ch'ing Yi Lu* (*The Sketch Book of Strange Events*), this Persian girl seemed to have come to China via Sinkiang with her merchant father. Anxious to please the royal customer, the Persian merchant offered his daughter to Prince Liu Ch'ang in exchange for some special trading concessions. When Liu Ch'ang first acquired her, the language barrier and her dark complexion slightly put him off. However, after having her for one night, the prince was thrilled with his new discovery. Without hesitation, he deserted all the other concubines in spite of their unceasing efforts to win back his favour. Infuriated, all these concubines decided to find out how this foreign girl managed to 'monopolise the bedchamber'. One night, they quietly gathered outside the rear window of the Persian concubine's suite to do some eavesdropping. To their surprise they did not have to strain their ears to hear what was going on inside. The shaking of the bed, the laughing and chanting of the Persian girl and the panting of the prince formed an assortment of sounds that made them blush.

Soon after, some of the prince's close friends tactfully but insistently, asked him to reveal to them some secrets about this woman. At first, Prince Liu Ch'ang merely smiled. But after a few drinks, he impulsively told these curious friends: 'It is so hard to describe these things. You just have to be in bed with her to know how wonderful she is. Sometimes, she is like a galloping steed, and yet the rider need not fear falling off. Other times, she can be as evasive as a little deer, and it excites me no end to be able to hold her tight and close, not to mention other things. In a word, she is different. Not just a woman, but many women in one.'

'How about talking to each other?' one friend asked.

'No trouble at all,' smiled the prince. 'Love needs no words. Anyway, I have already given her a pet name which she seems to like very much.'

'What is it then?' another friend cut in.

'The Bewitching Pig.'

Upon hearing it, all these friends applauded. After that, many people knew that their prince had a 'Bewitching Pig', though not all of them associated it with this Persian concubine of his.

'MY FRAGRANT PEARL'

However, it was not until the T'ang Dynasty (A.D. 618-904) that concubine-taking began to become a common practice among scholars and poets. Po Chu-I, one of the leading T'ang poets, was uninhibited enough to write poems describing the charm and beauty of his two concubines. In one of his poems, he likened one concubine's mouth to a 'red cherry' and the other's waist to a 'weeping willow'. For many centuries to come, 'cherry mouth' and 'willowy waist' have been frequently used to portray great beauties. This is also believed to have set the trend for Chinese men to prefer women with tiny mouths and slender figures.

Though another concubine of Court Official Yuan Tsai in the same Dynasty was not so well known as the poet's two concubines Fan Su and Hsiao Mang, her most unusual physical characteristics enabled her to captivate Yuan for years and years. Hsueh Yao-ying by name, she came from a very humble family. Ever since her baby-hood, her mother had been feeding her with pills made of the essence of various fragrant flowers, including peony, jasmine, orchid and magnolia. Whenever Yao-ying smiled or uttered a few words, a subtle fragrance would come out with her breath, lingering in the air for a long while. This made Yuan Tsai treasure her more than anything in the world. Proudly, but appropriately, he called her 'My Fragrant Pearl'. Needless to say, the name of 'Fragrant Pearl' led many roman-tic youths to dream of meeting her under more intimate circum-stances. But Yuan Tsai's watchful eyes were as sharp as a pair of glistening daggers; he would not even allow his closest friends to be near her a second too long, let alone these youthful day-dreamers.

It was also in the T'ang Dynasty that the two charming concubines of General Chang Hsiung won admiration in a totally different way, though their names remain unknown even today. After the rebel troops led by An Lu-shan had besieged the city of Suiyang for months the outnumbered garrison forces under General Chang were running out of food supplies. The worried general did not know what to do. He kept pacing the floor in his residence, sighing and murmuring. When the two young concubines realised what was worrying the general, they tiptoed to the rear Principal Hall and hanged them-selves, leaving a note urging him to cook their flesh to feed the famished soldiers, since this struck them as the only way to serve their country. Though broken-hearted, General Chang could not but comply with their wish. Unfortunately, the tragic sacrifice of these pretty women failed to keep the city from being captured. Nevertheless, General Chang and his soldiers did fight to the last man. To see things in perspective, his two self-sacrificing concubines had not really died in vain.

Naturally, not all concubines could hope to be half as glamorous, as famous or as heroic as these. Their roles were far more mundane and far less spectacular. Many were brought into the family only when the wife was barren, and, therefore, their chief concern was to bear an heir. Others were merely the husband's toys. They could be given away as presents, or used for the game of 'concubine-swopping' in a comparatively discreet or unobtrusive manner.

If and when a girl of humble origin was attractive enough to be included in a wealthy man's harem, she would have other worries. In an atmosphere full of intrigue and conspiracy, she must out-manoeuvre her rivals, or perish.

But as far as sex was concerned, she could easily seek fulfilment under the same roof. In those days, a big Chinese family house, with its annexes and gardens, was like a walled city in which dwelt hundreds of relations and servants. Most significantly, there were plenty of young unmarried males with roving eyes, only too willing and ready to prove their virility. Under such circumstances, a casual affair, if carried on with discretion, was seldom caught. Even if it were discovered, the imperative need to protect the family name would hush the whole thing up.

In fact, what worried the concubine most could be the favourite Chinese expression: 'A wife is never as exciting as a concubine; a concubine has nothing to compare with a casual affair or a prostitute —but most exciting of all is an inaccessible woman.'

CHAPTER THREE

The Origin and Evolution
of Prostitution

Prostitution in China owes its origin to the aristocracy in the Feudal Period (841-221 B.C.). In those ancient days, it was the vogue for aristocrats to keep huge numbers of courtesans, paid companions, actors and musicians, not merely for practical use but as status symbols. The courtesans were not necessarily picked solely for their ability to provide sexual pleasure. Some of them could be outstanding singers; some, excellent dancers. Nor would an aristocrat hesitate to purchase a courtesan for her culinary art, poetic gift or special talent in designing clothes or telling fortunes. In an aristocratic household, courtesans ranked below concubines but were far superior to maids and servants. Without bearing the surname of the master, like concubines, they enjoyed sexual freedom in a far more permissive way.

Even long after prostitution had gone 'public', the noble and the rich still kept their own courtesans. During the period of the Southern and Northern Empires (265-589 A.D.) Prince Ho-chien of Northern Wei kept as many as 300 courtesans of diversified talents to impress people with his wealth and 'generosity'. But his cousin, Prince Kao-yang, after becoming the prime minister, immediately acquired 500 courtesans of 'heavenly beauty and national fame' in order to outshine him.

Historical records show that Emperor Wu Ti of Western Han issued the imperial decree that introduced public prostitution. After that the number of privately-owned courtesans began to dwindle while prostitutes flourished.

THE FIRST PROSTITUTE TO BECOME A QUEEN

Ironically enough, it was no other than his own descendant, Emperor Ch'eng Ti (reigning 32-7 B.C.), who made a prostitute his

queen. Like her younger sister, Chao Ho-teh, the prostitute Chao
Fei-yen (Flying Swallow Chao) was working in a 'Song and Dance
House' when the emperor first heard about her beauty. A fascinating
dancer, she was so light in build that the story of her 'dancing on
the palms of men' spread like wildfire in the imperial capital. When
Ch'eng Ti paid her his first visit, he disguised himself as Marquis
Chang Fan's servant to avoid any possible scandal. Upon seeing her,
the emperor was so dazzled by her charm and beauty that he found
himself tongue-tied. Within a couple of days, he instructed Marquis
Chang to take her into the imperial palace and made her a lady-in-
waiting of the then queen.

That very night Ch'eng Ti summoned her to his Royal Bedchamber
to receive his favour. Still fascinated by her beauty, he fixed his eyes
on her for hours as if in a trance. When, at long last, he began to
enter her, he repeatedly bit her snow-white neck. During the process
of love-making, Fei-yen enchanted the emperor with her sexual technique—as if 'every tender movement obeyed an over-all rhythm and
tempo'. The emperor found that though intercourse was wholly effortless on his part, yet he achieved the greatest satisfaction. While panting slightly afterwards, he was even more thrilled to find his
underclothes stained with blood as 'scarlet as peach blossoms'. Fei-yen
respectfully offered to wash it off herself. But Ch'eng Ti would not
hear of it, telling her that it was his royal wish to keep the stained
underclothes as a souvenir.

Shortly after, the emperor made Fei-yen one of his royal consorts;
and as he found her so indispensable night after night, he had soon
downgraded his original queen and elevated Fei-yen to that status.
It was then that she got her younger sister Ho-teh into the palace,
so that the royal favour would not be shared by any other women.

Once she became queen, Fei-yen found the emperor too old to
satisfy her sexually, not to mention the fact that Ch'eng Ti by now
spent more nights with her sister Ho-teh than with her. However,
she was audacious enough to introduce some young men into the
palace through the agency of some eunuchs she could trust. With
these young men, she made love in broad daylight when Ch'eng Ti
was attending to state affairs. She did so also in the hope that she
might bear the emperor a 'son', since for years Ch'eng Ti had been
yearning for an heir.

When this had gone on for quite some time undetected, she did not even bother to post a eunuch outside her palace as a sentry. One day, the emperor suddenly descended on her with two of his personal eunuchs, after paying his tribute to the queen mother. It was not until he reached the palace door that Queen Fei-yen was hastily informed. Without time to freshen herself up, she left her bedchamber to greet the emperor at the Principal Hall. Her ruffled hair, flushed face and crumpled garments immediately aroused Ch'eng Ti's suspicion. Just then, he also heard a man coughing behind the heavy satin curtains. Infuriated, the emperor walked out without a word. He went to Ho-teh's palace at once, telling her everything. He also declared his decision to behead Fei-yen, cut off her limbs and throw her remains in a cess-pit. Frightened to the extreme, Ho-teh knelt down to beg for her sister's life. She even proposed to die to redeem her sister's unpardonable misbehaviour. The emperor sighed and promised to spare Fei-yen's life. Ho-teh secretly advised her to be more discreet.

But a few months later, Fei-yen had another affair with the son of a palace guard called Chen Tsung. When the emperor discovered this, he ordered the young man to be beheaded. As for Fei-yen, she did not lose her life because of Ch'eng Ti's previous promise to Ho-teh. After that, she made many attempts to win back the royal favour without any success, even though she enjoyed to the full the help and connivance of her sister.

PROSTITUTES MORE INACCESSIBLE THAN PRINCESSES

There were other well-known prostitutes in the Han Dynasty, but none of them could steal the limelight from the Chao sisters. More than 500 years later, in the middle of the T'ang Dynasty, the Golden Age of Chinese literature brought, as one of its incidental results, unprecedented prosperity to prostitutes as a whole, and fame to some in particular.

In the northern part of Changan, the imperial capital, the Peace and Prosperity District (Ping-Kang-Li) attracted many envious eyes and enthusiastic remarks with its huge mansions and well-cultivated gardens, especially along the Middleway and Southway. In these mansions dwelt the most famous prostitutes, much sought after by princes, dukes, high officials, scholars and poets. Under the watchful eyes of a 'foster-mother' (procuress), surrounded by maids and servants, some of these prostitutes were even more inaccessible than princesses. From the reign of Emperor Hsuan Tsung onwards, whenever scholars passed the Supreme State Examination in the imperial capital, it was the fashion for them to celebrate their success by giving banquets in the mansions of one of the leading prostitutes. To 'buy the smiles' they often squandered 1,000 taels of gold in a single night. Even so, they could still be turned down by a prostitute simply because she was not in the mood or 'indisposed'.

When Liu Chiao topped the Golden List (public announcement of the examination results) to everybody's admiration, he failed to see Cheng Chu-chu, the best-known prostitute of his time, after trying to date her no less than three times. Frustrated and helpless, he wrote a poem to console himself. However, three years later, Liu eventually had a chance meeting with Cheng Chu-chu at some friend's banquet. He sighed and told his host, 'It did not take me so long to top the Golden List as to meet this woman. But it is worth waiting for three long years to catch even a glimpse of her.'

Another famous prostitute named Ya-niang must have possessed a sadistic nature, for she liked to pinch or scratch the faces of her customers. Once, when the son of a certain prime minister spent a night with her, his face was clawed and his cheekbones broken, probably due to Ya-niang's burning passion. The following morning, he had to pay a tribute to the imperial examiner who had passed him. Shocked at seeing his messy face, the examiner asked him what had happened. He told the whole episode truthfully. Though many of his young colleagues present roared with laughter, they nonetheless regarded the incident as something very romantic.

The inaccessibility of these prostitutes will not appear strange if we examine the methods used to build up their fame. In those days, some 'foster-mothers' would not mind investing a large amount of capital to bring up a young girl of twelve or thirteen—if she had the potentiality—into becoming a most desirable maiden. She would be taught to sing, dance and play musical instruments by famous masters, once she had acquired the ability to read and write. In the case of the more talented ones, they would be made to master the art of calligraphy and poetry-writing. Witty conversation, poise and grace were the basic requirements. Having taken so much time and spent so much money in educating her find, the 'foster-mother' would not let any man come near the prostitute without her approval. She would wish to find her 'foster-daughter' a proper husband if possible, so that her own security in her old age could be ensured; but before the right man was found she would settle for the next best by getting the prostitute a steady customer. Therefore, it was not unusual for a 'joy-seeker' (a man who sows wild oats) to move in to live with a prostitute for two or three years until his means were exhausted.

A POET CAN MAKE OR BREAK A PROSTITUTE

To the popular poets in that period no prostitute would dare to show the slightest sign of disrespect, no matter how famous she might be. During the T'ang period poets were the 'favourite sons of the Heaven', their social status extremely high and their poems widely read and sung. Even princes and prime ministers would consider having a poet among their friends a great honour. And while most poets patronised some prostitutes, they turned to them more for platonic relationships than for sheer sexual pleasure. In the case of those prostitutes who could write poems, the poets never hesitated to treat them as literary friends.

Once a prostitute had a poem dedicated to her by a famous poet, her popularity would immediately soar. In one instance, a famous prostitute, Li Tuan-tuan, upset Tsui Huei the poet quite unintentionally. To let off steam, the poet scribbled a poem on the white wall of her mansion, deriding her ugliness. Overnight, the poem was sung everywhere in Changan. The power of the poet was so great that Li Tuan-tuan failed to retain even her regulars. Upon the advice of her 'foster-mother', she rushed to Tsui Huei to offer her apology. Flattered, the poet wrote her another short poem, likening her in one line to 'a sprig of white peony walking gracefully in the air'. (The peony is considered the king of all flowers in China.) In a matter of hours, Li Tuan-tuan's house was again crowded with customers, greater in number than ever.

In turn, some poets would enjoy hearing their poems sung by prostitutes or actors as an indication of popularity. In the imperial capital, most big restaurants kept twenty or thirty singing prostitutes to entertain their guests by singing popular poems. One snowy day, three famous poets—Kao Shih, Wang Ch'ang-ling and Wang Chih-huan—went to a leading restaurant for dinner. They had to take a small table in one corner for the main tables in the centre were occupied by a score of official actors (Emperor Hsuan Tsung gave all actors official appointments), joking and flirting with all the available singing prostitutes. Rather amused, the poets sipped their wine and enjoyed watching the snow-covered landscape outside the window. All of a sudden, they heard the singing prostitutes start to sing some of the popular poems of the day. The three of them agreed to see whose poems would be sung the most to decide the winner. After some time two of Wang Ch'ang-ling's had been performed and one of Kao Shih. Angered, Wang Chih-huan pointed to the most glamorous singing prostitute in the group and said, 'If she doesn't sing one of my poems, I will admit defeat.' No sooner had he finished his words than this prostitute started to sing one of his best-known poems. The tension was ended and the three poets burst out laughing simultaneously. When the official actors found out who these gentlemen were, they dragged them over to join their party, to drink and carouse until midnight.

As for prostitutes who could write poems, more were found in the T'ang period than in any other. Among them, Hsueh Tao seems to have enjoyed a lasting fame. Born to an official family in the Province of Shu (now Szechuan), she condescended to become a prostitute after the death of her parents. But once her poetic talent was discovered by Governor Wei Kao, he immediately appointed her an Official Compiler of Classics. In her old age, she became a Taoist nun and lived in the suburbs of Chengtu, in a small hut by a well. After her death, the natives named the well after her. Then someone with business acumen decided to make a profit out of her poetic fame. He used the water of the Hsueh Tao Well to make a specially-designed writing paper and called it 'Hsueh Tao's notepaper', claiming that it was most suitable for poetry-writing. It seemed that this man's commercial venture turned out to be a great success. For centuries and centuries, visitors to Chengtu never forgot to buy some of 'Hsueh Tao's notepaper' as a souvenir.

Another prostitute who has enjoyed equally lasting fame was Su Hsiao-hsiao* of the Southern Sung Dynasty (13th century). Even to this day, her tomb stands by the West Lake of Hangchow, one of the most famous of Chinese beauty-spots. She was so popular that one of her contemporary poets considered himself honoured to have been born in the same city, Chient'ang, as her.

---

*Another prostitute also named Su Hsiao-hsiao was of the Southern Chi Dynasty (5th century).

In many authorised Anthologies of Chinese Classical Poetry, a number of poems written by ancient prostitutes have been included for their literary merit. Take, for instance a poem (tzu) from *Tzu Tsung* (*An Imperial Manchu Anthology of Classical Poems*), which was written by an anonymous prostitute from Szechuan in the Yuan (Mongol) Dynasty:

> I wish I had more words to say;
> But alas, not today.
> While I was breaking every sprig of willow,
> You are about to set sail and go.
> So hard to tell when we will meet again;
> A man always goes off for his own gain.
> But he should not fade out like a dove,
> For nothing is more precious than love.
> If forget you really must,
> Let me pour the wine in the dust.

(In ancient China, people regarded the willow as the symbol of farewell. 'Pour the wine in the dust' means the ending of a love affair.)

THE 'PROSTITUTE SHOPS' IN CHANGAN

Naturally, not all prostitutes enjoyed popularity and fame like these mentioned above. In the T'ang Dynasty, also in the Peace and Prosperity District, the Northway contained the so-called 'prostitute shops'. In each of these places, the procuress kept no less than ten prostitutes whose ages and appearances varied. Looking like a small inn from the outside, the 'shop' was in no way comparable with the mansions in the Middleway and the Southway. But as the customers were able to take the prostitutes to bed on the very first night they wandered in, these far humbler institutions were not lacking in patrons.

As soon as a customer arrived, the procuress would, after a few words of greeting, tactfully find out how much 'night-spending-fare' he was prepared to pay. After taking the agreed sum from him, she would then lead him to one of the partitioned rooms, where a naked prostitute was lying in bed waiting. Under the dim candlelight, any woman would look passable. Moreover, the customer who came to seek sex here would not be too particular. The procuresses of the 'prostitute shops' were generally very good at sizing up the customers and so at finding them 'suitable' partners. In such places a customer needed the courage of an exhibitionist. His own love-making could easily be heard by the other customers, while he himself could clearly hear everything that was happening in the adjoining rooms. The prostitutes were 'as tough and strong as tigresses'. During the course of love-making, they swore, laughed loudly and bit the men's shoulders if they could not satisfy them. Some of them were compulsive gamblers; they would persuade the customers to have a game of dice with them. As the 'prostitute shops' were conveniently situated near wine shops and small restaurants, a lot of customers came after they had got drunk. Sometimes, a drunken customer might have his pockets cleared out and then be carried out to the street. But such cases seldom happened unless the customer deliberately made trouble under the influence of alcohol.

Meanwhile, the 'prostitute shops' were also a refuge for daughters of criminals, escaped concubines and even women of unknown background. They felt secure working there, since the garrison forces or police never bothered to search these places for a wanted person. But in fact, some strange incidents did take place there.

According to a short story included in the *T'ang Tai Ch'ung Shu*, once a very beautiful girl came to the procuress of one of these 'prostitute shops' offering her service. This was most unusual, for the procuress always bought her girls from their parents or relatives. Besides, this girl had class. It was only after her persistent persuasion that the procuress accepted her, also agreeing that she could leave at any time she liked. The girl's beauty naturally attracted a lot of customers. But none of them, after paying the money, was able to make love to her. When a customer came into her room, she lay naked in bed just like the other prostitutes, except that she kept her legs close together. She casually told every customer to force her legs apart so that he could make love to her. With such a naked beauty before his eyes, every single customer made the attempt to part her dainty legs—without success.

This went on for exactly one year. Then the girl suddenly told the procuress that she would have to leave. Having become very fond of her, the procuress asked her why she had lowered herself to become a prostitute. The girl said that this had been her method of spotting her father's assassin, who was reputed to frequent the 'prostitute shops' incognito to satiate his sexual desires. Shocked though the procuress was, she dared not breathe a word. A few months later, a high-ranking officer was found beheaded in his bedroom, while on the wall a bloody dagger held a piece of paper on which the words 'His victim's daughter did it' were scribbled with his blood. When the procuress learned about this, she almost fainted, for she knew that the murder must have been committed by that very girl once in her employment.

YANGCHOW AND THE 'BLUE CHAMBERS'

Later in the T'ang Dynasty, however, Yangchow, the pivot of river transportation, began to compete with Changan as the haven for 'joy-seekers'. Crowded with salt-merchants and iron-mine owners, Yangchow became the most wealthy town of the whole empire. Understandably, procuresses also hastened to join the gold rush there.

On both sides of the main street of the town, numerous newly-built two-storeyed houses, painted in blue and with verandahs overlooking the street, stretched in unbroken line for four miles. The main street, thirty feet in width, provided an ideal dual carriageway. But it was at night that the street looked its best, when lace lanterns of every imaginable colour were brightly lit on the verandahs of these houses, 'brightening up the whole street like a myriad of radiant stars'. From these houses emerged the delightful sound of soft music, punctuated from time to time by the pealing laughter of young girls.

Actually, these houses were none other than the residences of the high-class prostitutes fondly described by the contemporary poets as 'fairies' or 'jade girls'. Since these houses were all painted in blue, the poets appropriately called them the 'Blue Chambers', a name at once suggestive and elegant.

Among the Late T'ang poets, Tu Mu was supreme in youthful enjoyment of the pleasures of Yangchow. In his early twenties, he became the personal secretary of the governor-general of Yangchow, Niu Chen-ju, and remained there for ten years. Romantic and handsome, Tu Mu slept with practically every famous prostitute in the town. What he did not realise at the time was that the governor-general was a most understanding man. Night after night, thirty tough soldiers disguised in civilian clothes were ordered to look after the personal security of his poet-secretary. It was only when Tu was promoted to a higher official post in the imperial capital that the governor-general showed him the reports made by these disguised soldiers and advised the poet to be more discreet about his private life in Changan.

Years after, Tu Mu still cherished the memory of the good time he had had in Yangchow and not without a touch of sadness referred to it in the following two lines:

> Having awakened from my dreams in Yangchow after ten years,
> I hear them talking of my fickleness in Blue Chambers with tears.

GIRLS OF 'THE WINDS AND THE DUST'

Incidentally, the system of 'barrack prostitutes' seemed to come into existence during the T'ang Dynasty as well. To forestall the possible invasion of the barbarians from the north and the north-west, garrison forces were stationed at every strategic point along the Great Wall. With no fixed period of service, thousands and thousands of soldiers had to guard the border for as long as ten to fifteen years. Throughout all these years, they hardly had the chance of seeing a female figure. However, when one of these garrison commanders found out that the morale of his troops appeared to be constantly sinking he consulted his staff officers and so learned that the cause was mainly sexual deprivation. A few junior officers were immediately despatched to nearby towns to recruit prostitutes who would not mind coming to the border fortresses, to brave the winds and the dust. Quite unexpectedly, the special envoys brought back with them far more prostitutes than the general had expected. Needless to say, the morale of his men was greatly boosted in consequence, and in successive skirmishes they demolished the barbarians without the slightest difficulty.

The other garrison commanders followed suit; so the defence along the Great Wall became doubly efficacious without any need of reinforcements. As for the 'barrack prostitutes', they seemed to settle down quite happily in these outposts. Many of them even married the soldiers. In addition, they gradually learned to master the skill of using spears, swords and bows and arrows. In a sense, they were like auxiliary forces, though never formally organised. They must have inspired some of the poets of the times to call prostitutes the 'girls of the winds and the dust'.

But of course, with their fertile imagination, poets also created other metaphors applicable to prostitutes. They were called 'fallen flowers' to indicate their rootless and insecure life; they were likened to 'willows by the road and flowers on the wall' to suggest their accessibility. The prostitutes' way of earning a living was subtly described as 'leaning against the doorway to sell her smiles'. And, not irrelevantly, to visit a prostitute has since been referred to as 'buying the smiles'.

Prostitutes have also been called 'money trees' because of a tragic episode which occurred during the An Lu-shan rebellion against Emperor Hsuan Tsung of T'ang. When the imperial capital fell into the hands of the rebels, a palace maiden named Hsu Tzu-ho sank to becoming a prostitute. An expert composer and exquisite singer, she brought more customers for her 'foster-mother' than the other girls. Several years later, when she was on her deathbed, she smiled faintly at the procuress, murmuring, 'Mother, now your money-tree is about to fall down forever.' This was said not without a shade of sarcasm for she obviously realised why her 'foster-mother' had been shedding tears at the bedside.

It must be due to the greediness and ruthlessness of the procuresses that they have been contemptuously called the 'old pao'— a kind of Chinese bird, brownish-yellow in colour and with black markings believed to be very licentious. During the T'ang period, they were also known as 'explosive charcoals', perhaps because of their despicable ways of treating customers and prostitutes. Another most amusing name that was given to the gigolo of a procuress in that period was 'temple guest'. So far, no available sources have been able to offer a satisfactory interpretation for this seemingly irrelevant term. But we know that in ancient China, the doors of both Buddhist and Taoist temples were open to all. Therefore, this term could have been used to suggest the promiscuity of procuresses.

As to the background of procuresses, most of them were 'retired' prostitutes who had had their share of struggle. Perhaps this was why they were so ruthless and greedy, if only for the sake of avenging themselves.

THE EMPEROR, THE COURTESAN AND THEIR ORANGES

About half a century later, prostitution during the period of the Sung Dynasty (A.D. 960-1279) appears to have departed from the T'ang vogue. Fewer courtesans and prostitutes were then known as poets or artists, though there was no lack of romantic poets who patronised them. However, during the reign of Emperor Huei Tsung, the appearance of Li Shih-shih in Kaifeng, the then imperial capital, turned many an eye and touched off endless whispers. At the age of eighteen or nineteen, she excelled in playing the Chinese lyre and never ran short of witty remarks. 'Delicate as an orchid and graceful as a peony,' the courtesan captivated many court officials with a bewitching smile or a few tender words. But only those who had had the luck to sleep with her were able to tell what the 'delicate orchid' was like in bed. After having made love to Shih-shih, Prime Minister Li Pang-yen summed up his experience to a bosom friend in a few words: 'You feel utterly helpless when you make love to her. Her skin is as smooth as silk all over, giving you a delight the moment your body touches hers. She knows when to be gentle, when to be vigorous and when to let herself go. Once you enter her, you melt like a snow-lion by the side of a burning fire.'

It did not take Emperor Huei Tsung long to hear about this most attractive prostitute, for his chief eunuch, Chang Ti, before his castration, had been one of Li Shih-shih's regulars.

When the emperor first went to see Shih-shih, he disguised himself as a rich merchant, accompanied by Chang Ti and some forty plain-clothes palace guards. Beforehand, on behalf of the disguised emperor, Chang gave Shih-shih's 'foster-mother' two rolls (forty feet each) of imperial purple velvet, a pair of genuine pearls, two lamb's wool blankets and 400 taels of white gold as a 'token gift'.

Overwhelmed, the 'foster-mother' promised to make Shih-shih available that very night. However, things did not go as smoothly as expected. Upon his arrival, the disguised emperor was first entertained to a big banquet in the Principal Hall by the 'foster-mother'. Among the dishes served, Huei Tsung was surprised to find a few delicacies he had never eaten before. After that, Chang Ti was given a hint to leave while the 'foster-mother' led the emperor into Shih-shih's suite, where tea was served. Then he was led into the inner chamber to have a few drinks and some small snacks. Still, Shih-shih was not in sight. Impatient, Huei Tsung was about to say something when the 'foster-mother' whispered into his ear that he should take a bath first, for her 'daughter' was obsessed with cleanliness. At her beckoning hand, two young maids came to take the 'rich merchant' to the bathroom, where they bathed and scrubbed him.

After Huei Tsung had taken his compulsory bath, Shih-shih casually walked into the room. Without make-up and wearing a white silk dress, she greeted the disguised emperor rather coolly. After exchanging a few words, she began to play the lyre. At this point, dawn was breaking and the emperor had to leave to receive officials at the imperial court.

Two or three days later, Madame Li, the 'foster-mother', learned the identity of the 'rich merchant' and was scared to death. But Shih-shih told her not to worry. The courtesan was sure that Huei Tsung had already been baited. She advised her 'foster-mother' to rebuild the house, modelling it on the structure of a palace. The construction work was completed in less than three months.

Shih-shih's foresight was soon confirmed when Huei Tsung made his appearance again without any disguise. For the sake of security, the houses along the street between the imperial palace and Shih-shih's place were turned into barracks for the imperial guards. Not a single soul could walk along this street without a pass.

Disregarding the pleas made by some ministers and the jealousies showered on him by the queen and his royal concubines, Emperor Huei Tsung would unceremoniously come to make love to Shih-shih whenever he had the time. When one of his concubines asked him what was so different about the courtesan, the emperor told her frankly: 'None of you knows about the art of love. With her, I never have to labour, and yet she offers me so much pleasure. In bed, she is always so lively and so full of fun. Compared with her, all of you are like beauties made of clay or wood. Yes, she is very, very special!'

All this time Shih-shih kept on receiving some of her regular customers as usual. Nor did she try to hide this from the emperor. Her only discretion was not to let any of them come face to face with Huei Tsung.

But one night when she was drinking and chatting in her bed-chamber with Chou Pang-yen, the leading poet of the time, the emperor suddenly arrived, bringing with him a few oranges, a fruit then rare and available only to the imperial household. As Huei Tsung was already approaching the suite, Shih-shih had to push the poet to hide under the bed.

Calmly and easily, she sat the emperor down in his usual chair.

With a silver knife she cut the oranges and shared them with him. After that, they went to bed together.

For several hours Chou Pang-yen had to lie under the bed, holding his breath. But he could not help hearing everything imaginable. However, the next morning when he had the chance to stretch his numb arms and legs, inspiration drove him to write the following poem, entitled 'The Wandering Youth':

The knife from Pinchow glistens like water;
The salt from Soochow is whiter than snow.
With dainty fingers she cuts new oranges.

Over the city walls ring the midnight bells,
The frost is thick and the hooves may slip—
It is much better not to go!

Unfortunately, when the emperor came again a few days later, Shih-shih sang the poem to entertain him. Embarrassed and angered, Huei Tsung forced her to reveal the name of the poet and explicitly ordered him dismissed from his post as a tax official and banished.

However, it was again due to the courtesan's quick wit that the poet was spared his banishment. One afternoon, the emperor came to Shih-shih's place for a nap. But she was not there. A couple of hours later, she came back from outside. Curious, Huei Tsung asked her where she had been. Casually she told him that she had gone to the city gate to see Chou Pang-yen off. Before the emperor had time to say anything, she sang a new poem by Chou, in which he praised His Majesty lavishly and yet in good taste. A poet himself, Huei Tsung immediately called off Chou's banishment and promoted him to be the imperial poet.

The association between Emperor Huei Tsung and Li Shih-shih lasted seven years until he abdicated, to devote more time to the study of Taoism and poetry-writing. Moreover, increasing age prevented him from sowing more wild oats.

THE PROSTITUTE IS A DUCHESS
In less than ten years, after both Huei Tsung and his son Emperor Ch'in Tsung had been captured by the Kitan Tartars, another prostitute achieved historical fame as a heroine. By that time, the imperial

capital had moved to Linan (now Hangchow). The prostitute was Liang Hung-yu, who was then in Chinkou, a tiny town by the Yangtze River. As prostitution in Sung was partially under State control, Hung-yu, like other prostitutes, had to go to the Town Hall to pay her respects on the first and fifteenth day of each month.

On one occasion, when she was approaching the gate of the Town Hall, she suddenly caught a glimpse of a huge tiger lying there, snoring. Scared, Hung-yu was about to retreat, when she vaguely saw a soldier stand up and stretch his arms, while the tiger she had seen was no longer there. After paying her respects, she went back to her own place and told her 'foster-mother' about the whole episode. The 'foster-mother', always good to Hung-yu, happened to be an amateur astrologer. Upon hearing Hung-yu's story, the older woman became very excited. She told Hung-yu that the soldier must be the reincarnation of the Heavenly Tiger Star, and that when he was dozing off, the 'spirit of the Heavenly Tiger Star left his body to roam about'. While Liang Hung-yu began to wonder whether her 'foster-mother' was out of her mind, the older woman insisted on dragging her to the Town Hall to identify the soldier. As soon as they found him, the older woman invited him to their place for dinner, to the poor soldier's delight. At the dinner table, the 'foster-mother' asked for his 'Eight Characters' and worked assiduously on them.

His 'Eight Characters' confirmed her belief. She took Liang Hung-yu aside and advised her to marry the soldier with her blessing. With Hung-yu's agreement, she then told the soldier that he could marry her 'daughter' if he wanted to. The soldier could not believe his ears, muttering that he was actually penniless. The procuress told him not to worry about the money side, for she would let Hung-yu be his wife without charging him anything. She would give them enough money to travel to Linan where his luck would immediately change. Naturally the soldier accepted her proposal. Only now did she find out that the soldier's name was Han Shih-chung.

When Han Shih-chung took Liang Hung-yu to Linan, a nephew of Huei Tsung had been enthroned as Emperor Kao Tsung and was planning a counter-offensive against the Kitan Tartars. An extremely good warrior, Han joined the imperial forces as a sergeant in the infantry. After scoring numerous victories in less than three years, he rose to the rank of a general.

All these years, Hung-yu was with him in every battle and fought

the Tartars as bravely as a man. Once, in a battle on the Yangtze
River, the Sung rivercraft under the command of Han Shih-chung
were outnumbered by those of the Kitan Tartars. Their defeat was
imminent, and General Han began to wonder whether they should
temporarily retreat. But Liang Hung-yu, without a word, dashed up
to the upper deck of the flagship and beat the war drum vigorously.
When the Sung troops saw their commander's wife daring the Tartars' flying arrows like this, they fought like tigers. The Tartars were
summarily defeated, leaving behind them thousands of dead bodies.
To reward their bravery, the emperor made Han a duke and Hung-yu
a duchess. But unfortunately, as Prime Minister Ch'in Kuei was in
the secret pay of the Tartars, he advised the emperor to make peace
with the Tartars and Kao Tsung consented. Frustrated, Han retired
with Hung-yu to live by the West Lake. Frequently, people would
see the couple riding donkeys around the Lake, appreciating the
beauty of nature like hermits.

ORAL INSTRUCTIONS FOR PROSTITUTES

Strangely enough, the invasions of the Tartars were believed to
have exerted no little influence on the sex schooling of prostitutes.
A 19th century scholar under the pen-name of the 'Master of Plum
Blossoms' asserted that such schooling had started in the Southern
Sung Period (1127-1278), owing both to the strong influence of
Taoism and to the barbarous mass-rapings commited by the rampaging hordes of Tartars. However, as time went on, he continued, it
was enriched by procuresses and experienced prostitutes until sex was
elevated to an 'art'. In his *Memoirs of The Plum Blossom Cottage*, he
wrote a most candid account, putting the words in the mouth of a
procuress:

'As most males want to deem themselves potent and virile, your
primary concern is *not* to hurt their ego. Since they are your customers, your job is to satisfy their desires, not yours. Let them imagine
they have the initiative, though in fact it is in your hands. With
someone who does not have the stamina, you must feign satisfaction
even though he may discharge the moment he enters you. You can
still let his shrunk thing remain inside, embracing and caressing him
as if he were the most wonderful man you had ever had. With a
customer who has a tiny organ, you have to hold your legs tightly
together once he puts it inside you. This will give him the feeling that

his every thrust really hurts and yet thrills you.

'An older customer may find it difficult to be in erection; in this case you will have to fondle his thing tenderly and gently. Meanwhile tell some sexy stories to give him time to warm up. If this fails to arouse him, you will have to use your mouth to suck it. If sucking still fails, you should gently advise him to sleep first and then have intercourse whenever he wakes up. Generally, man is more potent after some rest. Never give him aphrodisiacs, for it will ruin his health. Besides, his inability is none of your responsibility, since you have tried all you can.

'But with a man who is really virile and has endurance, you have to rely on your techniques most. Do not let yourself be carried away even if he makes you enjoy it. For your own good, you have to make him discharge as quickly as you can. You must take the initiative without his knowledge. You can move your hips like a millstone in action, holding his waist tightly and stroking his spine near the waist gently but persistently. Meanwhile, you can tickle the upper part of his mouth with the tip of your tongue. If you do all things skilfully, he will definitely discharge at your will. But be sure to let him have some fun, or his ego will be pricked and you will lose a customer.

'Some customers may come after having taken aphrodisiacs; therefore, you must not forget to make them drink a cup of white chrysanthemum tea before you take them to bed. Also remember that some wines can counter the effects of aphrodisiacs.

'With a man who has a big weapon, there is no cause for worry. This does not necessarily mean that he is extraordinarily virile. But for your own protection, slip behind the bed curtains and anoint your private parts with a sufficient amount of rose-petal ointment. Make sure that he knows nothing about this, for most customers like to show off the bigness of their weapons and enjoy whatever pain they may cause you. When you want to make him discharge quickly, just use the millstone tactics. You can slightly bend your waist so that his member will not reach too deep inside.

'When you are lucky enough to have a "spring chicken" (virgin boy), you must be patient in coaching him. He is bound to be clumsy and may not be able to find the right path. Help him and make him overcome his initial shyness and lack of confidence. Sometimes, he can be more manly after his premature discharge. You must make him find both physical and mental pleasures in having sex. More often than not, you will find "spring chickens" most enjoyable after you have successfully coached them.'

In addition to enumerating sexual techniques, the document suggests ways of handling and hooking customers: 'Do not let customers think that you are after their money. Make them imagine that they always have rivals. When you ask them for jewelry, you have to do it cleverly. With a vain and generous customer, you can display a jade ring or a bracelet in a seemingly casual way, but make sure that it catches his eye. He is bound to ask you about its origin and you can them tell him it is from another customer, adding that it is not really of good quality. This will arouse his sense of superiority and vanity. He will offer to buy you something more expensive. Make him take you to the jeweller where you have had previous dealings, so that he will be shown the really expensive jewelry. While choosing a piece of jewelry, do not ask about the price, but emphasise its beauty and craftsmanship. When the customer disapproves of your taste, this means he cannot afford the item in question and you must be prepared to settle for a less expensive one. Once he has bought you a piece of jewelry, you must replace the old one with it in front of his eyes. Whenever he comes to visit you, you must put it on as soon as his name is announced at the door.

'With a jealous customer, you can apply the same tactic. But tell him that your old jewelry is loaned to you by a sister (fellow prostitute) who is lucky enough to have a wealthy patron. This will definitely work. But when you discover that he is really rich, you may make use of his jealousy. You can then actually borrow a piece of extremely expensive jewelry, and tell him it is a small gift from another customer who cares very much for you. He is then bound to have one of two reactions: (1) He will buy you a more expensive piece, if he is really fond of you; or (2) he will beat a retreat, if his miserly trait overcomes his jealousy. When a customer is both jealous and stingy, it is much better to lose him for good.

'With an older and respectful customer, who naturally has some sort of paternal instinct and is less possessive, you can afford to keep him as a regular and there is no need to squeeze money out of his purse with any tricks. Because of his rich experience, he will pay decently but not excessively. His constant contribution will amount to much in the long run.

'It is the young and smart-looking customers who will undo you. They can be classified into the following categories: (1) spoilt sons of wealthy families; (2) paid companions (Ch'ing Ke) of the rich; (3) big-headed young fools who think they can get free sex with their looks. To deal with a spoilt son of the rich is the easiest task. He won't mind spending money so long as he has it. Get rid of him tactfully once you find out that his means are exhausted. But remember that there is always a chance for him to come back once he succeeds in getting more money from his parents or inherits the family fortune.

'With a paid companion, you can give him plenty of lip service, but never get involved with him. This kind of person always comes with his patron, who foots all the bills. Even if he can afford to pay the night-spending fare once or twice, you must recommend him to one of your sisters who is not that popular. If you spend a night with him, it will lower your value in the eyes of his patron, who is your big fish.

'As to the third category of young customers, you can see through them almost at once. They are bound to be mean while tipping the maids, and they boast about their non-existent riches without batting an eye. You can easily expose them by asking for expensive jewelry point-blank. No matter how much they appeal to you sexually or in looks, cut them off decisively. Once your good customers learn about your associations with such kinds of low-class people, they will immediately stop coming, for no one would like to subsidise these blood-suckers through any woman.

'It is equally important not to associate with actors. High officials and rich people simply loathe them. Besides, we all know that a great number of actors are male prostitutes and therefore our rivals.

'Whenever a customer proposes marriage to you, you must immediately inform me. You must remember how much you owe me for having brought you up and making a success of you. Unless the customer who proposes to take you pays me enough money to compensate for my past expenses on you and my potential losses after being deprived of your earning power, you will have to remain with me. My *personal advice* regarding marriage is: never contemplate becoming the wife of a young man and be contented to become the concubine of a rich old man.'

The quoted instructions also cover such minor matters as drinking and eating: 'When you go out with a customer, watch the amount of wine you drink. Do not let your attendant (in those days, when a prostitute went out, she took one or two maidservants with her) leave you with him alone. Some customers may make you drink more than you can, so that they can satisfy their sexual desires free. Before going out, always have something to eat in the house, for you should never drink on an empty stomach. Bring with you a few handkerchiefs. Whenever you are forced to drain a whole glass of wine, you can pretend to laugh and cover your mouth with a handkerchief and spit the wine into it. After doing so, quietly pass it to your attendant. When you are offered some food, eat only a little bit of it to show that you have had better food before. When you leave the customer's house, you must not forget to tip his servants.'

Though the Master of Plum Blossoms wrote down these oral instructions nearly 100 years ago, there is no denying that the actual techniques and psychological factors set out in them still possess universal appeal even to this day.

CHAPTER FOUR

The Downfall of the
Last Imperial Court (Manchus)

Most Chinese historians agree that the downfall of the Ch'ing (Manchu) Dynasty was brought about by Empress Tzu Hsi, a woman who dominated the political scene from 1859 to 1909. But coincidentally, the Manchus succeeded in overthrowing the Ming Empire also through the aid of two women, Empress T'ai Tsung of Ch'ing and Ch'en Yuan-yuan—the favourite concubine of the most powerful Ming general Wu San-kwei.

Descendants of the Nu-chen Tartars, the Manchus took refuge in Manchuria after the Mongols conquered China and established their empire in 1206. For more than 300 years they were no more than a nomadic tribe of limited numbers, hunting and farming in a small region where the Sungari River and the Moutan River meet. In the earlier Ming Dynasty, they paid tribute to the imperial court in Peking like other submissive tribes.

It was not until 1616 that Nu-erh-ha-chih, their tribal chief at the age of twenty-four, subdued the neighbouring tribes with some 600 horsemen and created the Khan State of Later Chin. Two years later, Nu-erh-ha-chih the Khan invaded the southern part of Manchuria with barely 20,000 horsemen and foot soldiers, obliging the reinforced army of Ming, no less than 200,000 in number to encounter defeat after defeat. By 1621, the Khan captured more than seventy cities in Manchuria and established his capital first in Liaoyang, and then in Mukden.

With the Ming forces entrenched behind the fortified Great Wall, the Manchus concentrated on building up their military strength. Then, after another five years, Nu-erh-ha-chih led 100,000 troops to attack the Shan-hai-kuan Pass of the Great Wall. The Ming garrison forces under the command of General Yuan Ch'ung-huan, with the aid of Portuguese cannons, routed the invading Manchus and the Khan was killed in action.

Nu-erh-ha-chih was succeeded by his fourth son Huang-t'ai-chi, an outstanding warrior in spite of his debauchery. With an eye to overthrowing the Ming Empire and avenging his father's death, he changed the dynasty name to Ch'ing and called himself Emperor T'ai Tsung. But without the political brain of his younger brother Prince Tuo-erh-kun and the sexual beauty of his wife Empress Big Jade, he would not have been able to demoralise the Ming generals so efficiently and quickly.

EMPRESS BIG JADE AND HER SEXUAL CONQUESTS

Empress Big Jade was reputed to be the greatest beauty of Manchuria. She had been married to a tribal chief, who was killed by the Ch'ing emperor. As the Manchurian women were then far more uninhibited than their Chinese counterparts, they rode, hunted and swam like the men. While still in her teens, the empress was named Big Jade by her chieftain father because of her fair complexion. One day, when she and her younger sister Little Jade were bathing in a small river, a group of young men rode by. In the dazzling sun, these young men could not take their eyes away from the two mermaids whose 'sinuous bodies were more creamy than the purest white jade and more shapely than the Moon Girl'. Amused to see these dumbfounded young men, who were pulling their horses hard, the two sisters suddenly stood up in the water, allowing their admirers a few more moments to catch a glimpse of their pretty faces and voluptuous breasts. But before these young men had time to dismount and come closer, Big Jade and Little Jade simultaneously began to throw pebbles like raindrops to hit the eyes of their horses. Scared more than hurt, the horses galloped wildly. With their feet caught in the stirrups, some of these young men were dragged for miles before they could disentangle themselves, bruised and injured.

Soon Huang-T'ai-chi learned about this amusing episode. The temptation was too great for him to consider the feud between the girls' tribe and his own. Having found out the day when Big Jade and Little Jade went shooting, he tried to waylay them in the forests. Resourceful and brave, he left his horse in a cave and disguised himself as a tiger, hiding in the overgrown grass beside the path which the two sisters had to pass. When dusk was falling, the two sisters, with a bagful of hares, rode happily along the path, chatting and laughing.

All of a sudden, a 'tiger' roared and stood up like a man out of nowhere. Little Jade struck her horse and sped away like lightning. Helpless, Big Jade drew out her sword, since the distance was too short for her to use her bow and arrows. Just then, the 'tiger' shook off his skin and in front of her stood a young handsome warrior, full of smiles.

In two or three strides, he came to the side of her horse. Without a word, he snatched her sword and carried her off the horse and into the thickness of the grass. To Big Jade this was almost as incredible as a dream. But Huang-t'ai-chi had no time to waste. He kissed her passionately, fondled her breasts and then partly undressed her. For half an hour they made love on the natural mattress of grasses, with a few glistening stars as onlookers. Contented, Big Jade sat up and asked Huang-t'ai-chi who he was. Upon hearing his name, she sighed a desperate sigh.

Huang-t'ai-chi was about to advise her how to get around the tribal feud when the sound of approaching horses' hooves, the barking of mongrels and the reflections of burning torches made him dash for his horse, hidden in the nearby cave. Hastily Big Jade made herself look presentable and rolled back nearer to the path, feigning semi-consciousness.

Led by her father and Little Jade, some ten young fighters armed with spears and long swords eventually found her lying by the roadside. Full of concern, the father bent over her and kept asking where the tiger was, while Little Jade assisted her sister to sit up. Unwilling to say anything for fear that her father's suspicion might be aroused, Big Jade pretended to be too frightened to speak coherently.

Shortly afterwards, her father married her to a young chief of a friendly tribe. When Nu-erh-ha-chih the Khan started to wipe out the neighbouring tribes, Huang-t'ai-chi led his cavalry to attack the tribal chief whom Big Jade was married to. He slaughtered the whole male population and took Big Jade to be his wife. At the same time, he made his younger brother Tuo-erh-kun marry Little Jade, who had grown up to be a beauty comparable to her elder sister. The two brothers often swopped their wives secretly to seek more excitement and fun. But in fact, Big Jade found her brother-in-law Tuo-erh-kun far more potent, perhaps because he had not sown wild oats as much as Huang-t'ai-chi had.

In 1643, long after Huang-t'ai-chi had been enthroned as Emperor T'ai Tsung of Ch'ing, he launched a large-scale offensive against the Ming forces in Sungshan and captured their Commander-in-Chief, Hung Ch'eng-ts'ou. Having defeated the rebels led by Li Tsu-ch'eng in Shensi, Hung was considered the best strategist among the Ming generals. T'ai Tsung fully realised that it would speed up his conquest of the Ming Empire if he could make Hung defect to him. He housed the captured general in a luxurious mansion, where he was wined and dined and waited on by pretty maids. Determined to die for his country, Hung started fasting and refused to speak to anyone. The Ch'ing emperor was at his wits' end. But when Empress Big Jade found out about the cause of his frustration, she whispered a few words in her husband's ear.

The same afternoon, when Hung Ch'eng-ts'ou was sitting in his room with both eyes shut, he suddenly smelled something very fragrant in the air. Too weak to stir, he heard a female voice softly enquire after his health. Next, he felt someone breathing down his neck. Opening his eyes, he saw a woman in her early thirties, smiling at him sweetly. Judging by her attire, he could easily tell that she was certainly not one of the maids. But what impressed him most was her sex-appeal, such as none of his own concubines possessed. Immediately, he shut his eyes again, refusing to utter a single word.

But this did not discourage the mysterious woman. She casually held a cup of some sort of liquid against his lips, saying 'This is a cup of poison. Why don't you drink it to die for your emperor in Peking?'

Relieved, Hung gulped it down at once. But strangely enough, instead of feeling the effects of poison, he found his strength gradually restored. By this time, the mysterious woman had already sat down beside him on his bed, giggling. The captured general opened his eyes and asked her what she had given him to drink. She smilingly told him it was only a cup of ginseng tea to restore his energy. Hung demanded an explanation. She told him that he should think more of his aged mother and his young concubines, especially since the rebel forces of Li Tzu-ch'eng were now closing in from all directions to besiege Peking. Confounded as well as bewildered, the Ming general did not know what to say. The woman put an arm around his neck, consoling him with tender words. Hung burst into tears and she unhesitatingly wiped them off with her silk handkerchief. When her dainty hand touched Hung's face, he felt his heart miss a beat. Like a child, he found himself totally helpless. The woman signalled the maids to leave the room. No sooner had they gone than she started to help the captured general to undress. Then she stripped herself. At the sight of her naked body Hung could not help rubbing his eyes with his hands. Standing in front of him was a goddess carved of white jade, with two nipples as red as ripe cherries. She threw herself over his body and the general instinctively began to respond. Having had no woman for over a month, Hung was surprised by his own vigour and passion, of a kind that could rarely be found in a man of more than fifty years of age like himself.

The following morning, before the woman left, Hung had firmly promised her that he would serve the cause of Ch'ing. After his breakfast, two Manchu officials came to escort him to pay respect to Emperor T'ai Tsung. Then he was asked to raise his eyes and given a seat. His eyes met those of the empress who sat beside T'ai Tsung, and she smiled. But Hung was so shocked that he became speechless for a long while. For he identified the empress as the same mysterious woman who had spent a most passionate night with him. Not surprisingly, he served the Ch'ing Empire with greater devotion than any other defector and was eventually made the governor-general of the five provinces south of the Yangtze River, the most powerful post ever held by a non-Manchu in his time.

THE GENERAL'S CONCUBINE CHANGES THE FATE OF THE MING EMPIRE

Even with Hung Ch'eng Ts'ou's strategy, the Manchu troops could not have pushed beyond the Great Wall without the willing collaboration of General Wu San-kwei, the Ming commander who held the Shan-hai-kuan Pass, separating Manchuria from North China. When Li Tzu-ch'eng and his rebel forces captured Peking and Emperor Ch'ung Cheng hanged himself, unwittingly the rebel leader took Wu's favourite concubine, Ch'en Yuan-yuan, who had previously been one of the most sought-after prostitutes south of the Yangtze River. More than a great beauty, Yuan-yuan excelled in poetry, calligraphy and the playing of musical instruments. She used to befriend distinguished scholars such as Hou Ch'ao-tsung and Mao P'i-chiang. Mao once confessed to one of his friends that 'to sit next to Yuan-yuan and listen to her is already an ecstasy, all closer intimacy apart'.

Wu San-kwei first met Yuan-yuan unexpectedly. Before he was sent to command the garrison forces of the Shan-hai-kuan, the emperor's brother-in-law gave him a farewell dinner. To entertain the general, the host produced some of his concubines, including Ch'en Yuan-yuan, at the banquet. Wu fell for Yuan-yuan at first sight and bluntly asked the host to give her to him. At a time when Peking was under the menace of both Li Tzu-ch'eng and the Manchus, the host had no alternative. Once Wu had acquired Yuan-yuan, he ignored his other concubines. If it hadn't been for his father's advice, he would have taken her with him to his new military headquarters at the Shan-hai-kuan.

However, after capturing Peking, Li Tzu-ch'eng immediately sent a special envoy to seek Wu's surrender so that they could join forces to demolish the Manchus. Inspired by nationalism, Wu was prepared to accept Li's terms. Then the news that Yuan-yuan had been taken by Li reached him. Angered, he turned to the Manchus and sought their assistance to wipe out the rebel forces led by Li Tzu-ch'eng. At that time, Emperor T'ai Tsung of Ch'ing had just died and Tuo-erh-kun ostensibly promised to help restore the Ming Empire when he was first approached. Once the Manchu forces entered Peking and swept over North China, he immediately proclaimed Peking as the Imperial Capital of Ch'ing. Meanwhile Wu had been busily chasing the fleeing rebel troops from province to province, until he reached Yunnan.

Given the rank of a prince and allowed to govern Yunnan in his own way, Wu was reunited with Yuan-yuan. But sadly enough, Yuan-yuan had no more affection left for Wu, for she could not forgive his treason, even though Wu's only motive had been to recover her. She became a Taoist nun and declined the title of princess. If Wu had not sought assistance from the Manchus, there might not have been more than 200 years of Manchu rule in China.

THE LICENTIOUS EMPEROR AND HIS 'FRAGRANT' CONCUBINE

Like the Nu-chen Tartars and the Mongols, once the Manchus had conquered China proper, they indulged themselves in luxurious living and sexual pleasures. This was particularly true of the imperial family. Emperor K'ang Hsi had an affair with his own aunt and he openly made her one of his royal consorts. Since the Manchu royalty was forbidden to marry Chinese women, most of the Ch'ing emperors frequented prostitutes in Peking or had casual affairs with all sorts of Chinese women to satisfy their curiosity, if not for the sake of variety.

But it was Emperor Ch'ien Lung (reigning 1716-1795) who really went to the extreme. While still a young prince—known as Prince Precious—he was quite content to sow wild oats among the Manchurian women. His way of seducing his sister-in-law Madame Fu Heng was as ingenious as it could be. Having had an eye on her for a long time, he had so far found no way of getting around his own wife. But fortunately his personal eunuch, Hsiao-fu-tze, was highly resourceful. One summer day, Madame Fu Heng was summoned to see the princess in the Ch'ang-chun Yuan (Happy Spring Garden), the then summer palace in the western suburbs of Peking. This did not take Madame Fu by surprise, for the Princess was her husband's closest sister, who often asked her to spend a night or two in the imperial summer palace to enjoy its serene splendour and cool breezes. Upon arriving at a small lodge amid a grove of rustling bamboos, she was greeted by palace maidens who suggested that she could take a bath, since the princess would not be here for at least another half-an-hour. Madame Fu was more than pleased, for the sedan chair trip from Peking had made her perspire slightly on such a hot afternoon.

Respectfully, a palace maiden led her to the bathroom and helped to bathe her. After the bath, she was offered a transparent lace robe and led to an adjoining room to freshen up her make-up. While sitting in front of a huge mirror with her breasts half-exposed, someone suddenly appeared from behind her and put a flower in her hair. The reflection in the mirror showed her that it was Prince Precious. As the lace robe could hardly cover up anything, Madame Fu blushed and tried to grasp a towel. The prince immediately fell on his knees, drawing out his sword and threatening suicide.

Madame Fu was scared out of her wits; but she knew only too well that the young prince would soon be enthroned, since Emperor Yung Cheng was then quite ill. In a hushed voice she told him to drop the sword. At her command he jumped up and carried her in his arms to the couch. He tore off her lace robe and kissed her all over with his burning lips. Though covering her eyes with both her hands, she thoroughly enjoyed the vigorous way in which the prince made love. All the while, she felt deep in her heart a sensation no words could describe.

Needless to say, the whole escapade had been planned by Prince Precious's personal eunuch, Hsiao-fu-tze. After this unique experience, Madame Fu refused to sleep with her husband, who had to seek satisfaction from his four concubines, though none of them was as desirable as his wife in bed. From time to time, Madame Fu and the young prince would have a rendezvous somewhere in the summer palace. He was so good at love-making that she would willingly try every possible position with him for novelty and excitement. Early one afternoon, when the two of them were imitating different postures illustrated in a pornographic book that Prince Precious had secretly acquired, Hsiao-fu-tze breathlessly dashed into the bedchamber and announced the sudden death of Emperor Yung Cheng.

After ascending the Dragon Throne as Emperor Ch'ien Lung, the former Prince Precious spared no effort in seeking sexual fulfilment with women of different tribes. By that time, Madame Fu had borne him a son and entered her middle age. Ch'ien Lung often appeared incognito to patronise the leading Chinese prostitutes in Peking. But as emperor, he could not afford to do these things too freely. However, some of his court officials reported to him that in Sinkiang there was a great beauty among the Uighurs and that she had a bodily fragrance comparable to that of a musk deer. Though a daughter of Chieftain Ho-tso and married to a young Moslem tribal chief, she was fondly called the 'Fragrant Princess' throughout Sinkiang.

Incidentally, the Manchu forces were then carrying out a large-scale military campaign against all the minority tribes in Sinkiang. Ch'ien Lung despatched a special envoy all the way to the battle-front, orally conveying his royal wish to General Chao Huei that the 'Fragrant Princess' must be captured alive at all cost.

However, when the Uighur beauty was first presented to Ch'ien Lung in Peking after the military campaign, the emperor found himself tongue-tied. Slender and well-proportioned, she looked more like a 'western goddess' because of her Turkish ancestry. Apart from the delicate fragrance of her body, her fair complexion, cherry lips, blue eyes and long eyebrows were so fascinating that Ch'ien Lung sighed to one of his personal eunuchs: 'She must have been a fairy sent down to this world by Heaven.' As soon as the emperor got over his initial bewilderment, he conferred on her the title of the 'Fragrant Royal Consort'.

Homesick and broken-hearted over the deaths of her father and husband, the Uighur beauty refused to yield herself to his royal pleasure for quite some time. But Ch'ien Lung was not lacking in patience. He ordered the Precious Moon Palace to be specially designed and built for her, as well as an elaborate Turkish bath named the Hall of Bathing Virtues. He even took the trouble to build a replica of a Moslem town near the Forbidden City, complete with mosques, bazaars and Moslem residents. From the balcony of the Precious Moon Palace, the Fragrant Royal Consort was able to see all these things and gradually overcame her homesickness.

Deeply touched by Ch'ien Lung's thoughtfulness, she eventually submitted herself to him. Perhaps inspired by Emperor Yang Ti of the Sui Dynasty, Ch'ien Lung had many full-length mirrors mounted on the walls in the Precious Moon Palace. Whenever he made love to his Fragrant Concubine, the reflections in the mirrors gave him endless excitement, the more so since her shapely body neared artistic perfection.

A horsewoman, excelling in the art of the bow and arrow, she frequently accompanied the emperor on shooting or even hunting expeditions in Jehol, a part of Inner Mongolia. Since she was the favourite concubine of Ch'ien Lung, the fashionable court painter Giuseppe Castiglione (an Italian Jesuit) was instructed to do a portrait of her in armour and helmet.

One source claims that the Fragrant Concubine was ordered to be hanged by the queen mother, for she had been plotting to assassinate Ch'ien Lung. But according to the *Imperial Records of Ch'ien Lung*, the queen mother died in 1777 and the Fragrant Concubine in 1788. It seems that the story of this tragic death must have been concocted by some Chinese scholar for anti-Manchu reasons. Moreover, a historical romance with a tragic ending appeals more to human feelings, dramatic effect apart.

LITTLE ORCHID: EMPRESS DOWAGER TZU HSI

To expose the secret sex life of Empress Dowager Tzu Hsi, the woman whose greed for political power and stubborn conservatism sped the downfall of the Manchu Dynasty, it is necessary to trace her comparatively humble origins. When Emperor Hsien Feng (reigning 1851-1861), the great-grandson of Ch'ien Lung, succeeded to the Dragon Throne, the Manchu Empire had barely recovered from the shock and humiliation of the Opium War (1840), while the forces of the Taiping Rebellion constituted a serious menace in the provinces south of the Yangtze. But strangely enough, the young emperor left state affairs in the hands of his brother Prince Kung and a few Chinese officials, for he himself was too busily involved in seeking sexual pleasures. Obsessed with the sexual charm of bound feet, he often visited the Chinese prostitutes in Peking incognito. Still, these casual affairs could hardly satisfy him. To seek his royal favour, the Imperial Administrator of the Yuan-ming Yuan (Perfect and Brilliant Garden), the then summer palace, made a special trip to South China to handpick a few beautiful Chinese girls with bound feet from Nanking, Hangchow and Soochow, and brought them back to Peking.

But as the rules of the imperial household forbade any non-Manchu women to enter the Forbidden City, Emperor Hsien Feng had to settle his new Chinese concubines in the Perfect and Brilliant Garden, which included a Roman-style palace designed and built in the reign of Ch'ien Lung by the Italian Jesuit, Castiglione.

To maintain his virility, the emperor kept more than 300 deer in the summer palace. Every day, the eunuchs would let out one jade bowl of blood from these deer in turn, and serve it to Hsien Feng immediately. With the aid of the deer blood, the emperor made love to his concubines and palace maidens at random. It was not unusual for him to pick a palace maiden and strip her in front of other women and eunuchs. Then he would perform his love act under so many pairs of staring eyes, be it in the gardens or on the lawns.

However, his over-indulgence worried the empress, who was extremely virtuous but rather weak in character. In 1853, she pleaded with his majesty to select sixty-four Manchurian palace maidens in view of the fact that he had not yet had an heir.

Among these sixty-four Manchurian maidens, was one called Little Orchid, the elder daughter of a middle-ranking Manchu official. She was assigned to take care of a small cottage in the Yuan-ming Yuan. A healthy and charming girl of nineteen, Little Orchid was gifted in singing Peking Opera and all sorts of folk songs. Having travelled with her late father during his official posts in various parts of China, she was more worldly and sophisticated than the other Manchurian maidens. Moreover, she was not lacking in patience and was able to plan things far ahead. For months she spent her time in painting orchids and decorating the small cottage tastefully and elegantly. With her allowance saved, she was very generous in bribing those eunuchs who were in emperor Hsien Feng's close attendance. In return they would keep her informed of the emperor's activities and whereabouts.

A SEXUAL TRAP FOR EMPEROR HSIEN FENG

On one very hot afternoon two years later, Hsien Feng was carried by eight eunuchs in his royal sedan chair to see one of his Chinese concubines. Deliberately the eunuchs made a detour, under hundreds of leafy wutung trees, to pass by the small cottage in the charge of Little Orchid. As Hsien Feng had never seen this small cottage before, curiosity made him stop the sedan chair and wander in. In the small cottage he was most intrigued to see so many scrolls of painted orchids hanging on the walls. He was also impressed by the tasteful arrangement of the furniture and antiques. Walking towards the window, he saw a Manchurian girl in a pink silk Manchu dress sitting by the small pond behind the cottage. Fascinated, he walked through the rear door and intended to have a closer look at the girl. But the girl seemed to be unaware of his royal presence. Fanning herself gently, she kept on singing a Soochow folk song, which was extremely pleasing to the ear.

As soon as she came to a pause, the emperor hailed her and then stalked towards her. The girl immediately fell on her knees and murmured a plea for his forgiveness. Roaring with laughter, Hsien Feng lifted her face with his own hands. Her face possessed such charm that the emperor suddenly realised what a beautiful thing he had missed. Stroking her cheeks and then her arms, he discovered that her name was Little Orchid. Unceremoniously he told her that he felt like having a bath in the small cottage. Little Orchid was shaken with excitement. She had the bath ready in no time, and helped bathe the emperor.

After Hsien Feng had left, she immediately bathed herself with jasmine-scented water and then powdered her body with meticulous care. That very night, two eunuchs of the Imperial Bedchamber Affairs came to summon her for the royal favour. She stripped herself in front of them. Then they rolled her up in a blanket and carried her on their shoulders all the way to the palace where Hsien Feng was staying for the night.* The moment she was unrolled from the blanket and placed in the dragon bed, Hsien Feng, having just drunk a jade bowl of deer's blood, entered her almost without a word. By this time, he was somewhat tired of his Chinese concubines, who always exerted self-restraint. But Little Orchid was far more uninhibited; she responded, whispered endearing words and made no secret of how much she enjoyed the whole process. After the love-making, the two same eunuchs came in to carry Little Orchid back to the small cottage. The Emperor ordered them not to squeeze the royal sperm out from her vagina.† Next morning, she was promoted to be Royal Consort Orchid. Since then, Hsien Feng seldom went to favour his Chinese concubines, who were got rid of by the new royal consort one after another. And luck was certainly on her side. One year later, she gave birth to a baby boy, who later became Emperor T'ung Chih. Now that Hsien Feng had an heir-apparent, he made Little Orchid the deputy queen, second only to the empress.

HER AFFAIRS WITH TWO EUNUCHS

But as Emperor Hsien Feng had to rely on aphrodisiacs most of the time, though still in his late twenties, Little Orchid found herself still unsatisfied after receiving his royal favour. To her delight a eunuch named Li Lien-ying was assigned to her. Covered with pimples on his face, Li was nothing to look at. But he was an excellent hair-dresser and masseur. Crafty and observant, he could see how frus-trated Deputy Queen Orchid was. As it was his job to bathe and massage her, one day he hinted that he could satisfy her if she wanted him to. Lying in the bathtub, the deputy queen jokingly told him to go ahead. Li then slipped three fingers into her private parts, thrust-ing and moving until she reached a climax. At other times, he would use his tongue to satisfy her. This unusual relationship brought Li Lien-ying closer to her and she began to confide everything in him.

In 1860, the Franco-British troops invaded Peking and burned down the Yuan-ming Yuan to rubble and ruins, shortly after Hsien Feng, his empress and Deputy Queen Orchid had fled to the hunting palace in Jehol in three mule wagons. These recurrent humiliations

*In the Manchu palace, with the exception of the queen, all women had to be carried to the emperor in the nude.

†This was a common practice in the Manchu Dynasty, believed to be an effective form of birth-control.

caused the premature death of Emperor Hsien Feng. As Emperor T'ung Chih was enthroned at the age of seven, Empress Hsien Feng was made Empress Dowager Tzu An and Deputy Queen Orchid Empress Dowager Tzu Hsi—known to the Chinese as the Empress Dowager of the Easter Palace and the Empress Dowager of the Western Palace—to form a joint regency until T'ung Chih was old enough to attend to state affairs himself.

Widowed at the age of twenty-eight, Empress Dowager Tzu Hsi, though politically ambitious, found it difficult to overcome her sexual frustration. But for the sake of discretion, she had to wait for some miracle. However, the miracle happened much sooner than expected. A eunuch named An Teh-hai turned out to be more manly than most men. Not having been properly castrated, An, with the aid of a certain kind of Tibetan aphrodisiac made for Hsien Feng by some lamas, furnished for Tzu Hsi the real enjoyment of sex. Being a eunuch, he could openly stay in the Western Palace day and night without arousing any suspicion. Since Empress Dowager Tzu Hsi liked to compare herself to Empress Wu Tse-tien of the T'ang Dynasty, An Teh-hai must then be regarded as her 'Hsueh Ao-ts'ao'. Night after night, he made love to her majesty in such a vigorous way that even she had to call a halt. Though their affair soon became a palace scandal, the two of them simply paid no heed.

The one who felt extremely jealous was Li Lien-ying, especially after An Teh-hai had been made the chief eunuch by Empress Dowager Tzu Hsi. But there was little he could do. Unable to give the Empress Dowager the kind of sexual fulfilment that An did, Li was also more junior in service than the other eunuch. Being crafty and tricky, Li chose to bide his time.

As time passed, An became more and more haughty. His only object was to please Empress Dowager Tzu Hsi. Though Empress Dowager Tzu An was nominally superior to Tzu Hsi, An Teh-hai showed little respect to her. As for the boy Emperor T'ung Chih, about fourteen or fifteen now, he never bothered about how he behaved to him. But T'ung Chih was no fool; he knew all about his mother and this disgusting eunuch. One afternoon, he took a few of his personal eunuchs to wait outside the Western Palace where his mother lived. Inside the palace, Empress Dowager Tzu Hsi and An had been taking a 'nap' in her dragon bed. Now in her thirties, Tzu Hsi had become even more voracious for sex. Believing that an afternoon nap would be good for her fading beauty, she had to have An make love to her before she could doze off. This particular afternoon, the chief eunuch had to try a variety of positions to satiate her royal desire. When he saw that she eventually slumbered, he stalked out of the palace as usual. About twenty or thirty yards away, the boy emperor and his eunuch 'commandos' jumped at him, and he was dragged into the emperor's own palace. An, still regarding this as a young boy's prank, laughed contemptuously. But the precocious emperor summarily ordered his eunuchs to strip off An's trousers to examine him. Scared, An tried to struggle in vain. Fortunately for him, his member failed to rise, perhaps because of exhaustion resulting from his 'nap' with Tzu Hsi, or perhaps because of his fear for his life. Since T'ung Chih could not prove anything, An Teh-hai was let off.

That very night, he reported the whole episode to Empress Dowager Tzu Hsi. Angry though she was, there was nothing she could do about her own son. To cool things down, she sent An Teh-hai to Hangchow and Soochow to purchase a new wardrobe for her, hoping that his temporary absence would serve to pacify her son's anger and stop him from committing more mischief.

THE FORMER VICTIM OF THE 'PURPLE GRAPES'

To An Teh-hai, such a mission was more than welcome. In the past years, he had accumulated quite a sizable fortune by accepting bribes from the court officials. But to go to the richest provinces south of the Yangtze as a purchasing envoy could easily turn him into a millionaire. For his personal comfort as well as to collect more 'presents' from various local officials, he sailed southward along the Grand Canal. On his junk, he flew the Dragon and Phoenix standards of Empress Dowager Tzu Hsi. To attract more attention, he also displayed his personal standard on which was inscribed 'His Excellency Special Envoy An Teh-hai'. Bringing with him a host of singing prostitutes and a band of musicians, he stopped at every borough and county to receive tributes from the local officials. But since, according to the Manchu law, no eunuch was supposed to leave Peking except in the train of the emperor or some member of the royal family, some officials could not but suspect that An Teh-hai was in fact a confidence trickster. They hastened to send urgent reports to the governor of Shantung, Ting Pao-chen.

About the same time, Governor Ting received a personal letter from An Teh-hai, hinting that he would appreciate his hospitality in whatever form the governor thought fit. Actually, to Ting the chief eunuch was no stranger. A few years back, when he had been a court official in Peking, he had been selected by Empress Dowager Tzu Hsi as a potential imperial tutor for T'ung Chih. However, while awaiting the empress dowager to give instructions in the imperial study, Ting saw a jade plate full of purple grapes, looking inviting on a side table. As grapes were not yet in season, he picked one and put it into his mouth. To his surprise, he found the grape tasted like a candy. This must be some kind of preserved grape, he told himself. Then, all of a sudden, he felt the 'grape' produce a most unusual effect. His member became erect, almost bursting through his blue-lace official gown. He was desperate to make love to any woman in sight.

At this moment, two eunuchs rushed in to tell him that Her Majesty Empress Dowager Tzu Hsi was approaching the imperial study. Frightened about his unpresentable state, Ting feigned sudden illness, rolling on the floor as if in great pain. The empress dowager walked in with An Teh-hai in close attendance. She ordered a few eunuchs to carry Ting out, dismissing his sudden illness as something unfortunate. But observant as she was, it did not take her long to discover that one of the purple grapes was missing. Producing a big silk handkerchief as casually as she could, she wrapped up the whole plate of purple grapes and took them back to her own palace.

While reading the urgent reports and An's personal letter, this scene flashed back in Governor Ting's mind. He was determined to get rid of the chief eunuch. He sent a regiment of cavalry to ride along both shores of the Grand Canal, awaiting the appropriate moment to arrest An Teh-hai. One evening, when An's junk was but thirty or forty miles from the provincial border of Shantung, the chief eunuch celebrated his birthday. He sat in a chair to receive the kowtows of his subordinates, while in another chair beside him he displayed a dragon dress of Tzu Hsi, as if she were there for this special occasion.

Ting's cavalry came into action. They pushed aboard and tied up An and his followers with strong ropes, escorting them to the governor's office in Tsinan. Refusing to recognise An when the chief eunuch was being tried, Governor Ting submitted an urgent report to Peking, seeking the royal approval for An's immediate execution. Upon receiving the governor's report, Empress Dowager Tzu Hsi almost fainted. But both Empress Dowager Tzu An and Prince Kung, the then prime minister, insisted that An Teh-hai must be executed if only because he had violated the imperial law by leaving Peking on his own. For two days, Tzu Hsi kept on weeping and refused to sign the imperial decree of approval. Persuasively, Li Lien-ying convinced her that she should do so without hesitation, or the scandal would become nation-wide. Tearfully she signed the approval. After An had been executed, she had another shock. It was reported that An's body was exposed after his execution. Then another report relieved her mind. Actually, Governor Ting ordered another eunuch's body to be exposed, pretending it to be An Teh-hai's, for the rumours about An's affair with Empress Dowager of the Western Palace were spreading through the province of Shantung like wild-fire.

TZU HSI AND HER SON BY 'UNCLE' JUNG LU

Without An Teh-hai, Tzu Hsi's life became empty. Now the chief eunuch, Li Lien-ying, tried to incur her royal pleasure with his tongue and fingers once again. But the empress dowager found this surrogate hardly comparable with An's genuine love-making. She resorted to the Buddhist classics and a vegetarian diet for spiritual consolation; but she would still have sudden outbursts of anger from time to time. It was not hard for Li to guess the cause. With the acumen of a detective he had discovered that when the empress dowager was a young girl she had some sort of affair with her mother's cousin, Jung Lu. A dandy all his life, Jung Lu was by now a second-rate official in Peking. On one occasion, he tactfully suggested to Tzu Hsi that she might want to summon her 'uncle' Jung Lu to consult him on some state affairs.

The suggestion was gladly accepted. With her royal consent, Li Lien-ying then proceeded to rush Jung Lu into the Western Palace for an audience. While Jung Lu was waiting in the principal hall rather uneasily, Li Lien-ying reappeared and led him into the royal bedchamber. In casual dress the empress dowager was reclining on a couch, the French perfume she wore smelling intoxicatingly enough to make Jung Lu's heart beat vigorously. When he was about to kneel down as court etiquette required, Tzu Hsi signalled him not to bother. At this point, Li had already disappeared quietly. The empress dowager asked Jung Lu to sit by her on the couch, stroking his face with her newly-manicured fingers. In whispers she reminded him of those old days when they used to play the 'bride and groom' game in her father's back gardens. Jung Lu stammered, for he had not the slightest inkling of her majesty's revived passion for him. Tzu Hsi giggled happily like a little girl; she made her 'uncle' put his hands beneath her casual dress. Jung Lu's roving hands seemed to have some sort of magic touch, for the empress dowager hastily thrust her hand between his legs and asked him to proceed. A little nervous, Jung Lu cast a few glances around. 'You timid fool,' Tzu Hsi pinched his cheek with her other hand. 'How dare anyone come in at this moment?'

When they were both stripped, Jung Lu was amazed to see that her skin was as smooth as that of a young maiden. He pressed his lips all over her body to enjoy the silky sensation, sniffing at the same time the mixed fragrance of French perfume and her flesh. Itchy and eager not to wait any longer, the empress dowager separated her long, slender legs wide apart and put them around Jung Lu's waist. At this moment Jung Lu knew exactly where his loyalty lay. He pushed his expansive weapon into her almost with violence, only to be greeted with sighs of satisfaction. Thrusting rhythmically to the accompaniment of her endearments, he could feel under him the convulsive jerks of her naked body. At long last, she asked him to discharge, holding him tightly and panting.

As they lay side by side, caressing each other, the all-powerful empress dowager talked tenderly in whispers. She admitted to her 'uncle' that pleasure so intense had been previously unknown to her. In her mind she secretly compared his virility to that of Emperor Hsien Feng and that of An Teh-hai; neither of them was remotely comparable to the man beside her.

After Jung Lu had excused himself from her royal attendance, she began to feel the effects of exhaustion. Like a shadow Li Lien-ying floated in, carrying her into the adjoining chamber and laying her in the silver bathtub of scented hot water. He bathed her, rubbed her with dry clean towels and then massaged her with thorough care.

Revived, Tzu Hsi smoked two pipes of opium, thinking hard. Her pensive mood, however, did not escape Li Lien-ying's notice. As if talking to himself, he murmured that the post of Superintendent of Palace Affairs had been vacant for a considerable time.

The empress dowager immediately took the hint. Smilingly, she wrote a letter of appointment, asking Li to deliver it to Jung Lu without delay. As the Superintendent of Palace Affairs, Jung Lu now had free access to all the palaces as required by his duty. His frequent visits to the Western Palace hardly aroused any gossip, for after all Empress Dowager Tzu Hsi was his niece in everybody's eyes. Moreover, having devoted herself to Buddhist studies ever since Hsien Feng's death, Empress Dowager Tzu An habitually left everything to Tzu Hsi's care in spite of her seniority in position.

With her sex-life well looked after by her 'uncle' Jung Lu, Empress Dowager Tzu Hsi became less difficult, to the relief of all court officials. But as a Chinese saying goes, 'extreme happiness breeds sorrows', and she suddenly found herself in grave difficulty. Due either to sheer negligence or to uncontrollable passion, she had become pregnant. Having had a couple of abortions when An Teh-hai was alive, she instructed Li Lien-ying to find the same kind of medicine in the imperial dispensary.

With a long face Li came back to report that there was no more of it. Desperate, Tzu Hsi even considered the possibility of going to an ordinary herbal physician incognito. Both Jung Lu and Li strongly advised against this reckless act. With days growing into weeks, even the ever-resourceful empress dowager became resigned to her fate. One afternoon, when she was still racking her brains for a solution a eunuch came in to announce the courtesy call of her sister Princess Ch'un. The empress dowager was more than pleased; she hastily received this younger sister, to reveal her secret. Dumbfounded, Princess Ch'un sat there like a wooden doll. Tzu Hsi patted her shoulder fondly and came straight to the point. She instructed her to pretend pregnancy right at this very moment and summoned Li Lien-ying to break the news to Prince Ch'un. When the prince received Li the chief eunuch eloquently told him that his wife had deliberately gone to confide in the empress dowager about her pregnancy, since the two of them were so close to each other. Like all Manchu princes, Prince Ch'un kept quite a few concubines and he could not tell when he had last slept with his wife.

However, when Princess Ch'un's baby was due to be born, Empress Dowager Tzu Hsi moved to Prince Ch'un's residence for a few days to look after her sister. Attended by Li Lien-ying and a couple of court midwives, the princess 'gave birth' to a baby boy. She felt fine after the childbirth, though the 'supervising' empress dowager was pale as rice-paper. Two days later, both midwives died of food poisoning almost simultaneously.

THE BOY EMPEROR AND THE 'PLUM POISON'

As a result of this rather disquieting experience, Empress Dowager Tzu Hsi had to be more cautious. Though still having a rendezvous with Jung Lu from time to time, she was no longer able to enjoy their love-making so wholeheartedly. But while the empress dowager was seeking sexual pleasures more cautiously than ever, it was now the turn of her son Emperor T'ung Chih to go to extremes. Guided by his tutor, Wang Ch'ing-ch'i, T'ung Chih often disguised himself as the son of a wealthy merchant to visit prostitutes outside the Forbidden City. Almost sixteen at this time, he regarded himself as fit as a fighting cock. The two of them would slip out practically every afternoon to sow wild oats. Without sufficient time to patronise the high-class courtesans, they went to the cheapest prostitutes in the southern outskirts of the city to have quick sex. Like his father, the late Emperor Hsien Feng, T'ung Chih even went to the extent of seducing women of very humble background.

When Empress Dowager Tzu Hsi heard rumours of these escapades she discussed with Empress Dowager Tzu An the desirability of getting the boy emperor an empress. Four candidates were selected, and Tzu Hsi's niece was among them. Knowing that her son had an eye for beautiful girls, Tzu Hsi was confident about the chances of her own niece, who was both charming and beautiful. Unexpectedly T'ung Chih picked the fat and homely daughter of a Manchu official named Ch'ung Ch'i to be the empress-designate. Furious, Tzu Hsi demanded an explanation from her son. To make things easier, Empress Dowager Tzu An advised T'ung Chih to take the other girls as deputy queens as well.

On the wedding night T'ung Chih found his new empress so unattractive that he turned his back on her and had a sound sleep. Three nights later, Tzu Hsi's niece, now titled Deputy Queen Hui, was carried into his bedchamber by two eunuchs of the imperial bedchamber affairs to receive his favour. After she had been unrolled from the blanket wrapped around her, she climbed on to the far end of the dragon bed, lying quietly with her eyes and mouth tightly closed, as required by palace etiquette. Though T'ung Chih had had a lot of experience with prostitutes and women of loose virtue, he did not know how to deflower a virgin. However, he did make some efforts to warm her up, though with no response. Bored of the dumb show, T'ung Chih abruptly sat up and left the bed. Half an hour later, the two eunuchs knocked and came in to wrap up the naked deputy queen to carry her away, totally unaware of the fact that she was still a virgin.

The same procedure happened with the other deputy queens successively. The emperor immediately thought of those experiences of the old days that had so excited him. He again sought Wang Ch'ing-ch'i as a companion and resumed his former habits. As a consequence of this reckless indulgence in sex, he contracted syphilis, discreetly called by the Chinese the 'strawberry boils' or the 'plum poison'. But when the twelve imperial physicians were summoned to treat his illness, none of them had the courage to disclose the truth. Timidly they reported to the two empress dowagers that his majesty had contracted the illness of 'Heavenly Flower' (smallpox). It goes without saying that they were ordered to prescribe medicine accordingly.

Naturally T'ung Chih's condition worsened all the time. Suspicious, Tzu Hsi consulted her 'uncle' Jung Lu, who bluntly told her that all the symptoms sounded like that of the 'plum poison'. The empress dowager sent for the imperial physicians and forced them to reveal their true diagnosis. They confessed that they had deliberately made the wrong diagnosis to protect the emperor's prestige and reputation, and that they would now treat it as the 'plum poison'. But it was already too late to save T'ung Chih's life. He died shortly after, at the age of eighteen.

AN ACTOR IN EMPRESS DOWAGER TZU HSI'S BED

Empress Dowager Tzu Hsi, upon learning of her son's death, decided not to disclose the news instantly. Instead, she persuaded Empress Dowager Tzu An to summon the Council of Princes to nominate the next incumbent of the Dragon Throne, since 'the emperor was quite ill'. At the council, Tzu Hsi casually suggested that the son of Prince Ch'un seemed to be the logical choice. This was quite a shock for all the princes present, for according to the Manchu practice the pretender should be one of T'ung Chih's nephews. In an outburst Prince Ch'un stood up shouting: 'No, certainly not him!'

The other princes thought he was being modest, but Prince Ch'un had long discovered that his nominal son was actually the illegitimate child of Empress Dowager Tzu Hsi and Jung Lu. Paying no heed to him, Tzu Hsi insisted and all the princes agreed with her. It was at this point that she announced that T'ung Chih had just passed away. The date of the imperial funeral and the period of national mourning were then solemnly declared. Meanwhile, the four-year-old illegitimate son of Tzu Hsi was proclaimed Emperor Kuang Hsu. This enabled Empress Dowager Tzu Hsi to continue her powers of regency.

Though her political ambitions had again been fulfilled, Tzu Hsi, now in her forties, was keener on sexual pleasure than before. As her old lover Jung Lu had by chance seduced her niece, Deputy Queen Hui of the late T'ung Chih, she felt the need to have a younger man for her own use. Through Deputy Queen Hui she learned of the famous actor Chin Yu-lou, who was then the rage among the Peking women. On the pretext of celebrating Kuang Hsu's birthday, the empress dowager ordered Chin's Peking Opera group to stage a special performance in the imperial palace. After the performance, the famous actor was granted a special audience by Tzu Hsi in the Western Palace, which lasted a couple of hours.

A few months later, Chin's fans were disappointed to learn of the early retirement of the famous actor from the stage. But at about the same time, Empress Dowager Tzu Hsi, through the able arrangement of Chief Eunuch Li Lien-ying, had acquired as her personal attendant a 'Manchurian' woman who could be taken for the actor's twin sister. From morning to night, Tzu Hsi never let this personal attendant out of her sight. Between the empress dowager and her there seemed to be an intimacy which puzzled everyone in the imperial palace with the exception of Li Lien-ying. Even Jung Lu was wholly denied the chance of seeing her majesty.

One summer afternoon, when Tzu Hsi was having her nap, Empress Dowager Tzu An dropped in for a chat. Unable to find any eunuch or palace maiden to announce her call, Tzu An strolled into Tzu Hsi's bedchamber, without giving it a second thought. No sooner had she pushed the door open than Tzu Hsi poked her head out of the lace bed-curtains, her face as red as a sunset. Her slightly odd behaviour led Tzu An to believe that she was not feeling well. The kind-hearted woman, full of concern, walked up to her in order to feel her forehead. Only at this moment did she catch a glimpse of someone beside Tzu Hsi, in the process of rolling down from the other side of the bed, obviously in great haste.

Assuming it must be one of the palace maidens, Tzu An shouted at this person in anger. From behind the bed emerged a naked man with a woman's hairdo, prostrating himself and begging for his life, saying that he had had to give up his stage career at Empress Dowager Tzu Hsi's explicit order. Meanwhile, the ever-arrogant Tzu Hsi covered herself up with a bedsheet, speechless.

Though always lenient and hesitant, Empress Dowager Tzu An for once realised that she must take prompt action, for the reputation of the imperial family was at stake. She immediately sent for Chief Eunuch Li Lien-ying and ordered him to silence this naked actor as quickly as he could. With the assistance of a few eunuchs, Li dragged the trembling Chin Yu-lou out and beat him to death in the principal hall with sticks and rods.

To console Tzu Hsi, Empress Dowager Tzu An stayed on to offer some gentle advice regarding the moral standards required of an emperor's widow. Though furious and full of hatred, Tzu Hsi feigned remorse and promised her counterpart that hereafter she would devote herself to both state affairs and Buddhist studies. Her persuasive eloquence convinced Tzu An, who impulsively produced Emperor Hsien Feng's letter of authorisation for her to execute Tzu Hsi 'in case of necessity' and burned it before the latter's eyes.

THE ORIGIN OF CHINESE EUNUCHS

As soon as Tzu An was gone, Tzu Hsi and Chief Eunuch Li had a long session. A few days later, Li was sent by Empress Dowager Tzu Hsi to the Eastern Palace to present some of Tzu An's favourite pastry. After telling the chief eunuch to thank Tzu Hsi for her thoughtfulness, Tzu An ate the pastry while reading some Buddhist classics. That very afternoon she died of acute stomach pains before the imperial physicians could be sent for. In tears and choked with feeling, Tzu Hsi rushed over to pay her condolences. But when her eyes met Li Lien-ying's they exchanged a meaningful look, barely discernible. However, now that she was the sole empress dowager entrusted with regency powers, Tzu Hsi immediately gave the chief eunuch an honorary rank equivalent to that of a minister, enabling him to bully most high officials and accept bribes to his heart's content.

As far as eunuchs entrusted with immense powers were concerned, Li Lien-ying was by no means without precedent. During the reign of Hsi Tsung of the Ming Dynasty (1621-1627) the then chief eunuch, Wei Chung-hsien, being the lover of Hsi Tsung's wet nurse Madame Ke, dominated state affairs and slaughtered many patriotic scholars. Before Wei, another chief eunuch named Liu Chin, serving Emperor Wu Tsung (reigning 1506-1521), was so powerful that he was addressed by the Ming court officials as 'Your Royal Highness' ('Nine Thousand Years', to use the original term).

Chinese history reveals that the eunuch system was first established in the Chou Dynasty (1122-221 B.C.). At that time the duties which later became those of a eunuch were carried out by a 'domestic official' (Nei Huan). However, in the reign of the First Emperor of Ch'in (221-206 B.C.), the affair between the queen mother and Lao Ai made the emperor order all 'domestic officials' to be castrated, which set the precedent. After the enforcement of castration the same two characters continued to be used to denote a eunuch. In the Han Dynasty, castration was also adopted as one of the many forms of punishment. Ssu-ma Chien, the most eminent Chinese historian serving at the court of Emperor Wu Ti, was castrated because he had recommended General Li Ling, who defected to the Hsiung Nu invaders.

From the Han Dynasty to the Sung Dynasty, those who offered their services to be eunuchs had to be castrated by the imperial surgeons, and therefore the operations were properly performed. The eunuchs in those dynasties could be politically influential, but rarely caused a palace scandal.

But in the Manchu Dynasty, especially after the reign of Hsien Feng, the prolonged war with the Taiping rebels and the famine brought destitution and homelessness to countless people. Desperation drove some of them to seek work as eunuchs in the hope that they might be lucky enough to become rich after serving in the imperial palace, since bribe-taking was a common practice among many influential eunuchs. These applicants could have themselves castrated first and then be examined by those eunuchs already in the imperial household, sometimes perfunctorily if they were given a handsome amount of 'respectful money'. It was in this way that An Teh-hai succeeded in being selected to serve Empress Dowager Tzu

Hsi in the fullest sense.

Other eunuchs in Tzu Hsi's period of influence might not be as lucky as An Teh-hai or Li Lien-ying. But many of them frequented prostitutes, kept mistresses or even had wives, to public knowledge and as has been recorded by a number of contemporary scholars in their memoirs. After the downfall of the Imperial Manchu Court in 1911, many eunuchs in Peking started to earn their living by recounting their personal reminiscences of the Forbidden City for pecuniary rewards. Such narratives have helped Chinese scholars to fill many lacunae in their accounts of Manchu palace life—heavily guarded from public knowledge ever since the ruthless censorship initiated by Emperor Yung Cheng in 1723.

THE MANCHUS INDULGE IN HOMOSEXUALITY

That the Manchus should have resorted to homosexuality for another form of sexual fulfilment was no mere coincidence. Towards the end of the Ming Dynasty, homosexual practices were already in vogue. Many outstanding scholars and poets were known for their 'peach-sharing' romances. Apart from keeping concubines, they also bought young and handsome boys to 'look after their books', and these were discreetly called 'shu t'ung' (book-caring boys). In fact, many of these book-caring boys were used as females whenever their masters felt the urge, especially when they undertook long journeys without their concubines.

At the beginning of the Ch'ing Dynasty, the eminent poet Ch'en Ch'i-nien even wrote a poem to publicise his homosexual relationship with the book-caring boy Chih-yung (Purple Cloud), of his friend Mao Pi-chiang, a scholar as well as a wealthy man. The poem was written to celebrate Chih-yung's marriage to a girl.

As a less civilised tribe and a conquering minority, the Manchus could not help admiring the more 'sophisticated attitude' towards sexual pleasures, among other things, of these scholars. Moreover, as the Manchu leaders specifically forbade mixed marriages to maintain the 'purity' of Manchu blood, to commit homosexual practices with the Chinese was not regarded as an offence, and therefore the Manchus resorted to sodomy as a safety valve.

From the reign of Emperor Hsien Feng onwards, Peking Opera became a most popular entertainment and all the women's parts were played by young, effeminate boys. These transvestites, while offstage, were compelled to submit themselves to the desires of the court officials, if only to maintain their popularity and acting careers.

Though Hsien Feng had many women—including Little Orchid (later Empress Dowager Tzu Hsi)—to satisfy his sexual desires, he occasionally sought variety in homosexual practices. The leading actor of that time, Chu Lien-feng, who looked extremely beautiful when he impersonated a woman on stage, caught his royal fancy on one occasion. From time to time, Chu would be summoned to the Yuan-ming Yuan to be favoured by him. But before receiving the emperor's favour, the transvestite had already associated himself with a boy friend named Lu Mao-chung, who served in the court as an imperial remonstrant. When Lu learned about the emperor's affair with Chu, jealousy spurred him to submit a memorandum to Hsien Feng, insinuating that his majesty should devote more of his time to attending to state affairs and less to visiting transvestites. This infuriated the emperor and Lu was immediately banished. Already a victim of consumption in its advanced stage, Chu Lien-feng took his own life for fear that he himself might get involved, because of his association with the banished imperial remonstrant.

Not to be outdone by his father, Emperor T'ung Chih derived some pleasure from homosexual practices too. After his marriage, he suddenly found women boring and wanted to try something new. Disguising himself as the son of a rich merchant, he made the acquaintance of a young scholar from Hunan in a fashionable restaurant. The two of them hit it off almost instantly. Still hardly eighteen years of age, the emperor went to the young scholar's dwelling place and willingly played the part of a female. For some days they were often seen in public, hand-in-hand or arms around waists, like lovers. Soon the scandal reached Prince Kung's ears and the royal uncle sent a general of the Imperial Guards to search for the disguised monarch. T'ung Chih was located in a wine shop, carousing and fondling with the young scholar. The general walked up and, addressing him as 'Your Majesty', persuaded T'ung Chih to return to the imperial palace for the sake of his personal security. Embarrassed at the exposure of his identity, the teen-age emperor left the wine shop, albeit reluctantly. It goes without saying that the young scholar had the scare of his life. Immediately he packed up and went back to his native province Hunan, no longer daring to sit for the State Examination.

As for many of the court officials, they were more discreet about the practice. Though there were plenty of male prostitutes, with their houses open to homosexuals, these officials preferred to have their 'personal attendants' whom they could take everywhere, even when they were on night-shift in the Cabinet Office inside the Forbidden City. Many Manchu military commanders were equally fond of homosexual practices, partly because they had to solve their sexual problems during military campaigns. It was not unusual to see some generals surrounded by 'personal aides' wearing powder and rouge like women. The natives of Peking despised homosexuals, especially those who acted as females. They were disdainfully called 'rabbits' or 'hsiang ku' (mock women), with a social status even lower than that of prostitutes.

THE 'RABBIT' BECOMES A PRIME MINISTER

But one 'rabbit' must be singled out, for he was lucky enough to be favoured by Emperor Ch'ien Lung and eventually became his prime minister for years. This particular prime minister was Ho Shen, who caught Ch'ien Lung's eyes when he served as one of the bearers of the dragon sedan chair. A glimpse of his face so impressed the emperor that he decided that Ho Shen must be the reincarnation of his father's concubine, whom he had tried to seduce without success. He was even more convinced after finding out that Ho Shen had been born on the very day that that concubine of his father's was ordered to be hanged by his mother. At first Ho Shen thought Ch'ien Lung was crazy, then he resolved to indulge him. Frequently Ch'ien Lung would send for Ho Shen to sleep with him in the imperial study on the pretext of discussing state affairs. In this way commenced the advancement of the latter's official career until it reached the height of the premiership. Perhaps for the sake of discretion, the emperor encouraged Ho Shen to get married; and when his son grew up the young man was made the Prince Consort of Ch'ien Lung's youngest daughter, an honour seldom bestowed on princes or dukes. However, Ho Shen's downfall came after the death of Ch'ien Lung. By then, Emperor Chai Ch'ing had been enthroned for quite a few years. The new emperor had all along been aware of Ho Shen's corruption and embezzlement. But he refrained from taking action until after his father had been dead for some months. As soon as sixty-eight high officials petitioned to have Ho Shen removed Chai Ch'ing immediately had him arrested and put on trial. When Ho Shen was proved guilty, the young emperor allowed him to hang himself, in view of his 'outstanding service to the late Emperor Ch'ien Lung'. Even Chai Ch'ing was taken aback when he found out that the total value of gold, silver, jewelry, furs and real estate confiscated from the 'rabbit' prime minister was worth far more than the holdings of the imperial treasury.

THE BLACK MULE WAGON MYSTERY

Whereas the Manchu aristocrats sought sexual pleasures in every imaginable manner, their wives and concubines could not but feel neglected or even deserted. Frustration motivated them to look for some extra-marital 'comforts', if only to avenge themselves. The easiest way for them was to have casual affairs with their male relations or menservants. But in view of possible scandal, such arrangements could not be regularised in a satisfactory way. However, it was not until towards the end of the Manchu Dynasty that these frustrated princesses and duchesses became really reckless and audacious. With the aid of some eunuchs and servants they could trust, these noble women were able to enjoy both novelty and variety.

In those days, especially after the Boxer Rebellion (1900), the streets in Peking were mostly deserted at night. On many occasions, when a healthy-looking young man happened to be walking alone in some of these dimly-lit streets, a black mule wagon would suddenly drive by. Before he had time to step back, a couple of thugs would swiftly drag him into the wagon. Gagged and blindfolded, all he could apprehend was the rumbling of the wagon's wheels over the rugged roads.

One or two days later, this same young man would reappear, pale and exhausted. He would be evasive about what had happened to him, though looking rather pleased with himself. However, when similar cases continued to happen at a growing rate, some parents of the missing youths lodged complaints with the garrison commander of the imperial capital. But oddly enough, no action was taken by the commander, though he always promised to do his best.

Meanwhile, a lot of young men seemed anxious to be picked up by the mysterious black mule wagons. Some of them deliberately sauntered along the dark side-streets like adventurers. But their anxiety went unheeded. Everywhere in Peking people kept on talking about the black wagons, and yet the mystery remained unsolved.

One wintry night in 1902, a young scholar named Liang was trying to find his way back to the boarding-house where he stayed near the Drum Tower in the northern part of the city. He had just arrived from his home town in Kuangtung Province, to take part in the forth-coming State Examination. Still a stranger, Liang became a little nervous when he realised that he had lost his way. Just then a black mule wagon suddenly rolled by. Intending to ask the driver for direc-tions, the young scholar shouted at it. The wagon stopped and two well-dressed men poked their heads out, asking him what they could do for him. Liang hastened to explain, but his heavy Cantonese accent seemed to please the two men. They offered to give him a lift, which he gratefully accepted. When he got into the wagon, one of the men courteously passed him his snuff-box. Unwilling to be rude, the young scholar inhaled some of the snuff. A sudden drowsiness overcame him and he dropped into sleep almost instantly.

When he woke up, Liang found himself in a luxuriously furnished bedchamber by himself. Wondering whether he was in a dream, he bit his finger and it hurt him. He was about to stand up when a feminine voice sounded behind him. Instinctively he turned around. Before his eyes stood a woman in her early thirties, smiling at him. Though not exactly beautiful, she obviously possessed an aristocratic air. Liang politely asked her how he had got there. The woman told him that it was the God of Fate at work. Then she clapped her dainty hands and a young maid came in with two jade cups of tea. Thirsty and cold, Liang drank the proffered tea at once. The young maid quietly left the room while the woman unceremoniously sat next to him, putting a slender arm around his neck. At the same time Liang felt the effects of the tea already stoking up his passion. He could hardly wait for the woman to undress before he pushed her on to the bed. With unusual vigour he made love to her; she seemed to be very good at the game. He must have continued for almost an hour when the woman gently asked him to halt.

They slept in each other's arms afterwards. While still half-asleep, Liang felt a hand fondling the most sensitive part of his anatomy. Roused, he climbed on to the female body next to him and made love again. Only when he entered could he tell that it was another woman. At this point, it was too late to do anything but carry on. When they were both fulfilled the woman lit the lamp by the bed-side. She was slightly smaller in build than the other one, and younger too. Liang asked her a few questions and she smilingly quoted a line from an ancient poem: 'Seek as much pleasure as you can while still young.' She advised him to rest for a little while before she dressed and left.

But Liang had hardly had forty winks when he was awakened by a third woman. With more sex appeal, she was even more demanding than the other two. Fortunately, the young scholar was still virile enough not to disappoint her.

In the morning Liang rose and tried to open the door. But it was locked from outside. He also found that all windows were sealed. Putting his ear against one of the windows, he could hear the sound of rustling leaves in the wintry wind. He sensed that the suite he was in must be somewhere in a large garden.

The meals served by the same young maid were excellent, consisting of many delicacies he had never eaten before. To him the second night was most memorable, for all three women came to him at the same time. Prior to love-making, he was given a couple of 'nourishing pills' to be washed down with the same kind of tea he had previously drunk. With three naked women in bed with him Liang took care of them one after another. After the amorous night was over the young scholar was so exhausted that he dropped into a dreamless slumber.

Suddenly, the bed became as chilly as if it had been moved into the open air. Liang opened his eyes and found himself dressed and leaning against the gate of his boarding house. Too tired to think, he walked straight to his room to have another sleep. While undressing, he discovered a gold hair-pin in the pocket of his inner garment. Without giving it a thought, he put it under his pillow and slumbered away.

When he again woke up, the cleaner told him that he had not come back for three successive days and nights. Liang pocketed the gold hair-pin and went straight to see an old friend of his father's. After listening to him, his father's friend made him promise not to breathe a word about his experience as long as he was in Peking. Then Liang showed him the gold hair-pin and for the first time noticed some Manchurian words inscribed on it. Upon reading the inscription, the older man was speechless for a while. Then he determinedly commanded Liang to leave Peking straight away, not even permitting him to go back to his boarding-house to pack.

It was years later that Liang realised that he had spent three amorous nights in the residence of a certain Manchu prince who was very much in Empress Dowager Tzu Hsi's favour. He began to tell some of his friends this unique experience only after the downfall of the Manchu Court, though not without some relish and nostalgia.

CHAPTER FIVE

Shanghai—the Paradise of Sinners

At the turn of the century, after the Boxers had failed to throw out the foreign devils as Empress Dowager Tzu Hsi would have dearly wanted, the wicked old Manchu woman spent most of her time in the Yi-ho Yuan—the new summer palace built with funds originally appropriated for the navy—for recreation and relaxation since she was 'tired of handling political affairs'. To prolong her youthful looks and maintain her fair complexion, she took pearl powder as prescribed by the imperial physicians and bathed in goats' milk. Though having been addressed as the 'Old Buddha' by all eunuchs and court officials for quite some years now, she showed not the slightest intention of abandoning carnal pleasures or worldly cares. With her illegitimate son Emperor Kuang Hsu making feeble efforts to introduce minor reforms, the empress dowager, around whom the conservatives rallied, kept an eye on the happenings in the Forbidden City like an eagle hovering over the Western Mountains behind the summer palace, ready to snatch back the Dragon Throne any moment. The atmosphere in Peking was charged with tension and full of rumours.

It was at this time that Shanghai (Upper Sea) emerged as a paradise for those who could afford to seek a foothold there. Previously a fishing village under the jurisdiction of Pao-shan hsien (county), Shanghai was one of the five seaports opened to Western traders after the Manchus had been defeated in the Opium War. Girdled by the Whampoo River and situated off the East China Sea, Shanghai had been growing by leaps and bounds, especially since the Taiping Rebellion. With all foreigners sheltered under the protective umbrella of extra-territoriality in the International Settlement (under British control) and the French Concession, this gigantic city thrived on the conflicts and divided rule between the Chinese and the Westerners, notably the British and the French.

With plenty of legal loopholes provided by circumstances, both European and Chinese adventurers sought to make quick fortunes in this city of paradoxes. Their approaches might be different, but between the Boxer Rebellion and the 'liberation' by the Chinese Communists in 1949, for half a century these soldiers of fortune kept marching on. While civil wars, famines and calamities befell other parts of China, gold bullion and silver dollars poured into Shanghai all the time.

DIFFERENT CLASSES OF PROSTITUTES

In the eyes of the wealthy Chinese, the International Settlement and the French Concession in Shanghai were as secure as any foreign country. Winked at by the British and French authorities, the quick-profit seekers, with the collaboration of secret societies such as the Red Gang and the Blue Gang, staked their money on traffic in opium, gambling and prostitution. In little or no time, Shanghai replaced Peking as the 'joy-seeking arena'.

Before, the high-class prostitutes had adorned the southern city of Peking, reaping profits from princes, dukes and high officials. But after the Boxer Rebellion, they moved southward to Shanghai, settling down in the British-style terrace houses off Tibet Road in the International Settlement. These prostitutes, nicknamed by the Shanghainese 'ch'ang-san' (a certain piece in Chinese dominoes), were only accessible to customers of means. To patronise a prostitute of this class, one had to be introduced by some friend who had already become a regular of the 'house'. The friend would first take one there for a 'tea round'. On such occasions, the procuress would display all her 'foster-daughters' as though in a beauty parade. The prospective customer, though already having someone in mind, had to patiently view them all—and pay for each. Once he came across the one he fancied, he would ask her to have a cup of tea with him. At this point, the procuress would suggest that he and the introducer could go to this prostitute's room for a brief chat. When they left, he must leave a handsome sum for this cup of tea and a generous tip for the servants.

After that, whenever he was invited to a flower banquet given by a friend, he could send this particular prostitute a 'call-slip' through the restaurant where they were dining. If she were very popular, she would appear belatedly, sitting behind him for a few minutes and then excusing herself. If the customer wanted to see more of her he could ask her to make another 'call' after she had been elsewhere. Sometimes the prostitute would not reappear; sometimes she would. It all depended whether she regarded him worth her while.

Actually, the flower banquet came into vogue as early as the late Ming Dynasty. The banquet was so named because prostitutes were subtly called 'flowers'. In those days, poets and scholars mixed with prostitutes socially and openly. It was a dinner party in every sense, except that each guest would take his favourite prostitute with him. Apart from offering sexual pleasures, these prostitutes were proficient in poetry-writing, lyre-playing, painting or calligraphy. In many ways, they were the 'girlfriends' of these joy-seekers. Throughout the dinner these talented courtesans would paint, sing, write poems or make witty remarks. In the then capital, Nanking, a small river named Ch'in-huai ran through the southern part of the city—ironically enough, not far away from the solemn-looking Temple of Confucius and the State Examination Assembly Hall—and on it flower banquets were given on beautifully decorated junks night after night, as if to defy the Chinese sage.

In the period of the Manchu Dynasty, when famous prostitutes concentrated in Peking, the flower banquets were usually held in the prostitutes' houses, since the nobility and high officials had to be discreet about their wanton life. But in Shanghai it was a different matter. Thousands of miles away from Peking and somewhat similar to a foreign country, Shanghai offered the joy-seekers—be they high officials or millionaires—a haven where they could wholly relax. That was why the flower banquets were uninhibitedly held in restaurants or private houses.

A LONG WAY TO GO TO BED

To sleep with a first-class prostitute the interested customer had to do something special to give her 'face'. He had to throw a special banquet in her 'house', inviting his friends to play mahjong and dine there. A banquet like this could cost him thousands of dollars, though the food was nothing to compare with that at the restaurants. To help him win the 'heart' of the prostitute, his friends must all be prepared to pass on their winnings at mahjong to the 'hostess'. With a really popular prostitute, similar procedures had to be repeated many times before the customer could eventually spend a night with her. Then he would become a regular and a 'brother-in-law' to the other prostitutes in the same 'house'. It would not be right for him to be interested in his 'sisters-in-law'. From time to time, he was obliged to throw a party there. On Chinese New Year, the Dragon Boat Festival, the Autumn Moon Festival and the Birthday of the Fox Fairy he must manage to spend some time with the prostitute for her 'good luck', not to mention a great deal of money.

Fickle customers were much despised by the prostitutes and were disgustedly referred to as 'toothpicks'.* Once a customer had won such a title, he would probably be boycotted by all prostitutes of equal standing with his old favourite, even if he had plenty of money to squander.

However, these 'ch'ang-san' prostitutes soon found rivals in the rise of another class of prostitutes called 'yao-erh' (also a certain piece in Chinese dominoes, lower than 'ch'ang-san'), more easily accessible to customers who did not want to spend too much time in going through so many rituals before hopping into bed with the women they desired. Not necessarily cheaper in night-spending fees, nor less pretty, the 'yao-erh' prostitutes were merely more direct in providing sex for impatient customers.

As the higher a Chinese was in rank, the more he emphasised the need for subtlety and ceremony even in prostitute-seeking, the 'ch'ang-san' prostitutes appealed more to important officials and wealthier people, while the 'yao-erh' prostitutes suited businessmen, compradors and foreigners who were lacking in patience. Perhaps this was why the former class of prostitutes tended to regard themselves superior to the latter. The strangest thing was: once a customer had patronised a 'yao-erh' prostitute he would find it extremely difficult to patronise a 'ch'ang-san' even if he were willing to spend the time and money.

WHERE THE 'PHEASANTS' FLY

As for the ordinary people, in the alleys along Foochow Road there stood hundreds and hundreds of tiny terrace houses which were the headquarters of the low-class prostitutes, disdainfully called 'pheasants' by the Shanghai people. As soon as night set in, the whole

---

* At Chinese dinner parties all kinds of fruit were peeled and sliced into small pieces; one could use a toothpick to pick up the pieces one liked.

length of Foochow Road would be packed with 'pheasants' wearing cheap perfume and heavy make-up. Once they spotted a prospective customer, they would fight for him. Quite frequently, one lone sight-seer would be dragged into one of these terrace houses against his own wish. He could not count on the help of the patrolling Indian policemen, who actually received pecuniary subsidies in the form of 'red packets' from these hovering 'pheasants'. Moreover, when the policemen were off duty they could sleep with these prostitutes free, if they chose to forfeit the 'red packets'.

In addition, along the embankment of the Soochow River—a tributary of the Whampoo, embracing the major part of the International Settlement—one would see a lot of Chinese women unconventionally attired in any form of European dress, ranging from jumpers and skirts to evening gowns, leaning in the doorways of huge apartment houses, shouting in pidgin English: 'Come in and play. Wash, wash every day. No clean, no pay.' These were prostitutes who concentrated on attracting foreign sailors. Like street-walkers elsewhere in the world, they were 'experts' in quick sex and would refuse to spend a whole night with any customer. Their favourite expression was 'C.O.B.', meaning 'cash on bed'. As the Shanghai slang referred to quick sex as 'firing the cannon', and these prostitutes only catered for the sexual needs of foreigners, they were sarcastically called the 'foreign caissons'. Even the 'pheasants' along Foochow Road would unhesitatingly turn their noses up at them.

THE 'CHICKEN BLOOD' VIRGIN

High-class prostitutes were also classified into 'ch'ing-kuan-jen' (pure official attendants) and 'hung-kuang-jen' (popular official attendants), no doubt due to the fact that in the Manchu Dynasty their important customers were mainly high officials. The pure official attendants were supposed to be virgin prostitutes. If a custo-mer wanted to deflower a virgin prostitute, apart from spending a very sizeable sum of money and going through the rituals of 'tea rounds' and 'flower banquets', he would have to offer the procuress a small fortune to satiate her greed. The first night was suggestively called the 'lighting of big candles', as if it were a wedding night. When the customer went to bed with a virgin prostitute the procuress would have already given her 'foster-daughter' instructions regard-ing how to place a square of white silk under her and how to prove her virginity by wiping herself carefully to keep the stain of blood on the white silk. Customarily, the procuress herself would come in to congratulate the couple on the following morning when everything went right. The customer was allowed three nights to complete the deflowering process without having to pay additional money. But if the prostitute failed to prove herself to have been a virgin the customer had every right to claim back all his money. The procuress generally accepted this unfortunate incident with grace, though the prostitute concerned would most definitely be tortured afterwards.

These 'professional ethics' were strictly observed until the downfall of the Manchu Dynasty in 1911, two years after the deaths of Emperor Kuang Hsu and Empress Dowager Tzu Hsi within two days of each other. By then, the procuresses in Shanghai began to become more mercenary and tricky. The early years of the Republic brought Shanghai greater prosperity and its prostitution entered a golden era. The protective security of the International Settlement and the French Concession attracted endless streams of defeated warlords and corrupt officials to whom money was no object. Once they got there, they could hardly resist the temptation of the sexual pleasures of this sophisticated city.

Since some of these warlords were originally country bumpkins who happened to have had luck on their side during civil wars, the rank of general or marshal hardly altered their ignorance or stupidity. Like most superstitious peasants, they considered deflowering a virgin as something exceedingly lucky. When they started to frequent the prostitute houses they demanded virgin prostitutes as well. This posed a difficult problem for most procuresses, since there could not be so many virgins in their 'houses'. However, some of the more resourceful procuresses had their own ways. They coached their 'foster-daughters' to use chicken blood skilfully to fool these warlords. So the warlords had their good luck, while the procuresses had their good luck too—in the form of money.

Gradually, the procuresses began to apply the same practice to other customers who were obsessed with virgin prostitutes. After being caught red-handed on a number of occasions, 'chicken blood' virgins became a standard joke with joy-seekers.

THE 'THREE-LEGGED' GENERAL

With more civil wars won and lost, Shanghai was jammed with

ever-increasing numbers of warlords and politicians. Once they had set their feet in the paradise, these newcomers squandered their easily acquired money on wine and women without stint. Of these warlords, Chang Chung-ch'ang was often likened to the 'god of plague' by many prostitutes because of his crude and distasteful ways of seeking sexual pleasures. Of peasant stock, Chang started as a foot-soldier and eventually reached the height of military governor of Shantung Province. Once in a while, he would either go to Peking or Shanghai for some 'relaxation'. Perhaps an exhibitionist by nature, Chang liked to impress his fellow warlords with his virility and the size of his member. On one occasion in Peking, he and some other warlords were having a flower banquet in one of the best restaurants. Surrounded by numerous high-class prostitutes singing and flirting, Chang Chung-ch'ang suddenly suggested to his colleagues that they should compare their weapons to decide the champion. His suggestion was unanimously accepted, since none of the other warlords had a sense of decency. Chang ordered his bodyguards to bring in lots of silver dollars to be used as a measure. While Chang and his guests placed their members on the dining table to the shock of the prostitutes present, the bodyguards carefully and fastidiously stacked silver dollars alongside to find out their measurements in repose. Chang's weapon matched seventy-two pieces of stacked silver dollars in length and diameter and he won the championship. The story took wing overnight and he became known to the Peking prostitutes as the 'seventy-two-dollar cannon'. Most prostitutes would have refused to sleep with him but for his generosity with money and his cruelty in dealing with them if he were offended.

On one of his pleasure trips to Shanghai, Chang found to his immense delight that the 'seventy-two-dollar cannon' had already become common knowledge to the Shanghai prostitutes. Comfortably settled in a luxurious hotel suite in the International Settlement, he sent his bodyguards to round up the best-known prostitutes from 'house' after 'house'. When the scared prostitutes were brought into his suite he stood there already stripped below the waist. Beside him, piles of silver dollars were displayed on an enormous table; they varied between fifty and two hundred dollars. Without any preliminary remarks, he ordered all the prostitutes to strip at once. Then he made love to them one after another. Each was paid immediately after intercourse. The warlord picked one pile of silver dollars to give to each prostitute at random, irrespective of her 'service' or skill in satisfying him. Not without some pride, he called this the 'full house' game. Perhaps enlightened by his standing posture, some of the prostitutes conferred on him the new nickname 'the general with three long legs'.

THE FRENCH WAYS OF OFFERING SEXUAL PLEASURES

The booming trade of prostitutes in the International Settlement naturally invited the jealousy of the authorities in the French Concession. Fully aware of the profitable side of offering people sexual pleasures, the French started to introduce their 'innovations'. As a result of the October Revolution in Russia, the French Concession, consisting of elegant boulevards and attractive residential areas, became the haven for Russian refugees. After living a few years in exile, these White Russians had run through their means. To keep body and soul together, many of the former generals and colonels of the Tsar worked as bodyguards for the Chinese business tycoons and millionaires. But as far as the former princesses and titled ladies were concerned, their bodies became their sole capital. With the subtle encouragement of the French authorities, strip-tease clubs, dance-halls, restaurants and cafés shot up like mushrooms along Rue Joffre and Rue Lafayette—the Champs Elysées of the French Concession. These places elegantly decorated were vaguely comparable to some of their counterparts in Europe. But what attracted the Chinese customers most were the Russian dancing girls, waitresses and bar-maids. As it was hard for the Chinese to discern the difference between various European nationalities, these Russian women could safely pose as new arrivals from Paris, especially since most of them spoke French quite fluently. Once they spotted a good customer, they would not hesitate to name their own price. The customer was free to take his pick, driving her either to a nearby hotel or going to her apartment for the night. The Russians were particularly popular with the younger Chinese males, who despised the complicated procedures of having sex with Chinese prostitutes. Indeed, these white women might be less subtle than their Chinese rivals in the International Settlement, but it was equally true that they offered variety and a different form of excitement. The most refreshing part for the Chinese customers, however, was that they did not have to bother about throwing flower banquets on every imaginable occasion. Nor did they have to become a 'regular'. They could come whenever they had the time and the urge, so long as they had enough money for the night.

For people who could not afford to spend too much money, there were plenty of 'language instructresses' giving their addresses and the amount of 'tuition fees' in the classified advertisements of the local papers. These 'instructresses' all lived in the quieter areas in the French Concession. One would have to ring for an appointment beforehand, for they usually started to give their 'lessons' from afternoon to midnight. These Russian girls mostly spoke the Shanghai dialect very fluently and lived in tiny but clean flatlets in those impressive-looking mansions. The 'pupil' had to pay upon entering the room before the 'instructress' would commence to give her 'lessons'. The matter-of-factness and abruptness of the whole process tended to put a lot of Chinese off. If a Chinese were known by his friends to have had the experience of 'taking French lessons', he would quickly become a laughing stock.

'OFFICIAL RESIDENCES' AND LIVE PERFORMANCES

When the Russian novelty ceased to be an attraction, the French Concession again offered something new. In its most sought-after residential areas, one could occasionally spot a shining bronze plate inscribed 'So-and-So's Official Residence' at the gate of a detached house surrounded by mature gardens. But there was no need to be frightened off by these bronze plates—the 'in' people knew only too well what these 'official residences' actually were. These impressive detached houses were but the places of assignation for frustrated rich women and their 'temporaries'. A place like this was generally run by a woman with wide contacts as well as some association with a secret society such as the Blue Gang. Keeping comprehensive dossiers about both her male and female patrons, she was able to match them with every discretion. She would always first show the woman the picture of a man she had in mind for her, to make sure that he was not a friend or a relative of her husband's.

It is believed that such precautions were taken only after a couple of embarrassing incidents had happened. The case of a certain businessman named Wong was perhaps the most illuminating. Wong was a man-about-town in the early 1930s. Tired of prostitutes, dancing girls and actresses, Wong was delighted to hear about a certain 'official residence' in Rue Pétain in the French Concession. Equipped with a card of introduction from one of the 'in' people, he drove there in his Cadillac. Naturally the madame was very impressed by such a well-off customer. She courteously ushered him into the best room of the house, promising to bring him the most beautiful woman on her carefully compiled list. With a Havana lit and a large whisky on the rocks at his elbow, Wong was anticipating the most exciting encounter of his life. But when about half an hour later, an elegantly dressed young woman walked into the room, one look at her made Wong tremble with fury, for she was no other than his own favourite concubine. He was about to hit her, when his concubine charged at him and slapped his face, telling him that she, having been tipped off, had deliberately come here to catch him in the act. She sounded so convincing that he did not even have the benefit of doubt. But after they had both left, the madame was still a very frightened woman, for in fact Wong's concubine had been a 'regular customer' of hers for a long time. Had it not been for her quick wit in coping with the totally unexpected crisis, the madame would certainly have landed in trouble.

In pecuniary terms, to run such a house of assignation was most profitable. The expenses were perhaps slightly higher than running one's own house, but the madame was in the enviable position of receiving money from both partners of the temporary 'match'.

Some of these 'residences' had additional revenues. With well-concealed peep-holes in the walls of the bedrooms, the madames could charge a number of spectators an entrance fee to watch the live performances of couples who had already paid a generous sum for the use of the rooms. Completely unaware of what was happening beyond the walls of the room, couples seeking to satisfy each other often surpassed professional performers in vigour and endurance. This gave the peeping Toms great excitement and pleasure.

Such peep-shows took place in the International Settlement too. In some of the hotels along Tibet Road and thereabouts one could pay the hotel boys an insignificant amount of money to watch similar performances. As these hotels let their rooms on an hourly basis, many men and women tended to use these hotels for brief encounters. What they did not realise was that there were also many peep-holes in the walls of each room—the ingenious creation of the hotel boys for the source of their additional income. More often than not, a couple using a room in these hotels to enjoy sexual pleasures would unwittingly also serve to entertain observers. Experienced wild-oat sowers always refrained from using these hotels. However, if they had no alternative, they would turn off the light and draw the bed curtains of the four-poster, leaving nothing to chance.

As a whole, the victims were either newcomers to Shanghai or young students. To them one hotel was as good as another. Besides, the room charge on an hourly basis was naturally far more economical since they could not keep their women for longer sessions.

Once, however, a certain professor of social studies was investigating the social causes of extramarital affairs. He was advised by one of his friends to go to a certain hotel one afternoon to be an 'observer'. After paying the hotel boys the peeping fee, he was led into a room already packed with spectators eagerly waiting their turn, for there were no more than five peep-holes in the wall adjoining the next room. Like most academics he was not lacking in patience. Calmly he waited for his turn. At long last, he put his eye to one of the peep-holes. He almost fainted when he discovered the woman and the young man in the next room to be his wife and one of his favourite students.

HOW THE 'SOCIAL FLOWERS' BLOOM

Even in the offering of sexual pleasures, Shanghai frequently rang the changes. When the Nationalists came into power in 1928, the Shanghai tycoons immediately sensed a change of political climate. With Nanking now as the national capital—less than five hours away by the through night express—this paradise of sinners soon became the weekend resort of highly-placed politicians. Revolutionaries at that time, these bigwigs were far more discreet about their sexual adventures. To them, prostitute-patronising belonged to the 'old elite', nor would they visit sexual haunts openly. Here, the talented Shanghai speculators knew how to operate. One after another, a great number of exclusive clubs were hastily formed. These clubs, hidden from the public eye behind the iron gates of those elegant houses in the French Concession, offered every imaginable entertainment in utmost privacy. It was in these clubs that the 'social flowers' came in for the kill.

The 'social flowers' shot up from different kinds of backgrounds: some of them were self-styled debutantes; some, girls of slender

means but anxious to achieve a higher social status; some, famous
prostitutes now in new disguise. No matter how diversified their backgrounds might be, they were all gold-diggers with youth, beauty and
their bodies as their capital. To get what they wanted, most of them
were extremely tactful, discreet and yet, in many cases, ruthless.
They also had patience. Their patrons seldom had the wit or wisdom
not to become victims of their 'axing tactics'. These women never
talked about money. The men associated with them could carry on
living like lords for months and months. Then, all of a sudden, they
would be manoeuvred into the situation of having to make a very
handsome contribution. The old Shanghai hands jokingly referred to
these experiences as 'being axed', indicating the extent of their heavy
financial losses.

A typical case must be that of a prominent Nationalist politician
nicknamed 'The Prince' in the early 1930s. With an enviable family
background and a doctorate from an American university, 'The Prince'
associated himself with one of these 'social flowers'. Impressed by his
political status, she became his mistress and lived quietly in Shanghai.
Though unknown to the politician's wife, she was his 'Mrs. Shanghai'
to all his business friends. Through her, they were able to exert some
influence on him whenever they needed certain forms of political
assistance to advance their business. A few years later, however, the
politician acquired as his second mistress the widowed daughter-in-
law of a Yunnan banker. Politically ambitious and renowned for her
sexual virtuosity, this mistress of his frequently travelled between
Shanghai and Nanking. Their association was an open secret in political circles, especially since her influence on him was conspicuous
enough to turn many an eye.

For better or worse, this delicate balance between the three women
in his life seemed to have been tactfully maintained by this politician
until the fall of the Chinese mainland in 1949. Taking refuge in
Hong Kong with his formal wife on his way to America, he was
descended upon by his 'Mrs. Shanghai' with their teen-age daughter
demanding 'legal status' and maintenance. The politician naturally
avoided confrontation, while his formal wife had two alsatians
unleashed. The local papers had a field day. A law-suit soon developed.
But the politician was able to proceed to America as scheduled by
securing the help of some of his Shanghai friends to reach a settlement outside the courts with his 'Mrs. Shanghai'. Since the Chinese

Communists then in Hong Kong still occasionally saw things from the capitalist angle, they started to build up the Nationalist politician's illegitimate daughter as a film-star with quite a few pictures to her credit. As for the politician's other mistress, she did not cling to him like a shadow. Extremely youthful even in her early forties, she soon established herself in Hong Kong as one of the 'women of fame' from Shanghai. She had some casual affairs with a few men, perhaps merely to keep herself occupied. A grandmother by now, she is often seen flying between the United States and Hong Kong, with occasional brief stops at Taipei—but certainly not to see the aforesaid politician.

The best-known club in Shanghai at that time was run by Tu Yueh-sheng, the all-powerful leader of the Blue Gang. It was at 181 Rue Giraud, with a rear gate opening on to Rue Foche. The huge three-storey French-style house was surrounded by an enormous garden of several acres. With armed guards posted at both front and rear gates, the club could pass as the residence of some V.I.P. Night after night the iron gates would open only to admit cars familiar to the armed guards. On the ground floor, thirty-six roulette wheels kept spinning, while on the first floor there were eight luxuriously furnished rest rooms, where the distinguished guests could lie down to smoke one or two pipes of opium if they had not had much luck at roulette. The second floor was a different world, and only the very select guests had access to it. The suites on this floor were used by business tycoons and leading politicians to spend an undisturbed night with the women who struck their fancy. With the exception of the club manager and a couple of first-class chefs, the club was staffed with young and pretty girls. Someone who had frequented this club said that he simply could not find in any other part of the world a club 'up to this standard'.

Once a Szechuan warlord named Fan Shao-chen came to Shanghai for a quick fling. Being also the leader of the Szechuan underworld, he was entertained by Tu in this most exclusive club. As Fan couldn't do without a woman for a single night, his host found him a 'social flower' who used to be the most popular prostitute in Shanghai. She pleased Fan to such an extent that the warlord never bothered to leave 181 Rue Giraud during his Shanghai sojourn.

When General Fan eventually had to go back to Chungking, he praised her effusively to his generous host, who merely nodded and smiled. A few days later, however, when Fan had safely arrived at his grand mansion in Chungking, still reminiscing about his Shanghai adventures, he could not believe his own eyes when the first woman who greeted him at the door turned out to be the very prostitute who had conquered him in that exclusive club. Incidentally, his generous host Tu Yueh-sheng had chartered a plane to fly her to Chungking as a home-coming surprise for the warlord.

SEX IN CAFÉS AND PEDICABS

Those who could not afford to join such clubs had other ways to comfort themselves. Along Rue Joffre and Rue Lafayette, some French cafés boasted of their special seating arrangements. Dimly lit and heavily curtained, these cafés contained cubicles identical to the compartments of a railway carriage. When a man and a woman came in for a cup of coffee, they would be ushered into one of these cubicles. Once the waiter or waitress brought them their coffee, he or she would habitually draw the curtain of the cubicle to give the couple ample privacy. Inside the cubicle the two-seater was comfortable and wide enough, while soft music provided the right atmosphere. Nor did the couple have to worry about any possible intrusion or disruption, for unless the customers opened the curtain to order another cup of coffee, the waiter or waitress would never come near. In these cafés, a cup of coffee was dearer than a three-course dinner and one had to tip handsomely. Still, it was considerably cheaper than using a hotel room, the 'Parisian' atmosphere apart.

On rainy days, young lovers sometimes used pedicabs for their love-making. Slightly wider than a mini car and double the size of a rickshaw, the pedicab had its driver riding on the bicycle-like front part. Cycling through the heavy traffic the poor fellow did not have the chance to look back over his shoulder. With the convertible canopy and waterproof curtains up, the couple in the pedicab were invisible from the outside, especially in the pouring rain. When they deliberately hired a pedicab for a long journey from one end of Shanghai to the other, it could mean a couple of hours of intensive pedalling for the driver. Shut away from the outside world for such a long while, they could easily achieve what they had set out to do. This was particularly popular with some students of third- or fourth-rate universities, for this kind of adventure would not cost them as much as using a French café.

CHINESE-FASHION TURKISH BATHS

To satisfy the curiosity and needs of a different kind of clientele, the men behind the sex industry always had something new up their sleeve. From the mid-1930s onwards extravagant night clubs and dance halls flourished in both the International Settlement and the French Concession, projecting a new dimension of sexual pleasure both for the idle rich in Shanghai and for those who deliberately came to this paradise of sinners with the devotion of pilgrims. Needless to say, the dancing girls and female performers in these haunts all had a price, though nominally they were not exactly prostitutes.

In some of these night clubs, 'special performances' were staged for an élite group of customers after closing time. For an exorbitant admission fee, one could see lesbian acts, termed by the Shanghainese as the 'mirror-rubbing' show, as well as intercourse performed by women with dogs or monkeys. At that time the most welcome performer was probably a White Russian woman named Nina Nikolina. Apart from making love with her alsatian, she often demonstrated her special skill in smoking a cigarette with her vagina.

But Nina soon found a rival in Isabella, a Portuguese girl who performed in another secret night club off Rue Lafayette. When this girl stripped, she was able to make every bit of her naked body move to the rhythm of the music. The climax of her performance was the playing of a mouth organ with her vagina. She could also make it drink up a glass of whisky or any kind of liquid.

These performances constantly drew a packed house. But for those who preferred something more than mere watching, they were not exciting enough. This perhaps led to the mushrooming of Chinese-fashion Turkish baths in both the International Settlement and the French Concession. These baths could be found in many of the side streets, with neon signs attracting people's eyes at night. The proprietors mostly had some form of association with the underworld. Terrace houses were converted into bathrooms en suite. When a customer stepped in, he would be ushered into one of these bathrooms. From then on his every need would be attended to by girls wearing nothing but a bra and a g-string. Once he had sat in the bathtub full of steaming hot water, a girl would scrub his back and other parts meticulously. Properly dried with a clean towel, he would then be led back to lie down on the couch in the adjoining room. If desired, he could have some refreshments or drinks. The same girl would proceed to give him a massage from top to toe, ending with masturbation or fellatio. The customer could have intercourse with the girl if he found her desirable. After everything had been done, he would be given another bath to make him really relaxed, and would then have a nap. The whole process would cost him in the region of two U.S. dollars in those days. For people who happened to be passing through Shanghai and who wanted something different, these places became favourite resorts.

THE JAPANESE SEX RESTAURANTS

Not to be outdone by the sex industries in the International Settlement and the French Concession, the Japanese offered something different and cheaper. In the Japanese-dominated area of Honkew, one could find practically in every street signs of Japanese restaurants. Though the Chinese were never very keen on Japanese food, these restaurants nonetheless attracted unusually large crowds of customers. The attraction lay in the young Japanese waitresses who offered the customers everything. To a joy-seeker, the raw fish might not be very appetising and the sake hardly comparable to the Chinese Shaohsing wine; but it was what he could do with a Japanese waitress after dinner that mattered. The average Chinese went to the White Russian prostitutes in the French Concession out of curiosity or for a change. But in a Japanese waitress in these Honkew restaurants, he could find the tenderness and submissiveness of an oriental female, totally unobtainable in her Slavic counterparts.

To attract the playboys of some nearby universities, the Japanese also set up a great number of cheaper dance halls in Honkew, especially along North Szechuan Road. In these small but cosy dance halls, the dance girls were either Chinese or Japanese. The charges were about one-tenth of those at first-class dance halls along Nanking Road, Rue Lafayette or Lido Road. Knowing about the limited amount of money these university students could afford, some of these dance halls introduced a credit system, to allow these young customers ample time to pay their bills by instalments. But towards the end of each term, money collectors would be sent to school campuses to grab those who had failed to clear their 'dancing debts'.

In contrast to the attitude of these proprietors, most of the dance girls were actually very fond of their student-customers, perhaps because they were more refreshing than experienced joy-seekers.

The most unwelcome customers to the dance halls, big or small, were disdainfully called the 'dance hall rats'. They usually arrived at a dance hall at its peak hour. Taking advantage of the crowds, they had a few dances with different dance girls and sneaked away without paying their bills. Some popular dance girls kept boy friends. In the dance halls these were known as the 'trailers'. They had to remain faceless. Once a dance girl was found to have a 'trailer', she would immediately lose her customers.

'THE FAIRY'S JUMP'

The seasoned joy-seekers in Shanghai were always prepared to pay a reasonable price for what they wanted. In Shanghai, one just could not expect to get anything 'free'. The greatest risk a man could run was to be picked up by a woman in a café or any other public place. Over a cup of coffee or a drink she would tactfully suggest taking the man home. Her place might be an apartment full of splendour and grandeur. This would certainly give the man the illusion of having captivated a rich widow or a frustrated concubine of some wealthy man. Naturally, he could hardly wait to strip and hop into bed with his new find. But as soon as the woman was half undressed, a couple of thugs would burst into the bedroom, one of them claiming to be her husband. The poor joy-seeker would be punched and tied up with a rope, until he agreed to pay a sizable sum of money to save the 'husband' his disgrace. If he did not have that much cash on him, he would have to write an I.O.U. or make out a cheque before they set him free. At this point, he might realise that it was a put-up job by the woman and the men, but there was nothing he could do. This kind of sex blackmail, widely practised in Shanghai, was known as 'the fairy's jump'.

But there was an experience even worse than being blackmailed. One night in the late 1940s, a certain Mr. Li sauntered along the Bubbling Well Road after a dinner party. While crossing the road rather absent-mindedly, he would have been run over by a car if the driver had not braked in time. Unhurt, he was quite prepared to walk away when the driver apologised to him effusively. The feminine voice sounded so pleasing that he instinctively took another look at the car. A very sexy woman was at the wheel, alone. She insisted that he must come with her to her apartment for a drink, if he really had no hard feelings towards her. Tipsy as well as curious, Mr. Li accepted the invitation. After a few turns, he found himself in front of a pleasant detached house in a quiet road. He was even more impressed when this woman took him into a drawing-room which was elegantly furnished. The only odd feeling he had was that the house was unusually quiet. But this ceased to worry him when his hostess told him that both her sisters had left for Hong Kong in view of the military situation. After a few drinks, he and the woman undressed and made love on the studio couch. The woman impressed him with her sexual skill and they tried a variety of positions. Afterwards, they both dressed and the woman drove him to his hotel. Extremely pleased with his random conquest, Mr. Li was secretly hoping to run into her again.

Several days later, however, some of his friends suddenly started to call him 'our movie star' amid endless laughter. Annoyed, Li demanded an explanation. That very evening, one of his friends took him to see a pornographic film. Li was shocked to see the close resemblance between the male in the picture and himself. Then the woman turned her face, and she was the very one who had had the 'wonderful' encounter with him a few nights before. The poor man was too ashamed to stay to witness the end of his own performance.

Naturally, in those days in Shanghai, anything could happen. Like a kaleidoscope, this gigantic city used to appear differently in the eyes of each individual viewer. Some people may look back on it with a touch of nostalgia, others in anger. However, it is only fair to say that this paradise of sinners, with all its vices and fantasies, was the unique product of circumstances—the most un-Chinese city, which China once had to accept, willingly or unwillingly.

CHAPTER SIX

Sexual Fulfilment and Performance

No matter how firmly Confucian ethics may have built up a fence between man and woman in old Chinese society, there is no denying that for centuries and centuries countless romances and affairs have been going on behind the high walls of grand mansions and amid the mulberry trees by the riverside. With marriages regarded as life-long bonds and divorces unthinkable, love and lust have had to find their outlet through unconventional channels.

Until recently, a Chinese woman could be as tame as a sheep to her husband, who gave her social status, security and glory. But when it came to a lover, what she demanded of him was totally different. According to an old Chinese saying, to be a conqueror of the fair sex, a man must have the following five qualifications, abbreviated into five Chinese characters: 'Pan, lu, Teng, hsiao and hsien'.

'Pan' stands for Pan An-jen, an extremely handsome young scholar in the Hsi Chin Dynasty (3rd-4th century). Whenever he drove along the streets in the crowded city of Loyang in his open chariot, the women derived immense pleasure by catching a glimpse of him. They were so fond of him that their dainty hands never ceased to throw all kinds of fruit into his chariot. Faithful to his wife, Pan never fell for any of these women, though he must have been appreciative, if only for the endless supplies of free fruit.

'Lu' in Chinese means 'donkey'. This expression was a subtle way to suggest that a competent lover should have a member as big as that of a donkey. It is believed that this prerequisite had some remote association with Hsueh Ao-ts'ao, Empress Wu Tse-t'ien's 'face-head' whose weapon was comparable to a mule's.

'Teng' was the surname of multi-millionaire Teng T'ung during the reign of Emperor Wu Ti (140-87 B.C.) in the Han Dynasty. He owned an enormous copper mine, which his contemporaries enviously called the 'Copper Mountain'. As the Chinese currency in that period was in the form of copper coins, multi-millionaire Teng's wealth far exceeded that of the whole empire.

'Hsiao' is the Chinese equivalent of youth. A young man would have more vigour and greater endurance.

'Hsien' means leisure. Given a handsome appearance, a big weapon, wealth and youth, a man would still need leisure to chase after the woman he desired.

Armed with all these five qualifications a man could then be a Chinese Casanova. But judging by the order in which they are listed, it seems that handsomeness was of paramount importance, for it would be the first to strike the eyes of a woman if she were interested in having a man.

In the old Shanghai days, when a man had a handsome appearance, the prostitutes' favourite description of him was that he had 'hao chao hui', which means a 'good passport', a 'valid licence' or a 'special permit'. Taking everything into account, this must be considered a simile expressive as well as appropriate.

A PERFECT WOMAN IN RELATION TO SEX

As for a man whose sole aim was to seek sexual pleasures, his concept of a perfect woman naturally had much to do with that part of her anatomy. To sum up the characteristics of an ideal porte feminine (vagina) as listed in a number of ancient sex manuals, it seems that an experienced man always stressed the importance of shallowness, tightness, warmth and fragrance. Naturally these characteristics were seen as components of perfection from the man's angle, for, universally speaking, a man's chief worry in relation to sex is the size of his member. As to warmth and fragrance, they must be regarded as Chinese obsessions. To a Chinese man, the warmth inside reflected the woman's passion, while the demand for fragrance is believed to be relevant to the acute sense of smell of the average Chinese.

According to *Yu Fang Mi Chueh* (Secret Codes of the Jade Room), a Taoist sex manual written before the T'ang Dynasty, one can judge what a woman is like down below by looking at her face.

'A woman with a small mouth and short fingers has a shallow porte feminine and she is easy to please. You can be sure that a woman must have big and thick labia if she has a big mouth and thick lips. If she has deep-set eyes, her porte feminine is bound to be deep too. On the other hand, if she has protruding eyes, her porte feminine will be shallow. But if a woman has a pair of big, sparkling eyes, her porte feminine is narrow at its entrance, and yet roomy in the inner part. It takes a larger jade-stem (penis) to satisfy her. A woman with two dimples is tight and narrow down below. To have intercourse with her is an immense pleasure. But to look for an extremely sexy and responsive woman, one will have to bear in mind that short-sightedness is her predominant feature. If a woman has a narrow forehead and a small mouth, it indicates that the passage to the innermost part of her porte feminine is not that straight, and it will be extremely difficult for a man to make her reach a climax. Naturally, the rare find is a woman whose porte feminine can boast of tightness, shallowness, warmth and fragrance, and yet is sufficiently moist during intercourse to make the man enjoy the whole process.'

As regards the position of the vagina, it has been assumed that the nearer to the front its entrance is, the better. When this is the case with a woman, the man can come into her more easily. Moreover, the traditional and conventional way of love-making is for the man to be above the woman.

Apart from the above theories, it was widely believed in China that the shape of the woman's vagina varied from region to region. Tales went around about the women in Tatung, a county in Shansi Province, having 'double-door' vaginas. This claim of physiological difference can be traced back to the 15th and 16th centuries, when the Ming emperors concentrated more on seeking sexual fulfilment than running state affairs. Take Emperor Wu Tsung (reigning 1506-1521) for instance. He made a special trip via the Chu-jung Pass of the Great Wall to Tatung after he had been told of the physical characteristics of the women there. Disguised as a junior military officer, the emperor stopped at a small inn on the outskirts of Tatung. He seduced Feng-chieh (Phoenix Maiden), the younger sister of the inn-keeper, who apparently satisfied both his curiosity and desire. It seems that the erotic adventure of Wu Tsung inspired one composer of Peking Opera to write this episode into a delightful comic opera entitled 'The Wandering Dragon Teasing the Phoenix'. Witty in dialogue and subtle in sex approaches, it was most popular with the fans of Peking Opera until the outbreak of the Cultural Revolution.

But according to an anonymous Ch'ing scholar, the much-mentioned physiological difference of the women in Tatung was, in fact, the combination of fantasy and illusion. He claimed in his memoirs that since the women in this remote town were extremely skilful in the art of love-making, it gave the travellers from afar the feeling that they were different physiologically. To prove his point, he asserted that one would have the same feeling if one happened to make love to some woman in the small town of Yangliuch'ing, which is but a couple of miles to the west of Tientsin. Talking from personal experience, he stated that the women in both Tatung and Yangliuch'ing fascinated the men with 'their chanting in bed and the rhythmic movements of their hips during the whole process, which would make them seemingly different to men without previous experience'.

Convincing though his argument may sound to some people, yet many Chinese are of the opinion that climate and geographical features can cause the difference in the physical characteristics of people from various regions.

Naturally, in a vast country like China, geographical distances and the lack of adequate means of transportation in the old days tended to lead people to assume that their compatriots in the other parts of the country must be different in physical characteristics. In all probability, such an assumption is not completely without foundation. It is a fact that in North China and Manchuria the women are generally taller and bigger in build than their sisters in the South. Relevantly, they have larger breasts and broader hips. While in the provinces south of the Yangtze, the women are noted for their slender waists and delicate physiques. If the human body grows in proportion as we can all see, it is only logical to deduce that the women in South China are smaller in every part of their anatomy when compared with their counterparts in the North.

THE CULT OF BOUND FEET

Perhaps it was meant to compensate for the 'physical defects' of the Southern females in relation to sex that Li Yu, the poet-king of Southern T'ang (923-936), first introduced feet-binding. It all started with a palace maiden named Miao Niang, who was an excellent dancer. Out of sudden fancy, Li Yu thought she would dance more gracefully if she had her feet bound. She consented to this and it pleased the romantic king tremendously to see her dancing elegantly in a gilded wooden lotus decorated with pearls and precious stones. Since then the Chinese literary language has adopted the figurative term 'golden lotus' as a synonym for bound feet.

However, the instant impact of Miao Niang's success touched off the vogue of bound feet not only among other palace maidens, but also among the ordinary women in the Kingdom of Southern T'ang. Though Li Yu's kingdom was soon conquered by the Sung Empire, there were many supporters of his bound feet cult for centuries after his tragic death. It was claimed that a woman's figure improved greatly once she had her feet bound; her waist became slenderer, her breasts and hips bigger and more shapely. Li Li-weng, a Ch'ing scholar and playwright, discussed at length with his friends how the bound feet of a woman could arouse a man sexually. A womaniser himself, he firmly stated that the women in Tatung and Lanchow (now capital of Kansu Province) had their feet bound to perfection, 'good to look at and nice to hold in a man's hands'.

Among the Manchu emperors, both Ch'ien Lung and Hsien Feng seemed to be obsessed with bound feet. The former made six trips to the provinces south of the Yangtze for sexual indulgences with all sorts of women there, because of their bound feet, while the latter took concubines from that region for the same reason.

It was not until the establishment of the Republic in 1911 that the abolition of bound feet was proclaimed as one of the measures of women's emancipation, to the delight of the Chinese women. Meanwhile, it caused no little complaints from some bound-feet maniacs, including a few outstanding scholars.

A MATTER OF SHAPES

Having set down the standard of a perfect woman from the sex angle, the Chinese males were equally uninhibited enough to classify their own sex organs into three categories.

It was agreed that a member of the 'mushroom shape' would be ideal for any woman. Bigger at the top and slightly finer along the whole length during erection, it would give the woman a sense of fulfilment, since it could reach and keep in contact with every sensitive part inside her.

Next on the list came the 'cylinder shape'. With roughly the same diameter through its whole length, it was considered to be tolerably good for the average woman who was less demanding. But to a woman with a sharper appetite it could hardly be comparable to the 'mushroom shape'.

The 'nail shape' was never considered as an asset to a manly man. Pointed at the top and stouter towards the root, it would only serve to make a woman more frustrated during the process of love-making. Unable to keep in contact with the sensitive parts inside her, it could not be expected to give her any sense of fulfilment.

Interestingly enough, the Chinese have not in any sense stressed the importance of the size, though their male ego sometimes would prompt them to exaggerate. In actual fact, several competent sources have pointed out that the size in repose matters little. On the other hand they have attached much significance to its expansibility. To quote a Chinese slang expression, the male member is suggestively called the 'turtle's head', which obviously has something to do with the matter of repose and expansibility.

SHADOW BOXING, MEDITATION, ACUPUNCTURE AND SEXUAL PERFORMANCE

Since sexual fulfilment is dependent on sexual performance, many Chinese are known to have resorted to various ways to improve the latter. Discreet by nature, they have been taking measures which may seem totally irrelevant to sex in unsuspecting occidental eyes.

One of the most illuminating instances is the practice of 't'ai-chi-ch'uan' (shadow boxing). When one happens to see a Chinese spending no less than twenty minutes each morning in moving his legs and arms in a graceful and seemingly effortless manner, it seldom dawns upon one that this is, in fact, a strenuous exercise which can, among other things, improve a man's virility.

Shadow boxing was invented by a Taoist named Chang San-feng in the Sung Dynasty. Shutting himself in a mountain cave for meditation, he one day chanced to see a prolonged fight between a crane and a snake. Based on the offensive and defensive moves of both creatures, Chang worked out the series of movements that make up shadow boxing. Having practised it systematically for some years, he found himself able to control his breath, and his waist much stronger. The art of shadow boxing has since been carried on for centuries by some ardent followers.

The basic aim of this graceful exercise is to increase the strength of one's waist and enable one to breathe correctly. According to the

Taoist theory, the waist is the pivot of the human body and the fountain of strength, while the control of breath is essential to any form of exercise. Since love-making in its physical sense is a form of exercise, a man able to control his breath and equipped with a powerful waist can easily improve his vigour and prolong his endurance during the love act. Far-fetched as it may sound, this fact has been confirmed by those who have practised shadow boxing constantly.

If shadow boxing is a method of improving one's virility through physical exercises, meditation is a method of controlling one's will power in relation to sexual performance. Through meditation, one can gradually achieve an unprecedented calmness which, again, is vital to any form of performance. The Taoists of a certain school theorise that one's breath consists of two invisible 'forces' which can be harnessed into harmony. The two 'forces' are yin (negative) and yang (positive), complementary and productive when they are properly connected under a unified command. The Taoists believe that inside the human body, right under the navel, there is the 'power plant' which they metaphysically call 'tan t'ien' (the pill-forming field). To perform the Taoist meditation correctly, one must have a special wooden stool made. The measurements of the stool are determined to suit the build of each individual. When a man sits on the stool, his body forms two ninety degree angles—one behind his knee-caps and the other between the upper joints of his thighs and the part of his body below the navel. With his open palms placed downwards on the kneecaps, he half-closes his eyes and looks at the tip of his nose, which forms a thirty degree angle with his chest. Once he starts to meditate, he must forget everything including the existence of his own body. All he has to do is to breathe deeply and evenly. Meanwhile, he has to be relaxed mentally and physically. If he follows the instructions to the letter, after 100 days he should begin to feel in his 'tan t'ien' a certain warmth which indicates the 'endeavour of yin and yang to meet'. When eventually the feeling of warmth inside there becomes permanent, it means that he has successfully formed his 'inner pill', which is the foundation of his health and vigour. This will also enable him to assume full control in love-making.

Whereas both shadow boxing and meditation require the individual's initiative and application, the ancient medical treatment of acupuncture is believed to be an alternative method of improving virility, especially as a cure for over-indulgence. The concept of acupuncture is that internally throughout the body extend a number of meridians (or ducts), embedded in the muscles to form a fixed network, which can be spotted on 365 specific points on the skin. As these meridians harbour the ebb and flow of yin and yang, to correct either deficiency or excess of the two 'invisible forces' it is necessary to 'stimulate' the meridians by applying a set of acupuncture needles on the appropriate points on the skin. (A set consists of nine acupuncture needles, different in length, size and shape.) According to the acupuncture doctors, the kidneys govern one's sex functions and therefore, the victim of impotence can be cured by having those meridians related to the kidneys 'stimulated' through the correct use of these acupuncture needles. They assert that impotence is generally due to over-indulgence, which has necessarily caused the imbalance of yin and yang, and that once the imbalance is corrected, one's virility will naturally be reinvigorated.

However, the beauty of these three treatments lies in the fact that they are applicable to people of all ages, irrespective of their sex. Their primary common aim is to build up one's health and it takes time and patience to find them effective.

THE INTERRELATION BETWEEN FOOD AND SEX

Those who lack the initiative to seek remedy in one of the above three methods can make full use of the interrelation between food and sex, which has long been acknowledged by Confucius. Since a healthy diet is a key to the maintenance of one's health, the Chinese have always believed in the different values of various kinds of food. In relation to sex, many of them think that partly formed chicken eggs, quail eggs, kidneys, chicken blood, eels, lobster, oysters, scallops, all kinds of shell fish, the entrails of fish, roe, unprocessed honey, calamus, sesame, chestnuts, walnuts, dates, chives, leeks, garlic, onions, spring onions, celery, yams, carrots, litchi, mulberries, grapes, peaches and apples have their share of contribution to the improvement of virility, though in different degrees.

As far as meat is concerned, they attach much importance to lamb and venison. Among the seafoods, bêche-de-mer and turtle are high on their list. In North China, lamb stewed with chestnuts and garlic is a very popular dish in the winter, the season to build up a man's reserves of strength to cope with the forthcoming spring. The Manchurians are very fond of roast venison which, they believe, is full of hormones.

In the South, people tend to seek hormones in fresh and salt water fish because of their geographical environment. With the Shanghainese two dishes are particularly popular. One is stir-fried eels with diced garlic; the other is stir-fried river shrimp with fresh chives. Usually the southerners in China do not really like garlic, spring onions and chives; therefore, the use of garlic and chives in these two dishes is self-explanatory. In Shanghai restaurants, stir-fried fish entrails and steamed turtle are delicacies always included in a banquet. When a host urges his guests to help themselves to these two dishes, a roguish twinkle in his eyes can often be spotted. As to bêche-de-mer, it is a dish well prepared in every school of Chinese cooking. Though considered a delicacy in North China and the interior provinces, the Fukienese are lucky enough to have plenty of bêche-de-mer in their daily meals, for an inexhaustible supply of it can be found off the sea coast of Fukien.

Along the Yellow River, in some parts of both Shansi and Honan Provinces, the natives regard carp and red bean soup as a dish indispensable for newly-weds. The recipe for this very special soup dates back to the T'ang Dynasty, when a renowned gourmet-physician named Meng Hsien recommended it to people who were keen on having a happy married life.

In provinces such as Hunan, Szechuan and Kansu, the natives believe in the value of chili peppers as sex stimulants. That is why in both the Hunan and Szechuan schools of cooking, chili pepper is lavishly used in practically every dish.

The hormone value of chestnuts and walnuts has been widely recognised by the Chinese throughout the country. They use both nuts as ingredients in many meat dishes, among which stir-fried chicken with walnuts and chicken braised with chestnuts are included in both Shanghai and Peking cuisine.

But as far as the Cantonese are concerned, many of them are inclined to think that to improve virility, one has to do more than merely try to derive benefits from diet. Perhaps due to the subtropical climate and easier life, the Cantonese, especially the rich ones, are reputed to be more self-indulgent in sex. In many of their dishes they like to use herbs as ingredients. To name a few, fresh chicken with chu chi (reddish dried fruit like raisins) soup, pork with chu chi soup, fresh chicken with tung ch'ung hsia ts'ao (a special fungus) are among the best-known.

The Cantonese are also known for their fondness for eating cats and snakes. People generally attribute this to their obsession with gastronomic pleasures. But many Cantonese eat them with a view to the improvement of virility as well. They believe that both the cat and the snake are extremely sexy animals. This belief makes them include the meat of cats and snakes in their menu. In the leading Cantonese restaurant in Hong Kong, the 'Dragon and Tiger Stew' is a seasonal and most expensive dish in the autumn. It is, in fact, the meat of snake and cat stewed with a variety of herbs, which would take the chef at least two or three days to prepare.

As to the aphrodisiac value of dog's meat, the Cantonese are not alone in this conviction. In Hunan, Kwangsi, Szechuan and a few other provinces, people regard dog's meat cooked with garlic a delicacy in the severe winter. This does not mean they will eat alsatians, labradors and pekinese without discrimination. In China, there are the chow dogs, which yield plenty of meat and are believed to be exceptionally virile and sexy.

Among staunch believers in the usefulness of dog's meat, one deserves special mention. He is no other than Warlord Chang Chungch'ang, who won the title of the 'three-legged general' from the Shanghai prostitutes in the 1920s. According to a member of his entourage, Chang ate dog's meat almost every day, since he had so many women to handle all the year round. Therefore, in addition to his other nicknames, he was also known as the 'dog's meat general'.

THE USEFULNESS OF SOME WINES

Though the Chinese regard most wines and spirits as possessing destructive effects on one's health and virility, they put faith in several kinds of wines, which, if taken in moderation, are supposed to be helpful.

Ginseng wine is perhaps the most expensive of all Chinese wines. Actually, it is kaoliang (as strong as vodka) with the roots of ginseng soaked in its cask for at least three years. The correct dosage is to take a small glass as a nightcap regularly.

In North China, Tientsin is famous for its wukaipi wine. Wukaipi is the bark of a certain kind of tree believed to possess very high aphrodisiac value. Again, a quantity of it is soaked in 90% proof spirits for a considerable length of time, turning the original colourless spirits into a thickish brown liquid. Some people do serve it with meals, but most prefer to drink it in small quantities before bedtime.

In the north-west, however, the chu chi wine is held in high regard, perhaps second only to ginseng wine. Chu chi grows from a kind of tree with leaves slightly like those of the maple. It is a form of berry, red in colour when still fresh. Dried in the sun, it looks like raisins, though much redder. People use the dried berries to soak in spirits to make the chu chi wine. Chinese herbal physicians generally recommend it to older men in the belief that it may be too much of a stimulant for the young.

For those who go for milder wines, they can have mulberry wine, date wine, litchi wine, dragon-eye (a kind of sub-tropical fruit) wine and grape wine. These wines are produced across the country wherever the particular fruit is grown in abundance, are often used as dinner wines and are no stronger than claret or burgundy.

It must be noted that to derive benefits from food and drink for sexual purposes is not for the poor. Fortunately, however, walnuts, chestnuts, mulberries, garlic, spring onions and unprocessed honey are not beyond their pockets. In any case the poor do not go to the same extremes of indulgence as the rich. This reminds one of a Chinese saying: 'A well-fed stomach plus a well-clad body breeds lust in a man.'

CONCUBINES VS. MISTRESSES

Like people elsewhere in the world, the Chinese can be divided into different social strata, though class distinction in China has ceased to mean anything since the downfall of the Manchu Court. Therefore, it is not unnatural for people with a different background, upbringing and environment to differ in their attitudes towards life as a whole and sex in particular.

The Chinese people as a whole accept sex with matter-of-factness. To them it is a natural instinct, which has to be fulfilled. But it is not in their nature to go to the extreme of permissiveness or exhibitionism, the rich and the privileged excepted. Take concubinage for instance; it has undeniably created in the West the misconception that the Chinese are polygamists. But in fact, even in the old days, ninety-nine per cent of the Chinese males were monogamists. Many sociologists tend to condemn concubinage as a symbol of backwardness and of sex inequality in China. But they seem to have overlooked the fact that there were only a very small fraction of Chinese males who had the means to keep concubines. As for those Chinese who did have concubines, they were at least frank enough not to hide them from public knowledge. In a sense, concubines of the privileged Chinese are no more morally wrong than mistresses kept by wealthy Westerners. The difference, however, lies in the contrast between frankness and hypocrisy. Socially speaking, the children produced by concubines are at least accepted and protected, while in the West the number of illegitimate children is alarmingly large.

Of course, in the old China, some people did take far too many concubines. One of the well-known cases is a certain former Szechuan warlord who was in Chungking in the early 1940s. At that time, he was said to have about twenty concubines and each of them had borne him two or three children. He naturally did not have the chance to know all his children, not even by sight. Each year, he summoned all his children together on two occasions: Chinese New Year's Day and his own birthday. When his some fifty children formed a long queue to pay respects to him, each of them had to announce his or her name to the father, identifying himself or herself by saying, for instance, 'your number thirty child by so-and-so'.

The most amusing aspect of this former warlord's disbanding of his concubines was his endeavour to educate them. In early 1949, when the Chinese Communists were about to sweep over the south-west of China, he called an emergency meeting of all his concubines, giving each of them a golden handshake and telling them that they were free to do whatever they liked. But with a few young ones who had received some form of university education, he persuaded them to go to the U.S.A. to study for an advanced degree so that they would be better qualified to find 'new-fashioned' husbands. Some of these young women followed his advice and are now happily settled in America.

As for himself, he has lived in Taiwan in semi-retirement since 1949. Now in his eighties, he is still fit enough to do some mountain climbing. After moving to Taiwan, however, he has adopted a new system of concubine-taking for himself in the past twenty years. He now takes only one young concubine at a time, for a term of three years. Upon the expiration of her term, she is given ten thousand U.S. dollars to go abroad to study, plus the freedom to marry anyone she likes. This has unavoidably become the talk of the town in Taiwan. But he has made no bones of his usual practice however unusual it may seem to the world at large.

NUDISM WITH A DIFFERENT MOTIVE

Not surprisingly, nudism does not really interest the Chinese, except for those who have become Westernised in their concept of sex. Perhaps this attitude is tied up with Chinese dislike of exhibitionism, as well as their belief that sex is private and personal. But a hippy scholar in the Hsi Chin Dynasty (3rd-4th century) could have been one of the forerunners of the nudist movement in the whole world. Liu Ling by name, he was a great drinker and looked at everything with contempt. Sometimes he would walk about in the nude in his house. When some of his friends tried to dissuade him from doing so, he told them to stop worrying for he regarded 'heaven and earth as my house and my house as my clothes'. It must have been rather sad from his angle, for he remained an individual nudist without followers. However, the motive behind Liu Ling's nudist practice had nothing to do with either sex or health. He went nude to demonstrate his cynicism towards the establishment and the society of which he was an unwilling member.

The dislike of exhibitionism could have been one of the reasons why strip-tease acts are dismissed by most Chinese as 'low class and bad taste'. Even in the 'sophisticated' Shanghai in those days, strip-tease girls were mercilessly sneered at by prostitutes and women of loose virtue. It is equally true that many Chinese men have visited strip-tease clubs in other parts of the world. This is due more to their curiosity than to a desire to seek erotic pleasure.

By no means prudish, the overwhelming majority of Chinese enjoy healthy sex. To them, passion should only exist between man and woman and love-making is the physical expression of passion at its climax, perfectly normal and totally acceptable. The fact they seldom kiss or cuddle in public places does not mean that they are less passionate than their occidental counterparts. Realistic as they are, most Chinese deem it unnecessary to express their love and passion in words, let alone reveal them indiscreetly to the eyes of strangers. Subtle by nature, they know where and when to let themselves be carried away by their passion.

In love-making, both the privileged and the ordinary people do their best to seek fulfilment. But it is irrefutable that many Chinese men do fail to make their women enjoy sex as much as they do themselves. This is partly due to lack of sex education, though the traditional modesty in Chinese women is another factor.

It is worth mentioning that sexual indulgence exists only among the privileged class. With the aid of their wealth and influence, they are able to seek change and novelty in the opposite sex. But as for the ordinary people, they enjoy sex in the most natural and normal manner. To them it is a matter of need which should be met with moderation.

Accepting sex as a normal relationship between man and woman, the Chinese as a whole despise homosexuality and lesbianism. When a Chinese swears at another of his compatriots, nothing is more insulting than the expression 'rabbit' or 'rabbit's egg' (son of a homosexual). Towards lesbianism they seem to be slightly more tolerant, perhaps because the Chinese lesbians are but a drop in the human sea and are, in any case, extremely discreet in practising their perversion. As a matter of fact, the Chinese do not condemn homosexuals or lesbians on moral grounds. It is the unnaturalness and abnormality of the practice that angers them. That is why 'human monster' has been extensively used in China to indicate a homosexual or a lesbian.

CHAPTER SEVEN

The Art of the Bedchamber

Chinese love techniques, veiled under the name of the art of the bedchamber, owe their origin to one of the many schools of Taoism, which asserts that immortality can be achieved through the 'correct way of conducting intercourse, so that yang can benefit from yin and yin from yang'. As Tao means 'the way' or 'ways' and Taoists in China used to include metaphysicians, alchemists, mediums, magicians, astronomers, astrologers and many other non-conformists of Confucianism, Taoism has developed under a free rein and its influence has been more extensive than most people realise.

As early as the Eastern Han Dynasty (A.D. 25-220), a school of Taoists created the Yin Taoism which established the theoretical basis of immortality through sex. Understandably, the theory and the practice were snatched up by the emperors as the key to longevity, if not immortality, especially since their sexual indulgence could now be justified.

It was this school of Taoists who took pains to write volumes and volumes of sex manuals including *Su Nu Ching* (*Manual of Lady Purity*), *Yu Fang Mi Chueh* (*Secret Codes of the Jade Room*), the *Art of the Bedchamber* and *Yu Fang Chih Yao* (*Important Guidelines of the Jade Room*). To lend authenticity to their works and to exert psychological influence on the emperors, these Yin Taoists attributed the key points in their manuals to Huang Ti (the Yellow Emperor) and Peng Tsu, who reputedly lived to 800 years of age—born towards the end of the ancient Hsia Dynasty.

These manuals assert that the Yellow Emperor became an immortal after having had intercourse with 1,200 women and that Peng Tsu, through the 'correct way of making love to ten to twenty young girls every single night', was able to live to such a great age.

Obviously written from the man's angle, these manuals emphasise the importance for yang (the male) to assume the initiative and exert full control during the whole process of love-making. It is also stressed that though a man 'can make love to as many as thirty to forty women every night, he must be able not to discharge at all'.

As to the frequency of discharge, according to *Su Nu Ching*, Lady Purity gave the Yellow Emperor the following advice: 'At the age of twenty, a strong man can afford to "give" (discharge with control) several times each day; and a weak man, once. At thirty, a strong man once each day, a weak one once every other day. At forty, a strong man every three days, a weak one, every four days. At fifty, a fit man every five days; an unfit one every ten days. At sixty, a fit man every ten days; an unfit one every twenty days. At seventy, a fitman every thirty days; an unfit one must *not* "give".'

LADY MYSTERY'S THEORY OF LOVE-MAKING

Other than Lady Purity, the Yellow Emperor had another adviser in Hsuan Nu (Lady Mystery). In *Hsuan Nu Ching* (*Manual of Lady Mystery*), probably more ancient than the other sex manuals, a dialogue between the Yellow Emperor and Lady Mystery runs as follows: 'The Yellow Emperor asked: "I have learned something about the yin-yang technique from Su Nu, now would you enlighten me on the principle?" Lady Mystery replied: "In the universe everything abides with the principle of yin and yang. With the aid of yin, yang expands; with the aid of yang, yin flows. One yin and one yang are mutually complementary. Therefore, when the male feels strong, the female responds with vibration, thus enabling the interflow of seeds and secretion. Conducted with moderation, this process yields great pleasure and prolongs one's life." '

However, Lady Mystery went on to clarify the Yellow Emperor's doubt about the opportune moment to commence love-making. 'The Yellow Emperor asked: "When a man is not pleased during intercourse, his jade-stem does not stir up, nor does it stay strong. Why?" Lady Mystery explained: "Yin and yang attract and react to each other. Without the aid of yin, yang cannot arouse. Therefore, prior to intercourse, the man and the woman must both feel the need and anticipate the pleasure of it. Without mutual understanding and preliminary caresses, a spiritual harmony—the foundation of love-making —cannot be achieved. Under such circumstances, neither the man nor the woman is quite ready. Caresses and endearing words will stimulate the woman to respond to the man's desire. Her jade-doorway will vibrate and become moist, ready to greet his jade-stem. When his jade-stem enters her jade-doorway, it must combine slow movements with fast ones, sometimes gentle, sometimes vigorous. If Your Majesty follows these points with care, you will definitely derive both benefit and pleasure from it, no matter how strong your partner may be." '

When the Yellow Emperor turned to Lady Purity for further advice concerning actual technique, she said: ' "Before you commence love-making, you ask the woman to lie flat on her back and bend both her knees. While entering her, your opened mouth contacts hers and sucks her tongue. Let your jade-stem first of all knock about outside her jade-doorway for a while. Then push it in slowly and steadily. If your jade-stem is bursting, push it in for one and a half inches; if it is not yet in full erection, push it in for one inch and do not shake. Take it out and push it in more deeply this time. Once the jade-stem enters the jade-doorway completely the woman feels the warmth inside her and will respond by moving her body up and down in harmony with your thrusts, trembling slightly. As soon as the jade-stem reaches the depth of three and one-half inches, you should close your mouth tightly while thrusting. Pause after every nine thrusts and do not thrust any more after you have done so for eighty-one times.' "

THE NINE BASIC METHODS

Regarding the methods, Lady Mystery gave a list of nine:

(1) The Dragon Turns

The woman lies on her back and the man bends over her. She opens her jade-doorway to admit his jade-stem. He lets it reach the depth of five inches, moving and shaking slowly. While thrusting, his jade-stem goes not too deep for eight times and very deep for two times.

(2) The Tiger Slinks

The woman kneels on the bed, head down and hips up. The man kneels behind her and embraces her belly. He pushes his jade-stem into her, deep and tight. They must move in harmony, and he is to thrust for thirty-two times. Then stop and rest.

(3) The Monkey Wrestles

The woman lies on her back and the man places her legs on his shoulders and pushes her knees over her bosom. Her back and hips are raised to a suitable angle for him to push his jade-stem into her jade-doorway, as deep as three inches. The woman moves and shakes. He keeps on thrusting vigorously until she is contented.

(4) The Cicada Clings

The woman lies on her stomach, stretching herself, and opens her legs. The man lies over her back and raises her hips slightly. Then he pushes his jade-stem deep into her and thrusts for fifty-four times.

(5) The Turtle Stirs

The woman lies on her back and bends her knees. The man pushes her feet until her knees reach her breasts. He enters her, thrusting at random, sometimes deep, sometimes shallow. Responsive, she raises and moves her body automatically. When she becomes very moist, he pushes his jade-stem as far as it can go. Stop when the woman shows signs of content.

(6) The Phoenix Hovers

The woman lies with her face upwards and holds her legs apart with her own hands. The man kneels between her thighs, and pushes his jade-stem into her until reaching the depth of four inches. This will make her move rhythmically. He thrusts for twenty-four times and she will be exceedingly satisfied.

(7) The Rabbit Nibbles the Hair

The man lies on his back and stretches his legs. The woman kneels over his body, resting her weight on her knees and facing his feet, with her head lowered. He pushes his jade-stem into her, only one inch deep. The woman is bound to enjoy his random thrusts and will soon reach a climax.

(8) The Fish Interlock Their Scales

The man lies flat on his back. The woman sits lightly over his body, her thighs open to enable him to enter her slowly, no deeper than the point of two inches.

(9) The Cranes Entwine Their Necks

The man sits on the bed, bending his knees to the degree that the soles of his feet face each other. The woman opens her legs and sits on his thighs, holding his neck with her hands. He enters her as deeply as two inches and holds her hips to help them move rhythmically. The woman will naturally feel comfortable. Stop when she is contented.

PENG TSU'S PREFERENCE FOR VIRGINS

Peng Tsu's discourse on love-making, extensively quoted in both the *Secret Codes of the Jade Room* and the *Important Guidelines of the Jade Room*, lays more emphasis on the health aspect of intercourse. Unlike the Yellow Emperor, he expounded his theory while answering questions put to him by Ts'ai Nu (Lady Splendour).

He seemed to be extremely keen on having virgins, which is fully illustrated by his own words: ' "If a man wants to derive great benefit from intercourse, it is best for him to find partners in inexperienced females. He ought to make love to virgins and this will restore his youthful looks. What a pity there are not many virgins available! An ideal virgin is generally in the fourteen to nineteen age group. A woman under thirty is still all right, but she must not have given birth to a child. My late master observed these principles strictly. He lived to 3,000 years of age. One can become an immortal if one takes the right kind of herbs at the same time.

' "Still, to preserve health and prolong life through the ways of yin and yang, one cannot achieve one's aim by using one female. One will have to make love to three, nine or eleven women each night, the more the better." '

Regarding the problem of discharge, Peng Tsu discussed it with Lady Splendour: 'Lady Splendour asked: "Discharge is the pleasure of intercourse. Now if you refrain from discharging, how can that pleasure be obtained?" Peng Tsu answered: "After discharge, your body aches, your ears buzz, your eyes feel drowsy, your throat feels dry. The pleasure really does not last long. If you move without discharging, you will not have the aforesaid symptoms and your pleasure will be a lasting one." '

It seems that Peng Tsu attached more importance to the preliminaries. He said: 'The correct way of intercourse is, not surprisingly, difficult. You must be relaxed and calm. Remember to be as gentle as you can. You fondle her organ and ask for her tongue. When she responds, you will find her ears turning red, as if after a few drinks, and her breasts swelling, big enough to fill your open hands. She will also shift her bottom from time to time and her legs will tremble almost invisibly. This is the right moment for you to enter her, gradually and slowly. When she starts to hold you tight, you can then push your jade-stem to the very depth inside her. All the while, your mouth presses on hers, your tongue licks hers. It is good for you to swallow her saliva during the whole process, which is a natural tonic for your health. In this way, she will have an orgasm without your having to discharge.'

THE WOMAN'S STAGES OF DESIRE

Presumably from the female's angle, Lady Purity told the Yellow Emperor how to detect the woman's stages of desire. ' "When her face flushes, approach her gently. When her nose perspires and her breasts swell, enter her slowly. When she sounds husky and swallows her saliva, shake your jade-stem gently. When she becomes very moist inside, push your jade-stem as deeply as it can go. When her secretion overflows to the backside, guide it back to her jade-doorway." '

Concerning the woman's responses, she asserted: ' "When she wants it, she becomes short of breath and sometimes inhales hard. When she desires it, her mouth opens and her nostrils distend. When she wants more of it, she throws her arms around you. When she is about to reach contentment, she perspires all over. When she is extremely contented, she stretches her body and her eyes are fixed." '

Perhaps to enlighten the Yellow Emperor to a further extent, this mythical lady went on: ' "When the woman embraces you and rubs your body with hers, she is ready. When she stretches her legs, she wants you to rub her body from above. When she moves her belly, she wants you to discharge. When her hips shake, she enjoys the pleasure of it. When she raises her legs to pull your body closer to hers, she wants you to push your jade-stem as deeply as possible. When she interlocks her thighs, she is extremely itchy inside. When she wiggles sideways and shivers, she wants you to probe both sides of her flowery path. When she raises her body upwards against yours, she is extremely contented. When she jerks, she feels the pleasure even in her limbs. When her secretion overflows all over, she has reached an orgasm. If you are observant, you will be able to see the extent of her pleasures." '

FURTHER DEVELOPMENT OF THEORIES AND TECHNIQUES

At a later period, however, a Taoist named Tung Hsuan Tzu further developed the theories and instructions left behind by Lady Purity, Lady Mystery, the Yellow Emperor and Peng Tsu in his manual the *Art of the Bedchamber*.

Like all the Yin Taoists, he went to great lengths to convince people that immortality could be achieved through the yin-yang harmony, provided one knew how to make love to women with ample self-control and moderation.

In his introduction to his work he remarks: 'Of all creatures, man is the noblest and wisest. Of all human behaviour, intercourse is most sublime. It is based on the laws of Heaven and Earth, regulating the yin and the yang. If one can grasp its principles, one will be able to preserve one's natural strength and prolong one's life. If one fails to do so, one will be harmed and die young.

'Having made exhaustive studies, I am of the opinion that the methods left to us by Lady Mystery embrace all the essential principles. But as these methods are merely in the form of outlines, there is the need to fill in details and add some explanatory notes. It is for this reason that I have written my manual, endeavouring to throw some light on the key points hitherto unclarified.'

On the preliminaries Tung Hsuan Tzu asserts: 'The Heaven turns to the left and the Earth to the right. The man sings and the woman echoes. This is the law of nature. If the man stirs and the woman does not respond, or if the woman makes a move and the man does not oblige, it will be harmful to both of them. Therefore, the man must turn to the left and the woman to the right; he must descend from above and she receives him from below—this coincides with the union of the Heaven and the Earth.

'Prior to the intercourse, the woman sits first and then lies down, to the left of the man. After lying down for a while, ask the woman to lie squarely on her back, opening her legs wide and stretching her arms. The man covers her body, resting his weight on his two knees placed between her thighs. Then he proceeds to rub his jade-stem gently but persistently against the outside of her jade-doorway, like a lone pine standing proudly at the mouth of a mountain cave. While the rubbing process is going on, he opens her mouth with his and sucks her tongue. With his hands fondling her breasts or private parts, he can either look at her face or her jade-doorway. As soon as the woman shows signs of being entranced, the man can move his jade-stem more quickly, but still remaining outside. However, when the woman's secretion overflows like a flood, the man can throw his jade-stem into her jade-doorway immediately, discharging as soon as possible to enable the interflow of seeds and secretion. After discharging, he must carry on thrusting until the woman asks him to spare her. Then he can pull his jade-stem out for a short while, to be wiped with a piece of silk. When this is done, he must enter her again, thrusting shallowly for nine times and deeply for one. His movements should vary from time to time, sometimes deep, sometimes shallow, sometimes vigorous and sometimes gentle. After breathing in and breathing out for twenty-one times, the woman is about to reach another climax. The man must now push his jade-stem to the depth of five inches, thrusting quickly and rubbing against both sides of her flowery path. Again she will become extremely moist inside and feel very contented. At this moment, the man must withdraw at once to avoid discharging for a second time. If he is careless enough to discharge again, it is very bad for his health. Therefore, he must be very, very careful about it.'

THIRTY POSITIONS FROM HEAVEN TO EARTH

Tung Hsuan Tzu lists thirty positions of love-making, mainly based on the nine methods of Lady Mystery, though with more variety:

(1) The Cuddling Chat

The woman lies on the right side of the bed and the man on the left. They kiss, embrace and caress each other to kindle the flame of passion, whispering all sorts of endearing words.

(2) The Passionate Narration

The positions remain more or less unchanged. The man becomes more active with his hands, touching the woman's nipples, navel, and secret entrances, gently first and then with a quicker tempo. He sucks her tongue and she his.

(3) The Fish Exposes Its Gills

With all parts of their bodies in contact and the man's hands roving all over her, the woman is aroused and her jade-doorway vibrates and becomes moist with the overflow of secretion.

(4) The Unicorn Shows Its Horn

The man rises and hovers over the woman, who has by now instinctively opened her legs. He rubs and tickles the outside parts of her jade-doorway with his jade-stem to further arouse her passion so that he can enter her more smoothly. The above four postures and moves are all the 'outside-wandering' methods, which should be performed with subtlety and tenderness.

(5) The Silkworms Entwine

The woman lies on her back, raising her arms to embrace the nape of the man's neck, her two feet clasping his back. He kneels between her thighs, embracing the nape of her neck, and pushes his jade-stem into her.

(6) The Dragon Swings

The woman lies face upwards and bends both knees, keeping them together. The man kneels near her, pushing her feet with his left hand to make her knees reach her breasts. He uses his right hand to push his jade-stem into her jade-doorway.

(7) The Fish Eye to Eye

Both the man and the woman lie on their sides, face to face. She places one leg over his body and he stretches his legs in between hers. Using one hand to lift her upper leg, he enters her. Meanwhile, they open their mouths to suck each other's tongues.

(8) The Swallows of One Heart

The woman lies on her back and opens her legs wide apart. The man kneels across her stomach, holding the nape of her neck with his hands. She embraces his waist, to guide his jade-stem into her jade-doorway.

(9) The Kingfishers Unite

Ask the woman to lie on her back and bend her knees. The man kneels, with his legs apart, between her thighs. He embraces her hips and pushes his jade-stem into her, as deep as one inch.

(10) The Mandarin Ducks Play
Ask the woman to lie on her side and bend her knees as if in a sitting position. The man lies on his side behind her, lifting her upper leg with his knee and putting his other leg over her lower leg, and enters her.

(11) The Butterflies Somersault
The man lies on his back and opens his legs wide. The woman sits lightly on his thighs, resting her weight on her two feet on the bed. She uses her hand to guide his jade-stem into her jade-doorway.

(12) The Flying Widgeon at the Back
The man lies face upwards and opens his legs. The woman sits on his thighs, back to his face. She lowers her head to hold his jade-stem with both hands and put it into her jade-doorway.

(13) The Pine with a Drooping Top
The woman, lying on her back, raises her hips slightly by interlocking her feet high in the air. The man embraces her waist with both hands and she does the same to him. She pulls him towards her to admit his jade-stem.

(14) Approaching the Fragrant Bamboo
Both the man and the woman stand on the floor, face to face. They hold each other tightly around their loins. He enters her to the very depth of her flowery path.

(15) The Blue Phoenixes Dance in Pairs
The woman lies face upwards with her knees bent. The man squats over her with his jade-stem in the vicinity of her jade-doorway. He pushes his jade-stem into her, thrusting upwards and downwards.

(16) The Phoenix Cuddles Her Baby Bird
The woman is plump and big in build, while the man is small and short. He enters her from above—quite a spectacle.

(17) The Seagull Hovers

The man stands by the bed and lifts up the woman's legs. He pushes his jade-stem deep into her jade-doorway.

(18) The Mustang Hops

Make the woman lie on her back. The man lifts both her feet, so that they rest on his right shoulder. He pushes his jade-stem into her jade-doorway deeply.

(19) The Galloping Feet

Ask the woman to lie face upwards. The man squats by her, his left hand holding the nape of her neck, his right hand lifting both her feet. He then enters her.

(20) The Mare Shakes Her Hooves

Make the woman lie on her back. The man places one of her feet on his shoulder while she holds the other high with her own hand. He pushes his jade-stem to reach the utmost depth of her flowery path. Immense pleasure!

(21) The White Tiger Leaps

Make the woman rest her weight on her bent knees, face touching the mattress. The man kneels behind her, girdling her waist with both his arms. Then he pushes his jade-stem into her jade-doorway from that angle.

(22) The Black Cicada Clings

Make the woman lie on her stomach and open her legs wide. The man bends his knees and stays between her thighs. Holding her shoulders with his hands, he pushes his jade-stem into her jade-doorway from the rear.

(23) The Goat Faces the Tree

The man sits on the bed, bending his knees to make the soles of his feet face each other. He makes the woman sit on his legs, with her back to his face. She lowers her head to put his jade-stem into her; he holds her waist tightly.

(24) The Rooster Descends on the Ring

The man stays on the bed, half-squatting and half-sitting. He asks a little girl to hold his jade-stem and put it into the woman's jade-doorway, while another little girl holds the woman's skirt up from behind to facilitate the movements of her legs. Very exciting!

(25) The Phoenix Saunters in the Crimson Cave
Ask the woman to lie on her back and lift her legs with her own hands. The man kneels near her hips and rests his weight on both his hands, which are placed on the bed. He lets his jade-stem find its way into her crimson cave. Very pleasant.

(26) The Roc in the Firmament
Make the woman lie face upwards. The man puts her feet on both his arms and stretches his hands downwards to hold her waist to facilitate the entry of his jade-stem.

(27) The Crooning Monkey Embraces the Tree
The man sits with his legs forming a circle. The woman rides on his thighs, embracing him with both her hands. He holds her hips with one hand in order to enter her, using his other hand as a lever on the bed.

(28) The Cat and the Mouse Share One Cave
The man lying on his back stretches his legs. The woman lies above him and lets his jade-stem enter deep inside her. Then he makes her lie on her stomach and rises to get on top of her, pushing his jade-stem into her jade-doorway from her backside.

(29) The Donkeys in the Late Spring
The woman stands on the bed on all fours. The man stands behind her, embracing her waist with both hands and pushing his jade-stem into her at once. Extremely pleasant!

(30) The Dogs in the Late Autumn
Both the man and the woman are on all fours on the bed, hips to hips. He lowers his head and uses one hand to put his jade-stem into her jade-doorway.

TWENTY-EIGHT UNNAMED POSITIONS

In addition to the above thirty positions with fantastic names, Tung Hsuan Tzu gives twenty-eight unnamed ones:

(1) The woman lies on her back and holds her left leg up high. The man lies on his side to her left. He holds her left leg with one hand and pushes his jade-stem into her jade-doorway.

(2) The woman lies on her back and holds her right leg up high. The man lies on his side to her right. He puts his right leg over her left leg, holding her breasts with his right hand. Then he supports her right leg with his shoulder and pushes his jade-stem into her jade-doorway.

(3) The woman lies on her back and holds both her legs up high. The man lies on his side, next to her bottom, to form a right angle. Then he enters her.

(4) The woman lies on her back with her knees bent. The man sits next to her hips with his legs wide open. He pushes his jade-stem into her jade-doorway, no shallower than one inch and no deeper than two inches.

(5) The woman lies on her back, holding her legs closely together. The man lies above her, fondling her breasts with both hands. He can try to force his jade-stem to enter her jade-doorway.

(6) The woman lies face downwards, holding her legs closely together. Then she uses her hands to hold her posterior apart, while the man bends over her back and probes her jade-doorway with his jade-stem.

(7) The woman places the upper part of her body on the bed, with one leg lying on the edge of the bed and the other resting on the floor. The man stands by the bed and pushes his jade-stem into her.

(8) The woman spans the man's body, with one leg kneeling on the bed while the other is in a squatting angle. He raises his body to push his jade-stem into her jade-doorway.

(9) The woman places the upper part of her body sideways on the bed, bending her knees along the bedside, with her hips protruding for two or three inches from the edge of the bed. The man stands beside the bed and enters her from her backside.

(10) The woman bends over a table. She places one leg on the edge of the table while with her other leg she remains in a standing

position. The man stands behind her, holding her shoulders with his hands and pushing it in.

(11) The man and the woman stand face to face. She lifts one leg to clasp his waist and he supports her hips with both hands. Then he pushes his jade-stem into her jade-doorway.

(12) The man lies on his back. The woman sits on his thighs, opening her legs as wide apart as she can. Then her jade-doorway will be wide open to greet his jade-stem.

(13) The woman lies on her back, lifting her feet to reach her shoulders. The man bends over her hips and pushes his jade-stem into her.

(14) The woman lies on her back, holding her right leg up high with her right hand and left leg up high with her left hand, and bending them to reach her shoulders. The man bends over her hips to push his jade-stem into her. Or he can shift her near the edge of the bed and enter her while standing by the bed.

(15) The man lies on his back. The woman sits on him, putting his jade-stem into her jade-doorway. Then she uses her two hands as levers, spinning over him like a top.

(16) The man lies on his back. The woman squats over him. He pushes his jade-stem into her jade-doorway, and with the aid of the foreparts of his feet he moves it inside her in all directions.

(17) The woman lies the other way round on a couch with a slanting back, lifting her legs high and apart. The man enters her from the high spot where he stands.

(18) The woman lies on either side, stretching one leg and holding the other up high. The man lies forming a right angle to her thighs and pushes his jade-stem into her.

(19) The woman lies the other way round on the bed, stretching one leg and holding the other high. The man squats between her thighs, opening them and pushing his jade-stem into her jade-doorway. He embraces her upheld leg and thrusts incessantly.

(20) The man stands on the floor. The woman embraces the nape of his neck with her arms, her legs entwining his waist. The man holds her hips with both hands, putting his jade-stem into her and walking around the room.

(21) The woman stands on the floor, keeping her legs closed and stretching her hands to reach her toes. The man pushes his jade-stem into her jade-doorway from behind.

(22) The woman stands on the floor, bending her body backwards. The man reaches the floor backwards with his hands, then pushes his jade-stem into her jade-doorway from the front.

(23) The woman lies on her back, shifting her hips near the edge of the bed with her thighs wide apart. The man fondles her breasts with both hands and licks her jade-doorway with his tongue.

(24) The man and the woman lie on the bed, with her head between his legs and his head placed upon her private parts. She sucks his jade-stem and he puts his tongue into her jade-doorway, licking around.

(25) Make the woman squat on a chair or on the edge of the bed, with her hands holding the arms of the chair or the posters of the bed. She bends forward to raise her hips up high, her legs apart. The man stands behind her and pushes his jade-stem into her jade-doorway. She rotates her hips, sometimes slowly, sometimes quickly. Meanwhile, she alternately lets his jade-stem remain deep inside or rather shallow. He moves his jade-stem in harmony with the movements of her hips. Extremely pleasant.

(26) The woman stands on the floor, with her back leaning against something firm, or she can lie on her back. With both hands she lifts her left leg upwards so that her left foot can be placed on her right shoulder. The man faces her and pushes his jade-stem into her jade-doorway.

(27) The woman opens her thighs as widely as she can, bending forwards to an angle so sharp that her head almost touches the floor. She holds her ankles with both hands and her hips naturally go upwards, protruding. The man pushes his jade-stem into her jade-doorway from behind.

(28) The woman lies on her back, holding her left foot with her left hand and right foot with her right hand, and stretching them to reach her shoulder blades through the armpits. With both feet touching each other behind her back, her jade-doorway opens in an elevated position. The man bends over her and pushes his jade-stem to reach the innermost part of her flowery path.

POSITIONS FOR SPECIAL CASES

True, the fifty-eight positions listed by this Yin Taoist range from the easiest to the hardest and some of them actually require the skill of acrobats and contortionists. But, judging by his 'Heaven and Earth' theory, one can visualise that in his mind preference must have been given to the more conventional ones.

Moreover, some of his disciples do explain in their annotations to the Manual the reasons why their master went to such extremes. They assume that, 'due to the difference in length, depth, shape and position of their sex organs, some males and females have to resort to seemingly strange love postures as a remedy'.

To strengthen their argument, they assert: 'If a woman has a rather shallow jade-doorway and her man has a big jade-stem, it is advisable for them to adopt positions such as *The Fish Eye to Eye, The Mandarin Ducks Play* and *The Butterflies Somersault*. Otherwise, she is bound to find more pain than pleasure.

'If a man and a woman are both fat, it is only sensible to resort to positions such as *The White Tiger Leaps* or *The Black Cicada Clings*, so that their protruding stomachs will not be in their way.

'When a woman is pregnant, positions such as *The Goat Faces the Tree* and *The Seagull Hovers* should be adopted for the sake of safety. And if a man is exceedingly fat and heavy, it is far better for the woman to be on top of him.

'While with a woman who is slightly frigid, to enter her from the rear is possibly the best solution. The same position is applicable to a woman whose jade-doorway lies more to the back.

'To satisfy an extraordinarily sexy woman, *The Butterflies Somersault* as well as number 15 and number 16 of the unnamed twenty-eight positions are the answer ...'

SOME POSITIONS POPULARISED BY NOVELS

Historically speaking, love techniques and positions introduced by *The Art of the Bedchamber* and the other Taoist sex manuals only began to find their way into the sex life of ordinary people in the 16th century, when novels first became an accepted form of literature. As most novelists in those days wrote under pen-names, they felt at liberty to embellish love scenes with a wealth of erotic details without having to worry overmuch about their reputations. In some of these novels the writers were ingenious in devising suggestive metaphors and similes to describe this or that love position. But essentially, they were merely translating into their own words what they had read about in the above-mentioned sex manuals.

To prove this point, it is necessary to list a few positions of love-making fairly well-known to many Chinese:

(1) Tiger Climbing the Mountain
The woman kneels on all fours on the bed, with her hips raised. The man enters her from behind. Or she can bend over the bed while standing on the floor and he enters her in the same way. This position originates from *The White Tiger Leaps*.

(2) Old Fellow Pushing a Wheelbarrow
The woman lies on her back on the bed. The man stands at the bedside and holds both her legs while entering her. This position reminds one of *The Seagull Hovers*.

(3) Plugging the Lotus Upside Down
The man lies on his back on the bed and the woman is above him when love-making takes place. This position is similar to *The Butterflies Somersault*.

(4) The Jade Girl Playing the Flute
The man lies either on his side or his back on the bed. The woman sucks his jade-stem until he is satisfied. This is akin to number 24 among the twenty-eight unnamed positions listed in the *Art of the Bedchamber*.

(5) Mandarin Ducks Playing in the Water
The woman lies face upwards in the bathtub, her body partly covered by the water. The man enters her from above. This is but a varied version of *The Silkworms Entwine* or any other position with the woman under the man.

However, it must be admitted that two other positions seem to be more original, though their practicability remains doubtful:

(1) Twin Dragons Teasing the Phoenix
The woman lies on her side between two men. The one facing her enters her in the usual way while the other man uses her as a sodomite. The point is: both men should act simultaneously.

(2) Shooting the 'Arrow' While Galloping
The woman lies on a table or any other high object, with her legs

wide apart. The man runs towards her from some distance and aims at entering her at the first try.

SOME WAYS TO PROLONG THE MALE'S ENDURANCE

It must be reiterated that, though these ancient manuals may slightly differ in their explanations of certain love techniques and positions, yet their basic concept is the same. The male represents positiveness and domination and is the party to give fulfilment. Therefore, he must always have the initiative and exert full control throughout the whole process. As regards discharge, he can 'give', but only if he wants to. Reading between the lines, one can clearly see that these Yin Taoists are unanimous in advocating the concept that the man's fulfilment does not lie in discharge.

In the case of the female, none of these manuals overlooks her passiveness, slower response and reliance on the male for fulfilment. This accounts for the emphasis on caresses, kisses and other preliminaries before the actual intercourse.

In view of these factors, the prolonging of the male's endurance has necessarily become the chief concern of these ancient sex theoreticians.

As for how to refrain from discharging, the *Important Guidelines of the Jade Room* says: 'During intercourse, the moment you feel that the seeds (sperm) are trying to exude, quickly put the index and second fingers of your left hand on your groin and press it hard. Meanwhile, open your mouth to exhale heavily and then grind your teeth together for thirty to fifty times. In this way, the seeds will return to their fountain through the jade-stem.'

The same manual also asserts: 'While you are trying to benefit yang from yin during intercourse, and yet your seeds have the urge to exude, quickly raise your head and open your eyes wide. Look to the left, to the right, upwards and downwards. Meanwhile, contract the muscles of your lower abdomen. With this done, your seeds will immediately cease to abandon you.'

However, apart from the above advice given in this manual, there are two folk methods which have been proved by many Chinese men as effective. The one is: during the process of love-making, the man remains calm and relaxed; and it will be even better if he can keep his mind busily occupied with something else. But this form of 'psychological self-control' invites no little opposition, for it, in fact, strips love-making of its emotional element.

The other method sounds quite simple. It is recommended that before going to bed every night, the man should wash his private parts with cold water and soak his feet in hot water for some fifteen minutes. Naturally, the effectiveness of this cannot be assured unless it is practised regularly, without a single day's interruption.

CHAPTER EIGHT

Aphrodisiacs, Instruments and Devices

Basically, the ancient Taoist sex experts dissuaded people from resorting to any artificial means in order to achieve fulfilment, for they firmly believed that love-making, being a human instinct, must abide within the laws of nature. Peng Tsu is quoted in the *Secret Codes of the Jade Room* as saying: 'That a man's life is shortened by adulteries and licentiousness may not have been caused by spirits and gods. But if one puts some sort of powder into a woman's jade-doorway or carves a tusk into the shape of a man's jade-stem for use, he or she is bound to age quickly and speed up the descent of death.' Judging by these words, this mystic figure's objection to the use of aphrodisiacs or instruments is crystal clear.

But since the Taoists as a whole were convinced that 'immortality can be achieved by taking the right kinds of herbs to supplement meditation', their colleagues of the Yin School naturally turned to herbs believed to possess aphrodisiac value, with a view to the improvement of virility and intensification of sexual pleasure for both sexes.

As a result, quite a few 'exclusive prescriptions' have been left by them for posterity, to serve different purposes. But as Chinese herbs are diversified in both medicinal characteristics and chemical properties, each of these prescriptions consists of a number of herbs which, unfortunately, are mostly unobtainable outside China.

SOME PRESCRIPTIONS WITH TONIC VALUE

To maintain a man's potency, Wang Tao, a herbal physician in the T'ang Dynasty, includes in his *Collection of Secret Prescriptions* the following four prescriptions—based on Lady Purity's instructions —for spring, summer, autumn and winter uses:

(1) For the Spring:

(1 fen=0.36 grams)

Fu ling (and underground fungus)	4 fen	Fan feng (a kind of herb)	4 fen
Ch'ang p'u (Acorus calamus)	4 fen	Shu yu (yam root)	4 fen
		Hsu tuan (a kind of herb)	4 fen
Shan chu yu (a kind of plant)	4 fen	She ch'uang tzu (seeds of a kind of herb)	4 fen
K'u lou root (a kind of herb)	4 fen	Cypress seeds	4 fen
		Pa chi t'ien (a kind of herb)	4 fen
T'u ssu tzu (seeds of a kind of herb)	4 fen	T'ien hsiung (a kind of herb)	4 fen
Niu ch'i (a kind of herb)	4 fen	Yuan chih peel (milkwort)	4 fen
Ch'ih shih chih (a kind of mineral)	4 fen	Shih huo (a kind of herb)	4 fen
Dry ti huang (Rebmannia glutinosa)	7 fen	Tu chung (Eucomia ulmoides)	4 fen
Hsi hsin (wild ginger)	4 fen	Ch'ung jung (a kind of herb)	4 fen

Grind the above twenty ingredients into powder and use honey as the binding base to make pills as small as the seeds of wutung fruit. Take three pills before each meal, three times a day. The effect begins to tell after thirty days. If taken regularly throughout the spring, it is even better. But while taking the pills, refrain from eating pork, lamb and salads and from drinking cold water.

(2) For the Summer:

(1 liang=36.00 grams)

Fu ling (an underground fungus)	3 liang	Tse she (a kind of herb)	3 liang
		Shu yu (yam root)	3 liang
Fu tzu (azure monks-hood)	2 liang	Kuei hsin (cinnamon heart)	6 liang
Shan chu yu (a kind of plant)	3 liang	Hsi hsin (wild ginger)	3 liang
Tu chung (Eucomia ulmoides)	2 liang	Shih huo (a kind of herb)	2 liang
Mu tang (tree peony)	3 liang	Ch'ung jung (a kind of herb)	3 liang
Huang ch'i (milk vetch)	3 liang		

Grind the above twelve ingredients into powder and use honey as the binding base to make pills the size of the seeds of wutung fruit. Take seven pills twice a day. Refrain from eating spring onions, salads and pork and from drinking cold water.

(3) For the Autumn:

Fu ling (an underground fungus)	3 liang	Tzu wan (a kind of plant)	2 liang
Fan feng (a kind of herb)	2 liang	Niu ch'i (a kind of herb)	2 liang
Kuei hsin (cinnamon heart)	2 liang	Shao yao (dahlia)	2 liang
Pai chu (Atractylis ovata)	2 liang	Tan shen (salvia miltiorrhiza)	2 liang
Hsi hsin (wild ginger)	2 liang	Huang ch'i (milk vetch)	2 liang
Shan chu yu (a kind of plant)	2 liang	Sha shen (Fickle Lady-bell)	2 liang
Shu yu (yam root)	2 liang	Ch'ung jung (a kind of herb)	2 liang
Tse she (a kind of herb)	2 liang	Dry ginger	2 liang
Fu tzu (Azure monks-hood)	2 liang	Hsuan shen (a kind of herb)	2 liang
Dry ti huang (Rebmannia glutinosa)	2 liang	Ginseng	2 liang
		K'u shen (a kind of herb)	2 liang
Tu huo (a kind of herb)	2 liang		

Grind the above twenty-two ingredients into powder and use honey as the binding base to make pills the size of the seeds of the wutung fruit. Take five pills before meals. And before bedtime take five with wine. Refrain from eating deep-fried food, spring onions, peaches, plums, sparrows and pork.

(4) For the Winter:

Fu ling (an underground fungus)	2 liang	Mu chin tzu (seeds of a kind of plant)	2 liang
Pai chu (Atractylis ovata)	2 liang	Shu yu (yam root)	2 liang
Tse she (a kind of herb)	2 liang	Tu chung (Eucomia ulmoides)	2 liang
Oysters (raw)	2 liang		
Kuei hsin (cinnamon heart)	2 liang	T'ien hsiung (a kind of herb)	2 liang
Oysters (boiled)	2 liang	Jen hsin (a kind of herb)	2 liang

Shih ch'ang sheng (a kind of herb)	2 liang	Ch'ung jung (a kind of herb)	2 liang
Fu tzu (Azure monkshood)	2 liang	Shan chu yu (a kind of plant)	2 liang
Dry ginger	2 liang	Kan ts'ao (Ural licorice)	2 liang
T'u shih tzu (seeds of a kind of herb)	2 liang	T'ien men tung (shining asparagus)	2 liang
Pa chi tien (a kind of herb)	2 liang		

Grind the above twenty ingredients into powder and use honey as the binding base to make pills the size of the seeds of wutung fruit. Take five pills before each meal with wine or boiled water. Refrain from eating seaweed, vegetables, carp, spring onions, pork and deep-fried food.

If one wanted a prescription for all seasons, one of the ancient Yin Taoists offered 'Soul-consolidating pills', which consist of the following ingredients:

(1 chin = 576 grams)

Fu ling (peeled) (an underground fungus)	24 chin	Pine oil	24 chin
		Pine seeds	12 chin
Cypress seeds	12 chin		

First of all, boil the pine oil in a huge copper wok until it thickens. Then add the fu ling, pine seeds and cypress seeds (both finely ground) in that order. Mix the whole lot with twenty-four Chinese litres (about 24.84 litres) of white honey and stir it very thoroughly. Pour it into a clean copper wok and keep it simmering on a very low fire for seven days and seven nights. When it cools off, make it into pills the size of small dates. Take three pills each day, one at a time. If one continues to take these pills all one's life, this Taoist claimed, one will be as fit in one's nineties as a young man.

However, there is another prescription which seems easier to prepare:

Walnuts (shelled)	3 chin	Almonds	3 chin
Peanuts (shelled)	2 chin	Dried dates	2 chin

Soak the walnuts, peanuts and almonds in water until their skin can be peeled off. Stone the dried dates. Grind them together and use honey as the binding base to make pills the size of walnuts. Steam them on a very low fire for 24 hours. Take one before breakfast and another before bedtime regularly. Replenish the supply constantly before the old stock starts to run out. According to a Chinese legend, Ke Hung of the Hsi Chin Dynasty kept taking these pills and eventually became an immortal.

Upon examining the ingredients of these exclusive prescriptions more closely, one will see that these Taoist sex experts seemed to rely heavily on plants to acquire hormones. This is mainly due to their belief in the usefulness of the longer life-span of plants. Their theory is: 'Of animals, minerals and plants, the last named have the greatest benefit of absorbing the essence of the sun (Yang) and the substance of the moon (Yin).' Another interesting point is that these prescriptions share the common aim of building up one's health, which is the key to a healthy sex life. The Taoist experts thought of aphrodisiacs more in relation to their tonic value than to their function as stimulants.

APHRODISIACS IN THEIR TRUE COLOUR

Naturally, some other Yin Taoists held a different view about aphrodisiacs. Take the *Important Guidelines of the Jade Room* for instance, in which several secret prescriptions all concentrate on stimulating effects.

To enable a man to make love to more than ten women every night, the manual recommends: 'Grind equal portions of she ch'uang tzu, yuan chih (milkwort), hsu tuan and ch'ung jung into powder. Take one fan-ch'un-pi (ancient Chinese container, one square inch in volume) of it three times a day.'

For external use, it gives the following prescription:

(1 chien=3.60 grams)

She ch'uang tzu (seeds of a kind of herb)	2 chien	Ting feng (a kind of herb)	1 chien
Dog's bone	1 chien	Kuei hsin (cinnamon heart)	1 chien
Reburnt ash	1 chien		

Grind the above five ingredients into powder. Prior to intercourse, mix a tiny amount with saliva and apply the mixture to your jade-stem. The woman will enjoy your love-making thoroughly.

To stimulate the woman, the manual asserts that there are three very effective prescriptions:

(1) Sulphur	2 fen	Musk incense	2 fen
Chu yu (a kind of plant)	2 fen	Mu hsiang (a kind of herb)	2 fen

Grind the above four ingredients into powder. Mix a little bit of it with saliva and put the mixture into the woman's jade-doorway. She will immediately become very sexy and demand love-making.

(2) She ch'uang tzu (seeds of a kind of herb)	2 chien	plant)	2 chien
Chu mu hsiang (a kind of herb)	2 chien	Sulphur	2 chien
Chu yu (a kind of		Hsi hsin (wild ginger)	2 chien
		Chih shao flowers	2 chien

Grind the above six ingredients into powder. Take a tiny bit of it to mix with your saliva and put it into the woman's jade-doorway immediately before love-making. She is bound to feel extremely contented.

(3) Dragon's bone (a kind of herb)	Mu hsiang (a kind of herb)
	Yuan chih (milkwort)
Chu yu (a kind of plant)	Yu kuei (cinnamon)
Pomegranate peel	

Grind equal measurements of the above six ingredients into powder. Put a little bit of it into the woman's jade-doorway and use the 'nine-shallow-one-deep' way to make love to her. She will be extraordinarily responsive.

Each of these three prescriptions has a fascinating name: the first one is called 'The Beauty Holds a Man Upside-down', the second, the 'Happy Powder' and the third, 'A Beauty's Smile'.

THE CURES FOR FRIGIDITY

As far as the cure for a woman's frigidity is concerned, the manual offers the following prescription:

Dried lilacs	1 chien	Ground almonds	2 chien
Chen hsiang (a kind of		Sha jen (a kind of nut)	2 chien
incense)	1 chien	She ch'uang tzu (seeds of	
Chu yu (a kind of plant)	1 chien	a kind of herb)	2 chien
Yu kuei (cinnamon)	1 chien	Mu pieh tzu (seeds of a	
Pai chu (Atractylis		kind of herb)	2 chien
ovata)	1 chien	Hsi hsin (wild ginger)	2 chien

Grind the above ten ingredients into powder and use honey as the binding base to make pills as small as black beans. Before intercourse, break one pill to put into the woman's jade-doorway. She will become very responsive and sexy.

However, a simpler way to cure frigidity seems to depend on whether one can catch the right kind of bats. According to *Pei Fu Lu* (*Notes of the North Door*), in Lungchow (now in Kwangsi Province) a kind of 'red bat can be found resting in pairs amid the red flowers of banana trees'. 'When you catch one of a pair,' the notes go on, 'the other will follow you about. The natives kill these red bats, dry them in the sun and then grind them into powder. Use a very small amount of the powder on a woman externally. The effect is immediate.'

Regarding the woman's need to maintain vaginal freshness, the *Important Guidelines of the Jade Room* has the answer too. It recommends: 'Grind 2 fen of sulphur and 2 fen of dried sweet-flag flowers into very fine powder and keep it in an airtight porcelain container. Put 3 pinches of it in 1 sheng (1.035 litres) of hot water to wash your private parts every night before bedtime. After doing so for twenty successive nights, you will find yourself as fresh as a virgin.'

But in the old days, many, many Chinese women knew how to cope with this problem deftly. They usually put some alum powder in a tub of hot water for the nightly wash, especially after childbirth. It is believed that this simple method was handed down, together with feet-binding, from slightly over a thousand years ago.

HOW TO INCREASE A MAN'S DIMENSIONS

Not to be outdone by the aforesaid manual, the *Secret Codes of the Jade Room* has something to recommend as regards how to increase a man's dimensions. It asserts: 'Stuff a male dog's gall bladder with equal portions of Szechuan chili pepper, wild ginger and jou ch'ung jung (a Chinese herb) and hang it over your roof for exactly thirty days. Then take it down to rub your jade-stem. As a result, your jade-stem will increase its length by one inch.'

As for a temporary increase in dimensions, however, there is another prescription: 'Bake 1 earthworm on a tile until it dries up. Grind it with 1 fen of musk incense, 3 chien of ch'ung jung and 3 chien of chu sha (vermilion powder) into fine powder. Then use turtle's blood as the binding base to make it into tiny pills. Prior to intercourse, put one pill into the tiger's mouth (opening) of your jade-stem. You will find it grows bigger and bigger in all dimensions during intercourse. When you want it to resume its normal stature, just drink a teacup of cold water.'

But if one's preference is some herbal medicines for internal use, the *Important Guidelines of the Jade Room* recommends the following prescription:

Cypress seeds	5 fen	Pai chu (Atractylis ovata)	7 fen
Pai lien (a kind of herb)	4 fen	Cinnamon heart	3 fen
	Fu tzu (azure monkshood)	2 fen	

Grind the above five ingredients into powder. Take 1 fan-ch'un-pi of it twice daily after breakfast and supper. After twenty days, you will find your member increases considerably in all dimensions.

Not surprisingly Tung Hsuan Tzu, the author of the *Art of the Bedchamber*, also has his recommendation in this matter. In a very convincing tone he asserts: 'Obtain 3 fen of top quality jou ch'ung jung (a kind of herb) and 2 fen of hai tsao (a kind of seaweed) and grind them into powder. Find a white dog born in the First Moon of any year. Use the secretion of its liver to mix the powder into a form of paste. Apply the paste to your jade-stem three times. At dawn the following day draw some fresh water from the well and wash it off. Your jade-stem will definitely grow three inches longer.'

Other than resorting to the aid of herbal medicines, another ancient Taoist introduces in his *She Sheng Mi Pou* (*Secret Dissection of Health Maintenance*) some special techniques: 'For the person who wants to expand his turtle, he must do it between ten a.m. and noon, when yang grows to its full extent and yin subsides. He should sit squarely in a quiet room, with his garment draped over his shoulders. Maintaining tranquillity in order to breathe evenly, he swallows his saliva and imagines that it goes down through tan t'ien to his jade-stem internally. Meanwhile, he must rub his palms together until they become very warm. Holding his testes with one hand, he rubs his belly clockwise with the other eighty-one times. After that, he repeats the same process with hands changed. Then he holds his jade-stem by its root and strikes it against both legs numerous times. To achieve the desired effect, he must keep on doing so for a considerable length of time. However, patience and perseverance will reward him with an increase in all dimensions.'

THE 'LIVE LIMB' IS A BUDDHIST INVENTION

Where as the Yin Taoists enriched love techniques with their theories, their recommendations as to methods to be employed and their prescriptions for aphrodisiacs, the Buddhist monks made their own contribution with the recommendation of sex instruments during the reign of Empress Wu Tse-t'ien (A.D. 685-704). Historical records show that Empress Wu's imperial physician, Ming Ch'ung-yen, presented her with an instrument called the 'live limb' for her self-amusement in the royal bedchamber. The 'live limb', made of rubber, was brought to the imperial capital by a Buddhist monk from India via Tibet. A full description of it can be found in the Chinese version of one of the ancient Buddhist classics: 'It happened when the Buddha stayed in the city of Tranvancore, a nun named Singhchoor visited the princess to converse on Buddhist philosophy. In passing the nun asked: "When the prince is far away from home, how do you amuse yourself?" The princess replied: "Let me tell you, my saint. When the prince is away, I can amuse myself all right. I have asked a clever craftsman to make me a live limb of rubber. I am very contented after using it." After the conversation, the nun hastily went to the craftsman's wife, demanding: "My good woman, ask your husband to make me a live limb of rubber, like the one he has made for the princess." The wife retorted: "You are a nun, why do you need it?" "I have the need," insisted the nun. "In that case," the woman agreed, "I shall ask him to make one." Then she went to tell her husband to have it made.... When it was ready, the nun took it with her into the inner room. She tied the rubber live limb to her ankle and pushed it inside her by bending her knee and moving her foot, so that her carnal desire was satisfied.'

Judging by this vivid description, it is not hard to imagine what this ancient instrument looked like. It must have been about the same size and shape as the member in erection. There must also have been some strings or similar ligatures for tying purposes.

'MR. HORN', THE 'GOAT'S EYELID' AND 'BURMESE BELLS'

Much later, towards the end of the Manchu Dynasty, instrument-makers used rubber along the same lines, but in a more ingenious way. This was how 'Mr. Horn' came into existence. Modelled on the shape and size of the male member and based on the principle of the hot-water bottle, 'Mr. Horn' could be filled with hot water when the user felt the need. It was easy to tuck away when the water had been poured out after use. At first, there seemed to be only the portable version of 'Mr. Horn' and the user had to rely on her own hands to make it work. It was, in short, a tool of masturbation for women. Understandably, frustrated wives, rich widows and Buddhist nuns became the regular buyers of this instrument.

Then, in the early stages of the Republic, 'Mr. Horn' was further developed into two new models. One was the combination of hot-water bottle and hernia belt, which could be used by one female on another. The partners could swop their roles, so that both would be satisfied. The other was actually simpler and less expensive; it was like a hot-water bottle with tubes at both ends. By using it, two females could be fulfilled at the same moment. But this did not mean that the older model of 'Mr. Horn' was no longer in demand. It was true that the new models could give women the feeling that they were having real intercourse, but it required two for a performance. While with the older model, a woman could use it by herself, which was far more discreet.

Oddly enough, the older model of 'Mr. Horn' found a group of customers among men as well. These were either older men with concubines or younger ones who had lost confidence in themselves. Afraid that their women might seek other outlets, they acquired 'Mr. Horns' to be their 'aides-de-camp'. In other words, they would either use 'Mr. Horn' during the preliminaries or as a finishing touch after the main encounter.

When lesbian performances began to flourish in Shanghai in the late '20s and early '30s, all three models of 'Mr. Horn' sold like hot cakes. At that time, the Japanese manufacturers rushed their products into the ever-expanding market with great enthusiasm. Thenceforth, 'Mr. Horn' has had a 'dual nationality'.

An older instrument is the 'Happy Ring', which is also known as the 'Goat's Eyelid'. It was first introduced to the Mongol emperors by some Tibetan lamas as early as the 13th century. After a goat was killed, its eyelids were carefully removed together with the eyelashes. They were first put in quick-lime for a few days to dry up. Then they were steamed in a bamboo basket for no less than twelve hours. After they had dried, these 'Happy Rings' were again put in the quick-lime for a few days. The same process was repeated several times to ensure the durability and flexibility of these 'Goat's Eyelids'. The user had to soak a 'Happy Ring' in hot water for some ten minutes before he wanted to make love to a woman. He wore it around his erected jade-stem during the process of love-making. It is said that the goat's eyelashes gave the woman a tickling pleasure.

At present, in Hong Kong, Bangkok and Tokyo, plenty of plastic 'goat's eyelids' can be found in practically every chemist's, side by side with French letters, loops and other things of a similar nature. Coincidentally, the Japanese again are the mass producers.

If popularity is a criterion, it would not be superfluous to mention the 'sulphur ribbons' which were extensively used in the Ming Dynasty. In those days, the men often had 'sulphur ribbons' made by their women. To make one, one used a length of raw silk about a foot long and an inch wide. After the silk was sewn into a narrow tube, it would be filled with sulphur powder. A man would circle the root of his jade-stem with it prior to love-making. This ribbon, it was assumed, could help him to last longer, for his urge to discharge was supposedly lessened with that part of his anatomy tightly bound. The sulphur powder was believed to be instrumental in giving some kind of sensation, enjoyed equally by both partners. After each time of use, it could conveniently be replenished with a fresh supply of sulphur. At first, 'sulphur ribbons' were only known to the emperors and princes. But it did not take long for them to find their way to the homes of ordinary people, probably because of their inexpensiveness. For reasons unknown, they were no longer used after the collapse of the Ming Empire.

It was also in the Ming Dynasty that 'musical bracelets' came into vogue. These bracelets were not much different from ordinary ones except that they had a dozen tiny gold bells attached to them. A woman could wear two on her wrists and two larger ones around her ankles. During the love act, her every movement would make these tiny bells ring. The tinkling sound of different notes would give the man an additional pleasure. However, they were not as popular as the 'sulphur ribbons', since not many people could afford to have so much gold. Or perhaps music was not essential to everyone on such occasions.

Talking of music, the 'Burmese Bell' deserves special mention. It is a tiny gold bell, round in shape and slightly bigger than a marble. The bell is hollow inside and filled with particles of metal. When one shakes it, a rustling sound can be heard. It is said that when the woman puts a 'Burmese Bell' inside herself during love-making, she and her man will both experience pleasant sensations in those parts. Someone who has had the experience even claims that, while in action, he could always hear an almost inaudible sound when-ever his mistress puts such a bell inside her. As to its name, one source claims that it derives from its Burmese origin. But in all probability, it could have been the invention of the Pai Yi tribe near the border between Burma and the Yunnan Province of China. In the early '40s, these 'Burmese Bells' could be obtained in Kunming, the provincial capital of Yunnan. Incidentally, the Yunnan mistress of that Nationalist bigwig in the Shanghai days was then widely known for her possession of a set of specially made 'Burmese Bells'.

THE ROCKING BED AND THE 'ROMANTIC CHAIR'

In the bedchamber, naturally, the bed is of primary importance. Before the influence of the West found its foothold in Chinese interior decoration and furniture design, the old-fashioned Chinese beds were *objets d'art* in their own right. For a wedding couple, a new double bed would always be specially made. The bed, like a Western four-poster, was made of expensive wood such as mahogany and pomello, painted with red lacquer and gilded. Seven by six and not lower than two feet, it had half-panels on three sides. On these panels, one would find beautiful carvings of flowers, birds and the Gods of Harmony. A more elaborately-made bed actually looked like a shrine. It consisted of two parts: the low pedestal and the bed proper, both enclosed in the bed curtains. The pedestal was about five inches in height and two feet in width, as long as the bed itself. On the pedestal there was a bedside chest, in which undergarments and the woman's sleeping slippers were kept.

The emphasis of the bed was on privacy, rather than comfort. The bed curtains for winter use were made of red silk, while in the summer they were replaced with colourful lace ones. The bedding consisted of quilts of all weights and all patterns, since blankets were still unknown in China at that period. For the rich there were embroidered silk-covered quilts, but the ordinary people were quite happy with the cotton ones. As a Chinese saying goes, 'In bed you can behave like an ordinary creature, but be a gentleman once you are out of bed.' It is obvious that in those days the Chinese thought that love-making and its preliminaries should take place only in bed.

One supposes, however, that there were always some people trying to break the convention, especially when they had the means and freedom to indulge themselves. In the Ming Dynasty, a minister named Yen Shih-fan had a bed made of sandalwood. On the inside of the three half-panels, full-length mirrors were mounted. He enjoyed telling his close friends how the fragrance of his bed and these mirrors stimulated him during endless amorous nights.

Later on, when over-indulgence had its effects on his sleep, he was resourceful enough to ask some craftsman to make a rocking bed for him. Based on the idea of a cradle, the body of the bed was hung on four strong posts with silk ropes. Making love to a woman in this bed gave him some rhythmic feeling, as if aboard a small boat. The little bells of all sizes hung on the bottom of the bed clinked and tinkled all the time when he was in action, which undoubtedly gave him some kind of pleasure and excitement.

Another device one often reads about in Chinese 18th and 19th century novels is the 'romantic and comfortable chair'. This special kind of chair seems to have been a piece of furniture indispensable to leaders of outlaws and licentious landlords. By collating the descriptions of it in a number of novels, one can merely have a vague notion of what the chair was like. It sounds like a form of collapsible chair, with automatic clasps fixed on its arms and legs. When a woman was put in the chair, these clasps would spring up to hold her arms and legs and the chair collapsed and became a miniature bed. The outlaw leaders and landlords used them for raping purposes, and the possession of them was illegal even under the Manchu rule.

However, when the Chinese Communist regime launched its nation-wide land reform campaign in 1949, it was reported in one of the Party papers that in a landlord's mansion in Szechuan, such a kind of chair 'was found by the heroic poor peasants and burned to ashes after the landlord's crime had been confirmed'. Judging by the newspaper report, this chair could have been the last of its kind.

Needless to say, all these aphrodisiacs, instruments and devices have never been that important to—and have therefore remained practically unknown to—the majority of Chinese people. To them, a healthy sex life merely requires physical fitness and mutual love of both parties. It is inconceivable that a peasant boy or a worker would need any of these artificial aids to make up for his deficiency. Whenever he has the urge and need, all he has to do is to find a willing partner, either through the form of marriage or some sort of temporary arrangement. But as for the wealthy and privileged few, it is unavoidable that some of them should have considered these things as a form of sexual sophistication, if only to cover up their inability to satisfy their partners in the normal way without resorting to any outside help.

CHAPTER NINE

Sex Taboos, Customs and Superstitions

Until the recent Cultural Revolution carried out by Chairman Mao Tse-tung and his rampaging Red Guards for more than three painful years, traditions have pullulated in China. These traditions, permeated with Confucian teachings and intensified by Taoist and Buddhist influences, have found their expression, among other aspects, in the form of sex taboos, customs and superstitions which for centuries governed the love life of the Chinese people in various degrees.

By means of legends, the school of the Yin Taoists successfully introduced a set of restrictions on love-making as early as the first century. In the name of Heaven, they strongly advised people against having intercourse under any of the specified circumstances. In each lunar month, they warned, it would be very bad to make love on the first, the fifteenth and the last day, for 'a son conceived on any of these three days is destined to be deformed or accident-prone'. Nor was it advisable to 'unite yin and yang' when the thunder roared or gales blew, which indicated 'Heaven and Earth are not in the good mood'. Should a son be then conceived, he would be a victim of boils and tumours. Shortly after drinks or meals, a couple must refrain from making love. Otherwise, their prospective son was 'bound to be mental'. When the man had 'just urinated or moved bowels, it is wise not to conduct the yin-yang harmony, for this is the way to avoid having an odd child'. When either the man or the woman was tired from a 'long journey or work, it is best not to have intercourse, for a child conceived under such conditions will either be odd or deformed'. When the man had just taken a bath, his skin and hair still wet, 'intercourse must be avoided in order not to have an abnormal child'. When the man was not feeling well or not ready, love-making would 'definitely aggravate his internal illness'.

In the course of a year, these Taoists singled out the Twelfth Moon as most unfit for the yin-yang harmony, since spirits and gods are busy moving about and it is only sensible not to incur their displeasure'. And according to the *Manual of Lady Purity*, 'the sixteenth day of the Fifth Moon is the day for Heaven and Earth to have intercourse; therefore, no sensible people will ever make love on that day. If they do, they are bound to die within three years.' Other than this specific day, the *Manual* also lists the days in each lunar month unsuitable for love-making. Even to this day, one can still find in the Yellow Calendar (Lunar Calendar) all the 'forbidden dates' named subtly as 'unsuitable for setting the bed'.

The interesting point is that, if one looks through a copy of the Yellow Calendar, one will find that after adding all these 'unsuitable dates' together, in a year the man and the woman are only supposed to make love about 100 times. This precept coincides with Lady Mystery's theory that the average man and woman need three days to recuperate after each intercourse.

Another Taoist source assumed that certain natural phenomena must be taken into consideration before people make love. During the eclipse of the sun or the moon or the appearance of a rainbow, it would be harmful to have intercourse. For the same reason, love-making must be avoided while the earth quaked. The same source was also strongly against making love with the lights on, which seems rather strange.

However, leaving out the elements of superstition, one can clearly see that these taboos were aimed at moderation of sex. Meanwhile, they did not in any sense overlook the emotional and health factors. As for their emphasis on the effects on the offspring, this demonstrates the psychological acumen of these Taoists, for in those days the Chinese people considered the propagation of one's blood—especially having a son—as the most important of all filial obligations.

MOURNINGS AND 'PREGNANCY INSTRUCTIONS'

With loyalty to the monarch and respect for the parents as the main virtues, both Confucian teachings and laws stipulated that carnal pleasures should be abandoned during the period of national mourning for the death of the monarch or private mourning for the bereavement of either parent.

In the case of national mourning, it was certainly not possible to check every bedchamber in the whole country. As a result, court officials had the short end of the stick. Unlike the ordinary people, they must exert self-restraint to a greater extent. If an official were found to have a child born to him some nine months after a period of national mourning he would immediately be dismissed from office.

In the case of parental mourning, the sons were not supposed to indulge themselves in any form of pleasure for three years. This meant that if the wives of any of them conceived a child during that period or shortly after, he would be looked down upon by his relatives and friends and socially ostracised.

Many Confucian scholars went further. They would not consider love-making on the anniversaries of the deaths of their parents or grandparents. Nor would they make love to their wives or concubines on their own birthdays, for these days had been the days when their mothers suffered from labour pains. In Chinese literary language, one's birthday used to be mentioned as the 'day of my mother's suffering', which vividly portrays the children's love and respect for their mothers.

Perhaps to safeguard the health of women, old Chinese customs forbade love-making immediately before and during the women's menstruation; but 'it will invite ill luck' was the reason generally given to fend the man off. When a woman was pregnant, she must observe the 'pregnancy instructions' by living in a different bedroom. Throughout the whole period, she had to be in the right company, read the right books and observe a strict code of good manners. This was believed to be of great importance to the forthcoming child. She should not yield to her husband's desires under any circumstances. According to many Chinese herbal physicians, if a woman failed to observe the 'pregnancy instructions' strictly, the disastrous effects would be on the baby. They claimed that a baby born with 'boils on the face or skin diseases is the proof of its mother's self-indulgence during the period of pregnancy'. More than this, a woman after childbirth was not supposed to sleep with her husband until 100 days later.

There is no denying that these restrictions prove not only the importance attached to the future generation but also the relative care extended to their womenfolk by the Chinese in the not too distant past.

Old customs seemed to stress the importance of the right time and place for love-making. A couple would become a laughing stock if they were found to have made love in the daylight. While staying overnight in Buddhist or Taoist temples, the man was strictly forbidden to be intimate with any woman and vice versa. Other forbidden places included the coffin side, tombs and anywhere in the open air. Again, these restrictions, though aiming at decency and propriety, appeared to have taken mood and health into consideration.

THE 'HORSEBACK STROKE' AND 'WHITE TIGRESS'

Some taboos and superstitions sound stranger than others. In some provinces in South China, parents often discreetly hinted to their married children that they must not drink cold water or eat watermelons immediately after love-making. They would also advise against sitting in a draught or taking a cold shower. And to forestall over-indulgence, it was not unusual for elders to warn about the possibility of suffering from the 'horseback stroke', which means that the man is in a state of non-stop emission. The suggested cure is: 'The woman should let the man remain on top of her, with his member inside her, and give him the kiss of life while holding his waist tightly with both her hands.' Most people tended to accept such advice in a matter-of-fact way, without bothering to get to the bottom of it.

In some other regions, it was thought to be unlucky for a man to see a woman's private parts, especially in the morning. No available source indicates how this superstition first started. The best conjecture is that it could have originally been someone's clever device to discourage peeping Toms.

The same superstition could have made most Chinese women refuse to undress in front of their husbands, since to give their men ill luck would be the last thing they wanted to do.

It is true that superstitions often varied from place to place. Take for instance the question of pubic hair. In the coastal provinces south of the Yellow River, a woman without pubic hair was spitefully called the 'white tigress', the symbol of bad luck. It was not unusual for a bride to be returned to her parents for this physical characteristic. But in North China it was altogether different. Some men were even keener on having 'white tigresses' as wives. Evidently, they did not share the same apprehensions as their compatriots in the South.

The different attitudes towards the woman's pubic hair could have resulted from two conflicting theories. The ancient Taoist immortal Peng Tsu stated that a man should choose a young woman without pubic hair in order 'to benefit yang from yin'. This advice is pertinent to the age differences between the male and the female, for Peng Tsu theorised that 'a man at eighty or ninety must find a young maiden of fourteen or fifteen to be his sleeping partner'. Very possibly, a girl of such a young age may not yet have pubic hair.

Many centuries later, however, a famous fortune-teller (specialising in features and physical characteristics) contradicted what Peng Tsu had said. He claimed in his manual that 'Empress Lu Chih of the Han Dynasty had most unusual pubic hair, golden in colour and eighteen inches long. This special feature brought her husband Liu Pang good luck, on the strength of which he was able to conquer the whole Empire.' Quite possibly, the people in many southern provinces could have been more influenced by his assertion than by that of the Taoist immortal.

'EIGHT HORSES IN THE MUD'

But neither taboos nor customs had any binding power on the rulers. Their special privileges enabled them to set their own ground rules, which gave rise to some strange customs. In the Chou Dynasty, it was customary for the aristocrats to have some 'chamber music' before their bedtime to cultivate the mood for the ensuing love-making. This was by no means improper or exhibitionist in nature. Then, in the later dynasties, this 'chamber music' was turned into 'bedchamber music' functioning as accompaniment to the love acts of emperors and queens.

Of all these licentious royalties, it seems none could live up to Empress Wu Tse-tien's standard where 'bedchamber music' was concerned. Whenever she favoured one of her 'face-heads', a Chinese brass band consisting of gongs, cymbals and drums was ordered to play deafening tunes throughout. The reason was, according to one Chinese historian, that she had the habit of chanting and yelling throughout the whole process of love-making. Moreover, she was so full of life in bed that one would 'naturally associate her vigorous movements with the rolling of eight horses in the mud'. Obviously, for the sake of maintaining her dignity, she had to enlist the assistance of a brass band to drown her loud voice as well as the rumbling sound of the dragon bed.

Much later on, Emperor Shun Ti (reigning 1323-1368) of the Yuan (Mongol) Dynasty, established a strange sex practice which gave a number of Buddhist monks the chance to outshine their Taoist rivals in the art of the bedchamber. Shun Ti deliberately employed a number of Tibetan lamas to coach him and his concubines in practising 'Extremely Happy Zen' Buddhism, for being a Mongol he could not trust the Taoists who were all Chinese. Unlike their Taoist counterparts, these lama sex experts were the personification of anything but subtlety. To them, sexual fulfilment had to be demonstrated under the watchful eyes of the onlooking crowds. To perform the 'Extremely Happy Zen' the Yuan emperor stayed in the nude, surrounded by sixteen naked 'Heavenly Girls' who danced to the chanting of Buddhist sutras and the beating of gongs and cymbals. Meanwhile, the lama coach would make love to his 'women disciples', who were in their late teens or early twenties, to show Shun Ti how to do it. Like a sedulous ape, the emperor imitated what the lama had been doing to the sixteen 'Heavenly Girls' one after another. His assignment was to achieve the goal of coping with all of them at one go through constant practice. The secret techniques of these lamas were built on the basis of efficient breath control. Whenever Shun Ti failed, one of the lamas would step in his shoes to show him the authentic touch.

THE 'NOTHING MATTERS' PALACE AND BAMBOO CURTAIN

When the 'Extremely Happy Zen' was in its full swing, the emperor ordered his brothers to join in, so that competition would provide more fun and excitement. It appeared as if Shun Ti and his brothers never completely mastered their breath control, for soon the lamas had to take on the additional duty of making love to the royal women in front of their husbands' own eyes. Ironically enough, the emperor was not in the least hesitant to name this special palace for lovemaking 'Nothing Matters'.

But it did matter to the ordinary people in Peking, for these lamas, far from being satisfied by the imperial concubines and princesses, nonchalantly walked into private houses to make love to any women in sight. For precaution's sake every house in Peking began to hang a bamboo curtain on its door, so that the lustful eyes of these lamas would not be able to see the women inside.

Not surprisingly, everywhere in China at that period grand Buddhist temples were built after these lamas had been appointed to high posts such as the 'State Adviser' and 'Minister of Public Works'. And in some of these newly-built temples, the abbots and their associates suddenly changed sides. They gave up the traditional Chinese School of Ch'an Buddhism of self-examination, self-restraint and self-denial to follow the path of their Tibetan counterparts. No longer did they stick to a vegetarian diet and the study of Buddhist classics. They started to seek pleasures in this life instead of the next. In secret underground rooms they wined, dined and kept women, though in public they would still put up a front. Naturally, when they got tired of their kept women, these monks took advantage of the superstitions of the laymen to open up new resources. Under the pretext of 'transplanting the Buddha's seed', they made many barren women willingly offer to 'rub stomachs' with them. When a monk and a woman rubbed their stomachs together without a stitch on either of them, the consequences left hardly any room for doubt. This orgy went on in semi-secrecy for many more centuries after the fall of Genghis Khan's empire.

When the Ming Dynasty was first established, some Tibetan lamas still retained posts as sex advisers in the imperial palace. This could have been encouraged by Emperor T'ai Tsu, the founder of the empire, who had served as an apprentice Buddhist monk in his youth. Perhaps due to their past association with the Mongols, they were later replaced by a group of Yin Taoists, who staged their large-scale comeback during the reign of Emperor Shih Tsung.

SEX LESSONS FOR THE MANCHU MONARCHS

However, as soon as the Manchus conquered China, the Taoist sex experts were summarily dismissed from the imperial service because of their Chinese origin. Like the Mongols, the Manchu rulers took sex education from the constant stream of Tibetan lamas. During the reign of Emperor Yun Cheng, the Yun Ho Palace was built to enlighten emperors and heirs to the throne on the facts of life. In this palace, statues of the Happy Buddha having intercourse with mermaids and beautiful women with the bodies of animals were displayed in every room. And in the Hall of Devils, there stood the thirteen-foot statue of the King Devil. He had a human's body and the head of a dog with two horns. Beside him was the statue of a beautiful naked goddess. The two statues were entwined in a love-making posture and no details were omitted. In this hall and in every other room, figurines of men and women making love in various positions were strategically placed hither and thither.

Prior to his wedding, an emperor or heir to the throne would be conducted on a tour of the Yun Ho Palace, with the Tibetan lama in charge as his instructor. After the lama had explained everything, he could then put his theory into practice on his wedding night. It would not have been too strange if the instructions had merely continued to be given in this manner. But when Empress Dowager Tzu Hsi was in power, she sought to advance the sex lessons for emperors to a higher level. Thus the lama in charge was given a number of women assistants. When the emperor came to be enlightened, the lama, in addition to explaining everything to him, would make love to these women to make sure that he understood the lessons thoroughly.

But the time came when mere watching was apparently thought to be inadequate. According to the regulations of the Imperial Bed-chamber Affairs, an emperor or an heir apparent could and should derive some benefit from having pre-marital sex with hand-picked young widows of the royal family. As these widows might not be that experienced themselves, they had to 'coach' their pupil under the supervision of the Tibetan lama in charge of the Yun Ho Palace, where there was a marble room specially designed for this purpose.

On the day selected after consulting the Yellow Calendar, the emperor or heir to the throne would arrive at the Yun Ho Palace accompanied by two to four of these sex instructresses. After seeing all the statues with the lama in charge and his women assistants, the imperial novice and his instructresses would then be shepherded into the marble room by the lama, who might be anxious for action himself. Once they stepped into this heavily carpeted room, everyone immediately stripped. The lama would make love to his assistants one after another in different positions, while the imperial pupil scrupulously did the same thing with his instructresses. If the lama found his pupil's techniques under par, the session would go on for days and nights.

It seems that Emperor Kuang Hsu (reigning 1875-1905) must have been the most tragic victim of this type of sex education. When he was about to get married at the age of nineteen, Empress Dowager

Tzu Hsi hand-picked four most sexy widows from the mammoth-sized royal family to be his instructresses. She even saw to every detail, making sure that they were properly bathed and scented for the occasion. A handsome young man in every sense, Kuang Hsu aroused unusual enthusiasm in these four young widows. Perhaps to impress the young monarch with their undivided loyalty, they insisted on giving him more lessons. After going through this intensive cram course for several successive days, however, the imperial novice was over-exhausted and became impotent. This would not have been so disastrous if he had not had to marry the empress dowager's niece as his queen. After their wedding night, the queen hastened to inform her aunt of Kuang Hsu's impotence. Not unexpectedly, Empress Dowager Tzu told her not to feel sorry for herself, since there were plenty of men around in the Forbidden City. Like aunt, like niece—Kuang Hsu's queen lost no time in acquiring a young eunuch named Hsiao Teh Chang as her lover. Though her marriage to Kuang Hsu was never consummated, she did find some form of compensation, thanks to her aunt's advice.

THE BRONZE MULE TO CURE BARRENNESS

About the same time, some Taoist monks in Peking set out to double their efforts in making money out of the ordinary people's eagerness to have sons, especially since their predecessors had lost the place of honour to the Tibetan lamas in the Forbidden City. In the eastern suburb of Peking, the Tung Yueh Temple (Temple of the Mountain God of T'ai Shan) suddenly attracted endless throngs of female pilgrims from the imperial capital as well as many other big towns in North China. It was not the Mountain God himself who held so much attraction for these women. They came all the way to worship the life-size bronze statue of a mule which, according to Taoist legends, used to be the mount of the Mountain God in his human life. Still, the women pilgrims had something else on their minds when they came to see the mule. For some time word had been going around that a woman's barrenness could be cured once she came to the Tung Yueh Temple to touch the virile member of the bronze mule, provided she and her husband had first performed many good deeds.

Perhaps for the sake of discretion, the bronze mule was surrounded by red satin curtains in one of the halls of worship in the temple.

After a woman pilgrim had made her donation, she would be allowed to go into that hall of worship to touch the bronze mule's member without being seen by anybody.

Even in the late '30s, the bronze mule still commanded a sizable sum in 'touching fees'. Especially during the Chinese New Year he had to bear the gentle fondling of thousands and thousands of barren women. Naturally, it was very hard to ascertain the effectiveness and usefulness of this ritual. But it was only too obvious that the Taoist monks there must have made a fortune out of the bronze mule, for that part of his anatomy became far smoother and shinier than the rest of his body after so many years.

To compete with the bronze mule, other Taoist monks in the nearby White Cloud Temple claimed that the black bamboo shoot-shaped stone in their yard was equally useful, if not more so. They said that the stone was the surplus of the stock which the ancient goddess Nu Wuo, a legendary monarch after Emperor Fu-hsi, used to mend the broken sky. Having 'absorbed the essence of the sun' for countless years, these Taoist monks asserted, the stone 'emitted the strength of yang' whenever touched by a female hand. Their publicity campaign seemed to pay off, for year after year the stone was constantly touched by the anxious hands of numerous childless women. If some women's words were to be trusted, the stone seemed to have some stimulating effects on them. They firmly stated that the stone was always warm to the touch. This could have been what they imagined, or perhaps the suggestiveness of the stone's shape affected these women psychologically.

Even to this day it is believed that the legendary stone still stands there intact, though no more barren women make any attempt to touch it, for any act of superstition is strictly banned by the Peking regime.

THE DRAGON-PHOENIX LEGEND

As far as love legends go, the most enchanting one is perhaps the colourful romance between Nung Yu and Hsiao Shih (the Flute Officer). It is said that during the Period of the Warring States (481-221 B.C.), Duke Mu of the Ch'in State had a favourite daughter who was gifted in music. Nung Yu by name, she had her father's blessing to marry Hsiao Shih, whose flute-playing was unrivalled. After their marriage, the couple lived in a two-storey bamboo house specially built for them by the order of the duke. Day after day and night after night, Hsiao played his flute incessantly, while Nung Yu listened with ever-increasing interest. Twelve years later, the people of Ch'in suddenly saw a dragon and a phoenix descend on the roof of the bamboo house. To their greater surprise, however, Hsiao Shih mounted the dragon and Nung Yu the phoenix and amid the tunes of heavenly music flew beyond the floating clouds.

Since then the dragon and the phoenix combination has been used as an auspicious symbol in weddings. Usually, at a typical Chinese wedding, one can see the dragon-phoenix designs carved on the candles, embroidered on the bedcovers and painted on scrolls. This shows that this simple but beautiful legend has created in the minds of the Chinese people a lasting image.

Though not without some rather sad elements, the legend of the Weaving Girl and the Cowherd has, until recently, fathered some interesting customs among young Chinese girls. The Weaving Girl, according to the legend, was one of the daughters of an ancient goddess called Hsi Wang Mu. Unfortunately, she angered her mother by marrying the Cowherd without her permission. For punishment, Hsi Wang Mu transformed them into two stars to be separated by the Milky Way all the year round. However, they were allowed to see each other once a year on the seventh day of the Seventh Moon. In most parts of China, that day used to be regarded by young damsels as the most appropriate occasion to make wishes about matters of the heart. On that evening, they would stay under a square table and try to stick a piece of thread through the eye of a needle. If a girl succeeded in doing so in the dark she would find herself a good husband, it was believed. It was certainly not an easy task, but year after year most girls would spend hours in the shade of a table sweating the ritual through.

But the peasant girls in North China took a different approach to appeal to the Weaving Girl. On the seventh night of the Seventh Moon, they would quietly leave their cottages to pick cucumbers in the darkness. Their luck rested with the first cucumber they came upon. As soon as they got one, they would rush back to their own rooms to tell their fortunes by examining the cucumber. If it were shapely and the right size, the girl who had picked it was supposed to find the right man to be her husband within the year. But if a girl picked a cucumber of the wrong shape, she should stay clear of men until the next year. To city folks, one cucumber might look the same as another; yet in the eyes of the peasant girls of North China each cucumber told a different story about their future happiness. Why cucumbers were chosen for this special occasion nobody can really tell, in spite of the fact that a Chinese sex expert has eloquently associated the choice of the cucumber with the suggestiveness of its shape. On the other hand, some Taoist mythologists have taken pains to assert that cucumbers used to be the favourite vegetable of the Weaving Girl and that this belief has led people to use it to forecast their future happiness. In truth, it was the custom itself that really mattered. The endeavour to analyse an ancient legend from the point of view of today is often quite unnecessary.

THE TRADITIONAL ATTITUDE TO SEXUAL IRREGULARITIES

Whether in the category of superstitions or customs, one must now define the traditional Chinese attitude to sexual irregularities. Though the Yin Taoists may have done their share to enrich the sexual life of rulers and rich people, it is equally clear that they never encouraged extra-marital relationships. With the safeguarding of normal sexual relationships as one of their objectives, another school of conventional Taoists in the Ch'ing Dynasty published the *T'ai Shang Kan Ying Pien* (The Oracles of the Most Supreme), a combination of moral teachings and individual cases, for popular consumption. Throughout the whole book, the words of Lao Tzu (the founder of Taoism and the Most Supreme) are quoted and illustrated with individual cases. In matters of sex, incest, adultery and perversions are denounced with equal vehemence. Cases are given to prove how adulterers, adulteresses and the incestuous were punished both in their lifetime and after their deaths. The book moralises, in part, that 'if a man commits adultery with another's wife or daughter, his own wife or daughter is bound to fall the prey of someone else's adultery'. As for the incestuous, it lists a number of historical names and claims that 'these people are still detained in one of the eighteen Hells even long after their deaths'. To convince the readers to a further extent, the book asserts that the licentious monarchs and aristocrats in history never escaped their fate of 'serving their terms in different Hells appropriate to their respective offences'.

In fact, incest has always been considered the most serious sex offence in the Chinese eye. It must also be pointed out that, due to the big family system, the Chinese connotation of incest is far broader than the Western one. For instance, in the old China, if a man had an affair with the wife of his father's cousin three times removed, it still constituted a case of incest. In the countryside, when a case of incest was detected and confirmed, the offenders would be tied up and buried alive by their relatives with the full support of the villagers.

Nor was it then permissible for a man to have an affair with his friend's wife. In the old Chinese society, friendship was as important as brotherhood. If a man were known by others to enjoy liaison with the wife of one of his friends, both his reputation and career would take a deadly toll. Even after a man's death, it would be unthinkable for any of his friends to marry his widow. This applied to people of all walks of life. In the late 1920s, a distinguished educator of international fame in Peking tried to break the conventions by marrying the widow of one of his close friends; for years he was under a barrage of criticism from all sides. Both he and his wife were excluded from important social functions and even, in some cases, private parties.

To break this convention could also mean exile for life. At about the same period, an official in Fukien fell in love with his brother's widow. Without the courage to face the possible social censure, they sailed for Indonesia and got married there. For more than thirty years their marriage remained a closely guarded secret in their native town. And for all these years neither the husband nor the wife got around to disclosing their past to their children. It was also out of the question for either of them to take a brief visit home, despite their ever-growing homesickness.

That the old laws in China gave the husband a lot of leeway to protect his reputation is the necessary outcome of male possessiveness, coupled with the desire to uphold moral standards. When a man discovered his wife's unfaithfulness, he was at liberty to take whatever steps he thought fit. If he succeeded in catching his wife in bed with another man, he could behead both of them without being charged with murder or manslaughter. But he would be charged if he killed only one of them. This is why the Chinese saying 'catch the adulterer and adulteress in bed' has become a usage in everyday language. The basic concept of ancient Chinese laws is: 'Laws do not exceed the limit of human feelings.'

Though women were not the social equals of men, a chaste widow was in high esteem in the community. In those days, after a woman had maintained a widowhood of impeccable chastity for thirty or forty years, a monument would be built in her honour under imperial decree. She might be illiterate and penniless, and yet her social position would be greatly enhanced by the monument. Even when a high official passed by the monument or her house, he had to alight from his sedan chair or dismount from his horse.

On the other hand, a widow found out to have an affair would be mercilessly punished. In some parts of China, when a widow was caught in bed with a man all her in-laws had the right to bury them alive. She was punished for her 'betrayal of her late husband' and her lover for 'undermining the good name of a family'. Obviously, the Confucian concept of the family as the basic unit of an orderly state was a decisive factor behind this measure.

It goes without saying that all these taboos, customs and superstitions have largely ceased to exist in the China of today. Naturally, nothing could be easier than to condemn them in a sweeping manner. But if one examines the social and historical factors behind them with a certain amount of objectivity and tolerance, one will realise that people in the past were as fallible as we are now. Therefore, it would be imperceptive, if not dogmatic, to assume that they should have been able to rise above their circumstances and social trends.

CHAPTER TEN

Eroticism, Pornography and the Arts

It has been assumed by some sources that Chinese pornographic paintings were first started in the Sung Dynasty (A.D. 960-1279), when Emperor T'ai Tsung set up an imperial studio to include the leading portrait painters of his time. Like royal photographers of today, these painters were to record activities and functions in the imperial palace. Moreover, it was also their duty to execute a set of paintings illustrative of love-making in different positions for use in the sex education of heirs to the throne and princes. For the sake of discretion these pictures, called the 'Secret Games of the Spring Palace', were kept tucked away by the responsible palace officials for most of the time and were only shown to heirs and princes prior to their wedding nights. Though none of these pictures seems to have survived the rise and fall of the many ensuing dynasties, the term 'Spring Palace' has since been used by the Chinese to denote pornographic paintings.

But according to *Han Shu* (*Historical Records of the Han Dynasty*) Prince Kuan Ch'uan during the reign of Emperor Hsuan Ti (71-48 B.C.) was actually the first promoter of pornographic paintings. It is said that 'the prince, having commissioned a couple of famous painters to paint the palace ceiling with vivid pictures of men and women making love in a variety of positions, gave a banquet to entertain his uncles, elders and sisters there. While drinking and carousing, he asked his guests to look up at these pictures.'

Without any doubt, Prince Kuan Ch'uan might have acted in this manner since his indulgence in irregular sex practices was notorious. He even committed adultery with his own sisters. However, he ceased to hire any painter to do pornographic paintings after one incident. His favourite concubine, Tao Wan-ching, a great beauty in her early twenties, had a shapely and voluptuous body. Conscious of her own physical attractions, she liked to stay in the nude most of the time.

Once, when a painter was summoned to the prince's palace to execute a set of pornographic paintings, Tao Wan-ching, 'with her body powdered', watched him paint at close range. Out of a sudden urge, she ordered the painter to have intercourse with her by 'copying the positions in the pictures'. Infuriated, Prince Kuan Ch'uan drew out his sword and 'cut her body into eight pieces'.

Nonetheless, the fancy for pornographic paintings did not die with this licentious prince. When Emperor Ch'eng Ti succeeded to the throne, he outdid Prince Kuan Ch'uan by commissioning some famous painters to paint a huge screen. The panoramic picture showed 'King Chou-hsin entering Tachi from above, while around them hundreds of naked warriors and palace maidens made love in every imaginable position amid tigers and leopards, with the Wine Lake and the Meat Forest in the background.'

Later, towards the end of the Nan Ch'i Dynasty (A.D. 479-501), Duke Tung Hun (a dethroned emperor) was equally enthusiastic about pornographic art. He ordered a number of painters to execute erotic murals on the walls of his palace, so that he and his numerous concubines could be in a 'constant state of excitement and improve their performances considerably'.

It was during this period or thereabouts that pornographic paintings began to flourish in the households of the noble and the rich. Once they were in vogue, even scholars and literati could not but become their connoisseurs and collectors.

EMPERORS AS MODELS FOR
PORNOGRAPHIC PICTURES

But it was not until the T'ang Dynasty (618-907) that pornographic paintings embarked on a more daring approach. This started with Emperor Hsuan Tsung, fondly called Ming Huang (the Enlightened Emperor) by his subjects, who used his favourite concubine Yang Yu-huan—better known as Yang Kwei-fei because of her title—as a model for such paintings. A patron of musicians, actors and painters, Emperor Hsuan Tsung kept the outstanding portrait painter Chou Fang in his constant company. It was no sheer coincidence that Chou should be so high in his favour. Apart from his skill as a painter, he was also the son of a governor-general. Uninhibited as Hsuan Tsung was, he asked Chou Fang to paint Yang Kuei-fei stepping out of her bath. Obviously, the artist's work must have pleased the emperor tremendously, for he was later asked to do the famous painting 'Secret Games in a Spring Night'. In this painting Chou portrayed Hsuan Tsung in the company of five beauties, the one engaged in intercourse with him looking exactly like Yang Kwei-fei. Unfortunately, though we have vivid descriptions of these scenes by a number of scholars of successive dynasties, the pictures themselves cannot be found anywhere in China now. But judging by some portraits done by Chou Fang, now well-kept in the Palace Museum of Taiwan, one can visualise how superb those lost pictures must have been.

Naturally, Emperor Hsuan Tsung could not have anticipated that after a lapse of more than 200 years another monarch would follow his precedent and pose for a pornographic painting. In the Sung Dynasty, an unnamed painter of the imperial studio painted Emperor T'ai Tsung in the process of favouring the captured Little Queen Chou of Li Yu, the poet-king of Southern T'ang. According to a Ming scholar, the picture presented 'T'ai Tsung half-naked and wearing a turban. Dark and stout, he makes the dainty Little Queen Chou knit her eyebrows during the slightly painful process, though she is supported by several palace maidens.' One source claimed that the painter actually painted the emperor live when the love act was taking place; but another source stated with equal firmness that the picture was done by some painter after T'ai Tsung's death, despite the fact that he had served under him. Though they disagreed as to whether T'ai Tsung did actually pose for the picture, neither of them attempted to refute the more important point that the picture was executed by a Sung artist.

Apart from these two emperors, Emperor Ch'ien Lung of the Manchu Dynasty was also a model for pornographic paintings. During his reign, the pictures already mentioned were, according to the records of the *Imperial Collection of Pictures and Scrolls*, still in perfect condition. Perhaps inspired by them, Ch'ien Lung ordered a few royal painters to use him as a model when they executed pornographic paintings to his specifications. In these paintings, he was always depicted in a situation of coping with several anxious women. This could have been contrived deliberately by the painters to flatter his male ego; or he may have given an explicit order for such a subject to give himself a psychological lift during his old age.

FROM DARING TOUCHES TO SUGGESTIVENESS

In all fairness, it must be stated that Chou Fang is regarded as one of the greatest painters in Chinese history, with or without his pornographic paintings. Mi Fei, a famous painter in the Sung Dynasty, held Chou in the same class as Ku Kai-chih (one of whose surviving masterpieces is kept in the British Museum), Lu T'ang-wei and Wu Tao-tzu. The women in Chou's paintings are all on the plump side, which is believed to be relevant to the notion of feminine beauty in the T'ang Dynasty. It is also worth mentioning that in his pornographic paintings, Chou Fang tended to exaggerate the size of male organs. His influence can be traced in Japanese pornographic paintings, probably because Japan sent quite a number of students to China in that dynasty.

In contrast, Chou's influence on Chinese pornographic paintings did not last long. From the time of Emperor Huei Tsung of Sung onwards, this kind of painting increasingly departed from the emphasis on dramatic effects and daring touches. Instead, suggestiveness and subtlety became pronounced characteristics. This was especially true of the works by the leading Ming painters such as T'ang Yin, Wen Chen-ming, Ts'ou Shih-chou and his daughter, known by the pseudonym of Tu Ling Nei Shih.

In one of T'ang Yin's paintings there is a door depicted in the middle. On one side of it a man and a woman are busy with the preliminaries of love-making, while on the other side a young girl is peeping through the keyhole. It was through the expression on the young girl's face that T'ang tried to convey to the viewers the infectious effects of the burning passion of the couple.

Ts'ou Shih-chou, in a way, was even more subtle than T'ang Yin. Most of his pornographic paintings were done on squares of silk, roughly one foot by one in size. One of his surviving pictures shows a man and a woman aboard a small row-boat amid the reeds by the river bank. The man is trying to proceed with love-making while the woman is shaking her head. A few feet away in the river, however, a wild duck raises its head and looks surprised. Obviously, the artist let the duck tell the story and left the rest to the viewers' imagination.

His other famous picture portrays a stout man, with his cape over his shoulders, about to climb on to a bed half-hidden behind a marble screen. A woman is shown bending her body over on the edge of the bed, full of expectation. But behind her, a small baby boy is crying and she turns round to hand him a toy. And in front of the bed a wooden tub half-full of water has a towel in it. It shows that the woman has hardly finished bathing the baby when the man suddenly has the urge. Thus has the awkward situation arisen.

As far as suggestiveness is concerned, Wen Chen-ming seems to be the pastmaster. In one of his paintings, all one can see is the closed bed-curtains moving like waves. Underneath them, a pair of red satin female shoes and a pair of men's boots appear to have been thrown down in great haste. The finishing touch, however, is a pair of cats in heat, entangling with each other on the floor. It is said that this painting is now kept in the Tokyo Museum, highly treasured by many Japanese connoisseurs of art.

Though the daughter of Ts'ou Shih-chou is believed to have made many pornographic paintings, it is extraordinarily difficult to identify them, for she did not even sign her pseudonym on any of her pictures. One art critic in the Ch'ing Dynasty wrote that her style was akin to that of her father and yet 'more refined in minor details'. To illustrate his point, he did attribute a few pictures to her, which aroused some controversial remarks.

But evidently she was not the only woman painter of pornographic pictures. From the Ming Dynasty onwards, in Peking and in a few other towns in North China, there have been numerous women who did these pictures for pin-money. Their identity has never been discovered, yet their works have commanded a good market. Even in the late 1930s, one could discreetly ask a hotel porter in Peking or Tientsin where to buy the 'spring pictures' done by some housewives. In most cases he would be directed to go to such and such an address to buy them himself. When he arrived at his destination he would be surprised to find the matter-of-factness of the transaction. All he had to say was the number of pictures he wanted. The woman (or women) he saw would tell him the price. As soon as he had paid, she would have the pictures wrapped for him to take away. He was not supposed to look at them until he had left the house. Throughout the whole process neither the buyer nor the seller would mention a word about the nature of the merchandise. If a man wished to have pictures depicting love positions he would have written them down beforehand and would quietly pass the slip of paper to the woman who received him. His request would be fulfilled to his satisfaction.

PORNOGRAPHIC COINS IN THE FIRST CENTURY

Understandably, paintings are but one form of pornography. According to a Sung scholar, 'spring coins' first came into existence as early as the Han Dynasty. These coins, rectangular in shape, had words of good omen on one side, while on the other a god and a goddess performed a love act. It was claimed in those days that these coins could disperse the evil spirits in any household; and as a result, parents habitually gave them to their children on their wedding nights in the hope that, without being disturbed by the supernatural, they would be able to bring a healthy and intelligent third generation to the family.

This custom continued well into the Sung Dynasty. By that time, the coins became round in shape and the designs on them offered a variety of love positions. No longer were they called 'spring coins', for the people of Sung liked the name 'bed curtain-spreading coins' better. They formed an integral part of the dowry when one's daughter was married. On the wedding night, these coins would be scattered in the bridal bed before the wedding couple retired. This clearly demonstrates the real usefulness of these coins, no matter what pretext the people in that period chose to use.

As time passed, pornography found a new form in the carvings of jade and ivory. An eye-witness in the Ming Dynasty described at length in his memoirs the 'Happy Buddhas' he had seen in the Ming Palace. 'The two Happy Buddhas were carved out of two huge pieces of flawless jade. With their sex organs in close contact they gave the viewers the basic concept of the man-woman relationship. The eunuch in charge told me that these jade figures were actually left behind in the palace by the Mongols after their downfall. He also said that they had been used by the Mongol imperial family to enlighten their descendants about the facts of life. It is believed that after our empire had been established, these figures continued to be used for the same purpose during the reign of our first few emperors. However, I cannot help congratulating myself secretly for having the good luck to see these finished products of artistic perfection.'

It was also during the Ming Dynasty that ivory was extensively used for pornographic carvings. Figures and figurines in various love-positions could be purchased from craftsmen who had frequently spent years on carving a few masterpieces out of ivory of the best grade. Incidentally, it was in the province of Fukien that one would be most likely to obtain collectors' pieces if one had an artistic taste. In Fukien, these ivory figures were not only better finished, but more vivid in expression as well. Furthermore, the vital parts of the anatomy were often dyed pink, which added no little authentic touch to the figures. As far as the sizes were concerned, some figures could be as tall as three feet while the smallest figurines could be easily kept in a match-box. The most unusual point of all is that the workmanship of both big and small objects maintained the same highest standard of artistry. This must have been due to the clever hands of the natives.

PORNOGRAPHIC DESIGNS ON VASES AND PLATES

To most people's knowledge, pornographic designs were used for porcelain ware by the Manchu emperors such as Ch'ien Lung and Hsien Feng, as a form of sexual sophistication. Some art collectors in China and abroad have succeeded in acquiring vases, bowls and plates of such designs, though not necessarily genuine pieces. But archaeological diggings, carried out in some parts of Honan province in the 1920s, revealed that these designs had been painted on earthenware in the first and third centuries. Some leading Chinese archaeologists assert that in that period both the Han and Wei monarchs, on the advice of their astrologers, had these earthen bowls and plates buried underground in places where 'future rebel leaders or rulers might be born'. In those ancient days it was a common belief that earthenware with erotic designs on it would bring ill-luck to the future rulers and thus forestall possible uprisings.

This belief was certainly not shared by Ch'ien Lung and Hsien Feng, whose main concern lay in sexual pleasure. Apparently the workers of the imperial kilns did not restrict themselves to using these pornographic designs merely for the royal porcelain ware, for a great number of similar vases, bowls and plates have since continued to appear on the market for those who could afford them.

Towards the end of the Manchu Dynasty, the kilns in Chingtechen, the Chinese porcelain manufacturing centre in Kiangsi province, started to make porcelain peaches, apples, oranges and all kinds of fruit with love-making figurines concealed inside. These porcelain fruits look like those plastic ones now manufactured everywhere in the world. It is only when one opens them that figurines in different love positions appear before one's eyes. The designs may not be as artistic as those on bowls, plates and vases, but certainly they are not lacking in authentic touches. Many of them have been made in miniature sizes, which can be put in one's pocket to carry around unobtrusively.

Cheaper than these porcelain figurines, and yet equally real, were those made of dough which used to flood the streets of Peking and Tientsin. Even in the late 1950s, one would occasionally find along the Peking streets these dough toy-makers with wooden boxes strapped on their shoulders. Their customers were mainly little children, who would ask them to make dough figurines of heroes and beauties in Chinese history. In a matter of minutes these toy-makers could make a figurine with dough of various colours. Sometimes, they would be approached by some adult customers in a rather cautious manner. After bargaining in whispers, they would oblige the customers by making tiny figurines in love positions in match-boxes with equal efficiency. When a customer wanted more elaborate figurines he would have to pay in advance or at least put down a deposit.

FIRST BRASSIÈRE TO SAVE FACE

The emphasis placed on carnal pleasures by the Manchu rulers also had an influence on the art of embroidery. When Empress Dowager Tzu Hsi was in power, the women of the royal family first set the pattern by embroidering pornographic designs on their handbags, tobacco pouches and brassières.

Actually, the now almost extinct Chinese brassière was more like a small apron than its occidental counterpart. The woman who first introduced the use of these brassières was none other than Yang Kwei-fei, the aforementioned concubine of Emperor Hsuan Tsung of T'ang in the eighth century. Buxom and full of sex appeal, she would not have dreamed of covering up her breasts but for a mishap. Behind the emperor's back she had an affair with General An Lu-shan, who belonged to the Hu tribe. One day after making love with the Hu general, Yang Kwei-fei was shocked to find one of her breasts full of love bites and scratches caused by her lover. Fully aware of the possibility of receiving the royal favour that night she ordered her palace maids to make a small red silk 'apron' to cover her breasts while in bed. It must have been a stroke of luck that Hsuan Tsung did not in the least suspect anything. Instead he regarded the apron as an ingenious piece of invention and was effusive in singing its praises. Naturally, the women in the imperial palace then all rushed to have brassières made. The fashion soon caught on with ordinary women as well. After that Chinese females kept on using them as brassières until they were mostly replaced by their Western-style counterparts in the 1930s and subsequently. Still, this does not mean that these Chinese-style brassières can no longer be found in remote villages or border towns in the north-west and south-west, which have always been comparatively free from the impact of Westernisation.

When Yang Kwei-fei resorted in the eighth century to the wearing of brassières to save herself from disgrace she could hardly have imagined that, more than one thousand years later, brassières would be embroidered with pornographic designs by her fellow country-women as an erotic means to arouse their men.

Before her unintentional introduction of brassières, Yang Kwei-fei was also responsible for making semi-topless dresses the fashion in the T'ang palace. At that period the dresses of Chinese women were akin to the Japanese kimonos of today. One morning in the spring, however, when the imperial concubine was combing her hair in front of a mirror one of her breasts emerged from the collar of her robe, to catch Hsuan Tsung's fancy. Pleased with the effects, Yang Kwei-fei had all her new dresses made with extremely low necklines. In all of these dresses her half-exposed breasts would catch the roving eyes of the romantic emperor to his immense delight. To compete for the imperial favour the other women in the palace lost no time in wearing dresses of similar design. But due to moral inhibitions, these dresses never became popular outside the imperial palace.

EROTICISM IN POETRY

As regards eroticism, it is necessary to note that quite a number of Chinese poets and poetesses in the past centuries, either out of sudden passion or for the sake of seeking sexual sublimation, have contributed to a wealth of pornographic literature. A few random examples of such poems may suffice to illustrate the subtle and yet frank expressions liberally employed by these literary talents, who lived in a far from permissive society.

Take the T'ang poet Wei Chuang (A.D. 836-910) for instance. A minister at the court of Wang Chien in Szechuan, he is mainly known for his political achievements. But it is the same Wei Chuang who wrote the following poem:

> I wander about in a spring day,
> My head covered with apricot blossoms.
> Along this country path any chance
> To find a young man full of fiery passion?
> I would much like to wed one—
> Or there will be no real life.
> Though fickle he may one day become,
> It's certainly no shame on me.

The poet put these words in the mouth of a country girl, to challenge the conventional reticence about love and passion.

Ou-yang Hsiu (A.D. 1007-1072) of Sung, apart from his successful political career, is one of the eight greatest prose writers of the T'ang and Sung Dynasties. However, as a poet he seems to have had no compunction in revealing the romantic side of his character:

> The brook before my house is high these days,
> By boat you've come secretly to see me a few times.
> Though small your boat may be,
> It cannot sail into my red bedcurtains.
> Both helpless, we feel sorrows loom over us
> Amid the shadows of those lotuses.
>
> I only wish to be a red, red lotus
> Remaining in the autumn river year after year.
> You could then be a ripple underneath
> And nothing would stop you from embracing me.

Naturally, men in those days were less inhibited in expressing their emotions. But Li Ch'ing-chao (1084-?), probably the greatest woman poet in Chinese history, could be equally frank:

> The fragrance of red lotus lingers
> And the bamboo mattress feels cold.
> I gently take off my silk skirt
> To board an orchid-boat and row.

Will words of love be sent
To me down from the clouds remote and high?
The west pavilion is bathed in moonlight
When the wild goose* at last returns.

The flowers are falling and the streams flowing fast.
Our mutual longings grow while we are kept apart.
My sadness clings and deepens:
It may not show on my eyebrows,
Yet grasps my heart so very tight.

This poem was written when her husband had been away from home for some time, and Li Ch'ing-chao did not hesitate to express her physical desire by saying something about the cold mattress.

But another anonymous woman poet in the T'ang Dynasty went further. She wrote a short poem to describe her mixed feelings when her lover turned up at last but drunk:

When my little dog barks at the door,
I know it's he who has just come.
In stocking feet I rush down the stone stairs,
Only to find the devil drunk.

I help him enter the bedcurtains,
But he would not be unattired.
Let him remain drunk as he is—
Still better than to sleep alone.

Li Yu, the poet-king of Southern T'ang, was no less frank in describing his rendezvous with his sister-in-law, who later became his queen:

The fragrant mist veils the bright flowers
And dims the moon;
This is the night to go to him.
Descending the doorsteps in haste,
I walk in my stockings and carry my shoes.

(*The old Chinese folk stories describe the wild goose as a 'bird of fidelity', never deserting his mate.)

At the south side of the main hall
I dash into his outstretched arms
And keep on trembling a long while.
As it is hard to find another chance,
Let him caress and love to his heart's content.

It seems probable that Huang Ting-chien (A.D. 1045-1105), the distinguished scholar and calligrapher of the Sung Dynasty, must have shocked his contemporaries by describing the love act in one of his poems:

No more strength left in her body.
She feels so weak after pleasuring her lover.
The flower has fallen off her hair
And the golden hairpin dropped.
Upon her shoulders spreads
The dishevelled cloud of hair.
The staring lamp makes her perspire
As if after too much drink.
'Sleep, sleep, I want to sleep,'
So whispers she.

Centuries later, the Ming poet Shen Mao-hsueh was no less audacious in using the same theme for a poem of his:

Enshrouded in the bedcurtains of lace,
She is so fair and shapely in the nude.
The heart of the peony* is crimson red—
Almost as red as rouge.
So fragrant, she melts like the snow.
'You reckless devil, do not crush
The sprig of flower in my hair!'
She fondly blames my growing vigour.

When the Manchus conquered China, political frustration drove some poets to write about nothing but sex. Peng Hsieh-men even wrote a poem on the famous pornographic picture executed by T'ang Yin:

(*A metaphoric expression for the vagina.)

Against the pillows of red satin
Her cheeks shine bright like creamy jades.
She knits her dainty long eyebrows
To bear the pain of joy bestowed by him.

Through the door hinges the peeping eyes
Catch the love scene without missing a thing.
And in the shade of the lamplight
Her snow-white arms turn pink around his neck.

Another poet of the Manchu Dynasty known for his erotic poems
is Mao Yu-shen. In the following poem he describes how a couple
happened to make love in the garden, with utmost economy of words:

Amid the flowers she unfastens her silk skirt
When sudden passion sets them aflame.
Afterwards softly she tells him:
Beware of your naughty little sister
And put those pictures somewhere safe.

THE RISE OF PORNOGRAPHIC NOVELS

Though poets had for centuries portrayed sexual love in verse,
pornographic literature did not appear in the form of novels until
the early 16th century, during the reign of Emperor Shih Tsung of
Ming. That this came about then was no sheer coincidence. In that
period, for everyone from the emperor down to junior officials,
sexual pleasures were of paramount importance. The Taoist monk
Tao Chung-wen was made a minister and an earl by Shih Tsung
after he had presented the emperor with aphrodisiacs of various
kinds. Many other scholars obtained high offices through their contribution to the sexual art. Therefore, it was only natural for writers
to apply their literary skill to the writing of pornography.

Of many books written at that time, only a few have survived.
They are *Hsiu Ta Yeh Shih* (*A Tale of the Embroidered Bed*), *Ju
Yi Chun Chuang* (*The Biography of Mr. As-you-wish*) and *Chin
Ping Mei* (*The Story of Golden Lotus, Little Vase and Spring
Plum*).

A Tale of the Embroidered Bed is set in the Spring and Autumn
Period (722-481 B.C.). It describes at length the sexual adventures of

Hsia Chi, a great beauty of that time. A widow in her forties, Hsia Chi still looked like a young maiden in her late teens. She excelled in the art of the bedchamber and conquered one young man after another. Her wanton life angered her son Chen Shu, a knight in his early twenties. As a result, the conflicts between the mother and the son led to a tragic end. However, the writer failed to treat the conflicts in a convincing manner and the whole book consists of nothing but fragmentary scenes of love-making.

The Biography of Mr. As-you-wish deals with the affair between Empress Wu Tse-tien and Hsueh Ao-Ts'ao. From beginning to end, it concentrates on elaborate descriptions of the ways Hsueh made love to Empress Wu. The reader soon finds its reiterations boring and monotonous.

Compared with these two books, *Chin Ping Mei* is far superior in literary technique. It is often regarded as one of the outstanding realistic novels of all times. It was written by Wang Shih-chen, a distinguished 16th-century scholar, with the aim of avenging his father's death. As the man who had killed his father was a high official who enjoyed reading pornography, Wang devoted a number of years to writing this novel. Knowing that the high official had the habit of licking his fingers to turn the pages of a book, he tainted every page of his manuscript with poison. Once the high official heard about Wang's new work, he demanded to read it as soon as possible. After he had done so with great enthusiasm, he instantly died from poison.

The background of the story is set in a provincial town in the Sung Dynasty. Hsi-men Ching, the main character, is a rogue under the camouflage of businessman and local official. He acquires his concubines and women in a most despicable way, poisoning and assassinating their former husbands without the slightest inhibition. The title *Chin Ping Mei* is derived from one of the two ideograms which form the names of his concubines, Golden Lotus and Little Vase, and his chambermaid, Spring Plum. Of these three women, Golden Lotus appears to be the most wicked. Apart from striving for Hsi-men Ching's favour, she also has an affair with his son-in-law, Chen Ching-chi. The love scene between Hsi-men Ching and Golden Lotus under a grape arbour is thought to be a gem of pornographic literature:

'When Golden Lotus was about to join the other women to go

into the house, Hsi-men dragged her by the hand, saying, "You little smooth-tongued bitch, I won't let you get away." He dragged her along so hard that she almost fell.

' "You strange thing, what do you want me here for?" said the woman.

' "Let's stay near the rock. Get some wine and have a game of darts," Hsi-men Ching said. He then sent Spring Plum to get it.

'After Spring Plum was gone, Golden Lotus suggested to Hsi-men Ching that they should go over to the grape arbour to play darts. Shoulder to shoulder, they walked down the steps, passed by the Emerald Pavilion and reached the grape arbour. There were four stone stools and a special vase made for the dart game. While she and he were engaged in throwing darts into the vase, Spring Plum came with the wine and Autumn Chrysanthemum with eight plates of fruit and sweetmeats.

'Golden Lotus drank more than ten glasses of grape wine in a row after Hsi-men Ching had scored a number of successful throws. Her face began to flush and she eyed him coquettishly. Upon her insistence, Hsi-men Ching asked Spring Plum to tell Autumn Chrysanthemum to bring the bamboo mattress and pillows for Golden Lotus to lie on.

'After a long while, Autumn Chrysanthemum came with the bedding. Golden Lotus told her to set it down and to go to close the corner door of the garden.

'Hsi-men Ching took off his jade-coloured lace robe and placed it on the railings. He went to relieve himself somewhere near the flowers under the Peony Platform. When he came back, Golden Lotus had already stretched herself comfortably on the bamboo mattress. Her breasts were fully exposed and below the waist she had nothing on. Her shapely legs lay wide apart and the red satin sleeping slippers on her dainty feet looked most inviting. With a glass of wine in one hand, Hsi-men Ching sat himself beside her and started fondling and caressing her. Golden Lotus wiggled her body slightly, burning with desire. Suddenly Hsi-men Ching demanded that she explain why she had said so many rude words about Little Vase. Still tipsy, Golden Lotus refused. Angered, Hsi-men Ching raised his hand to slap her. She stretched one arm to intercept his oncoming hand, and made the wine spill from his glass. Now even more angry, he pulled off her embroidered sleeping slippers and unrolled her feet-binding cloth, with which he then tied her separated feet to the grape arbour.

'At this moment, Spring Plum came with some more wine. Upon seeing the scene, she rapidly went away. Hsi-men Ching chased after her and dragged her back to drink with him under the grape arbour. He embraced her with one hand and his other hand got busy too. In between sips of wine, he picked up a grape and threw it at the moistened crimson cave of Golden Lotus between her legs. Itchy as well as uncomfortable, Golden Lotus begged him to spare her. Spring Plum also urged him to untie Golden Lotus' feet from the grape arbour, saying that this unsightly scene might be witnessed by someone who happened to come that way.

'But Hsi-men Ching would not hear of it. He kept on drinking his wine and soon dozed off in a bamboo easy-chair. He woke up about two hours later. Only then did he untie the feet of Golden Lotus from the grape arbour. As her legs were numb and she could hardly walk by now, Hsi-men Ching asked Spring Plum and Autumn Chrysanthemum to assist Golden Lotus to go back to her own bedchamber. He spent that night with her. Thrilled, Golden Lotus did everything she could to please him in bed. They did not get up until noon the following day.'

TWO EARLIER WORKS OF EROTIC LITERATURE

Chin Ping Mei seemed to set a trend for pornography in fiction. In the 17th and 18th centuries, *Jou Pu Tuan* (*The Prayer Mat of Flesh*), *The Apricot Blossoms Sky*, *The Monk of Lamp Wick*, *The Biography of a Silly Woman* and *Yeh Sou Pu Yen* (*The Frank Words of a Rural Old Man*) came out in a rush. As far as literary merits are concerned, none of these works is comparable to *Chin Ping Mei*.

From the viewpoint of eroticism two earlier works are extremely well written. One is *Cha Shih Mi Hsin* (*Secret Sketches of the Han Palace*) and the other *Kung Ho Chien Mi Chi* (*Secret Sketches by the Supervisor of the Imperial Guard*).

In *Secret Sketches of the Han Palace*, written by an anonymous scholar in the Han or Wei Dynasty, the passages about the physical examination of a prospective queen are notable for their vividness and frankness:

'In the fourth year (A.D. 150) of Emperor Huang Tsi's reign, Madame

Wu was instructed to visit General Ch'eng Shang's residence together with Eunuch Ch'ao, for His Majesty, having heard about the virtue and beauty of the general's daughter, was considering whether he should take her as a royal consort. The mission of Madame Wu was to give the prospective consort a thorough physical examination, without omitting the slightest detail.

'When Madame Wu and Eunuch Ch'ao arrived at the general's residence, the whole family greeted them with great joy. While dining with the general, they saw Nu Ying, the general's daughter, gracefully walk into the room. Following the points listed in the Imperial Decree, Madame Wu and Ch'ao scrutinised her demeanour and deportment and were most impressed.

'With Ch'ao remaining in the outer chamber, Madame Wu went with Nu Ying to her boudoir. The maids were dismissed and the door was closed: The sun shone on Nu Ying's face. Like snow in the glow of morning, she looked radiant. Her eyes were as clear as calm waves and her eyebrows long and shapely. The white teeth formed a strong contrast with the tiny, red mouth; her nose and ears added more charm to her facial features. Madame Wu took off Nu Ying's hairpin and undid her hair. Shining like black satin, it reached to the floor and over.

'After feeling the hair, Madame Wu asked Nu Ying to take off her underwear. The young girl blushed and refused. But the older woman insisted, telling her not to disobey the imperial order.

'Nu Ying shed tears and then shut her eyes, turning round to face the other side of the room. Madame Wu gently undressed her and lifted her naked body against the sun. Her bodily fragrance wafted over the air and smooth and creamy was her skin. Her breasts were firm and each enough to fill a hand and her navel was deep enough to contain a pearl half an inch in diameter.

'Finally, Madame Wu, delighted with the shape of Nu Ying's slightly raised private parts, opened her thighs and found her jade-doorway crimson like a glowing fire. "She is really a pure and chaste virgin!" exclaimed the older woman.'

If the *Secret Sketches of the Han Palace* excelled in its description of how to examine a virgin, the *Secret Sketches by the Supervisor of the Imperial Guard* emphasised the sexual indulgence of Empress Wu Tse-t'ien with her 'face-heads'. It was presumably written by a T'ang scholar named Chang Mu, though some sources claimed that

Yuan Mei (1716-1798), the Ch'ing scholar and poet, did some rewriting of the original text. The most interesting part of the book is perhaps the discussion between Empress Wu Tse-t'ien and her favourite daughter Princess Tai-ping (Peace) about the characteristics of an ideal penis:

'After the empress had been favouring Huai-yi the monk for a number of years, Huai-yi became so haughty that he was slapped in the court by the then prime minister. Unhappy about the whole thing, Empress Wu sent for her daughter Princess Tai-ping to have a chat over drinks. She casually asked her daughter: "Do you realise that I don't really have the right man to be with me?" The Princess bowed and said: "I have realised this situation for a long time. I did not dare to say anything, for you had never mentioned it. However, I have discovered a young man named Chang Ch'ang-tsung, the nephew of a former vice-minister. Not older than twenty, he has a fair complexion and beautiful face like Princess Ts'ao La."

'Empress Wu lowered her head and said nothing. The princess whispered to her: "Your Majesty must not worry. I have actually found out what he is like down below. The other day I gave a dinner party at the Emerald Green Pond. Afterwards, I ordered the guests to take a bath. Behind the glass screen, I peeped. Chang Ch'angtsung is so different from other men. He has a flawless, fair and yet muscular body. That thing of his is most impressive, plump at the top and slightly finer along the stem. It does not look that big in repose, but its expansibility is evident, especially in view of the crown-like part at the top."

'The empress looked pleased and asked: "Have you tried him out?" "How dared I?" the princess hastily replied. "But I did ask a maid to try him out in order to give you a factual report." Then she ordered her maid to tell the empress everything.

'The maid knelt down and whispered: "When your slave first had Ch'ang-tsung, his thing was like fresh litchi from Canton, tender and smooth. After a few thrusts, it became bigger and bigger inside and gave your slave the sense of fulfilment. He was also so thoughtful, leaving the tempo to your slave. And when it was over, the pleasure lingered."

'Empress Wu was delighted. She smiled to her daughter, "You are really clever to have found him for me. Huai-yi is strong, but he always exhausts me. A man's member should not be full of sinews and muscles. In love-making, tenderness is a prerequisite. It seems that Ch'ang-tsung is the right man." '

Admittedly, these samples of ancient Chinese pornographic writing may be too concise and sketchy for modern taste; but it is undeniable that their authors chose to be subtle and suggestive in order that the reader could give his own imagination free rein.

When Westernisation began to spread over China more extensively in the early 1920s, its impact did not exclude pornography. At that time, a returned student from France called Chang Ching-sheng hurriedly produced in Shanghai the volumes of his so-called *History of Sex*. Written in colloquial Chinese and claiming to be the truthful records of the individuals he had interviewed, these pulp booklets were, in fact, no better than those now often hidden under the counters of some Soho bookstores. Chang's venture soon led many hack writers to hash up books even worse than his. Unfortunately, they spread like prairie fires among young students and less educated people in practically every sizable town of China. The vulgarisation and crudeness of the writing turned out to be an asset. As a strong measure, the then authorities banned all books on sex indiscriminately. Even *Chin Ping Mei* and the *Prayer Mat of Flesh* did not escape the same fate. Still, these books were by no means unobtainable, though one had to be prepared to pay an exorbitant price.

CHAPTER ELEVEN

Sex, Humour and Imagery

As a people, the Chinese may have impressed the outside world with their industry, cleverness and tenacity. But few have realised that humour is also a Chinese national trait. When the Chinese are together, they probably crack far more jokes than any other people. They can laugh at others, nor do they mind being laughed at. Since sex has always been regarded as an essential of life by the Chinese, there is naturally no shortage of sexual jokes, though language differences makes most of them untranslatable. However, a few examples may help to reveal this side of the Chinese character.

In the past, the relationship between an emperor and his court officials used to be extremely formal and pompous. But an emperor in the Hsi Chin Dynasty apparently made an exception to this rule. One day, after a son had just been born to him, he summoned his ministers to break the good news. Then, to commemorate the happy occasion, the emperor gave each of his ministers a generous reward. Overjoyed, they knelt down to thank him. However, one minister humbly refused to accept his reward. Surprised, the emperor asked for his reasons. The minister respectfully explained: 'According to ancient teachings, one should not accept a reward without making any contribution. I am afraid I do not deserve Your Majesty's reward for I have made no contribution at all.' 'My goodness,' the emperor roared with laughter, 'you can make contributions to many other things. But I certainly do not expect to receive your contribution regarding this matter. How could you have helped me make the queen pregnant?' He had hardly finished his remarks when all the court officials forgot etiquette and burst out laughing in unison.

Though the virginity of the bride has generally been regarded as a very important factor in a happy marriage, a popular joke about three friends' different experiences on their wedding-nights could have been invented by someone with an unconventional view of this matter.

Some years ago, the story goes, there were three young scholars who all insisted that they must marry only virgins. They drove their matchmakers mad by passing over one girl after another. At long last, they succeeded in finding their ideal brides and decided to get married on the same day. To make sure that they did get virgins, the three scholars agreed to get together after the wedding night to report their experiences, especially since none of them had had sex before. On the following morning, they dashed to their meeting place full of joy.

Being most senior in age, Wang was the first one to narrate his experience. 'My bride must have been a virgin,' he smiled contentedly. 'When I started to make love to her, I did not really know how to do it. But she guided me with her hand. After a little while, she told me to put two pillows under her hips so that we could both enjoy it better.'

'How could she be a virgin?' his two friends exclaimed simultaneously. 'She even knew the trick of using pillows—no virgin would have told you that.'

Deflated, Wang waited for Li to tell his experience. 'I am sure about her virginity, for she did not ask me to put pillows under her,' Li said, nodding. 'Anyway, it was I who took the initiative all the time.'

'Is that all?' asked Wang. 'How about afterwards?'

'Afterwards,' Li said, 'she asked me to give her ten dollars.'

'Good gracious, she must have been a prostitute!' the third friend, Liu, shouted. 'It seems I am the only lucky man. My bride did not tell me to use pillows, nor did she ask me to pay her.'

'Don't be too sure,' Wang and Li cut in. 'Let us hear your story.'

Proudly Liu proceeded: 'Last night, when I made love to her, she lay there motionless, just like a virgin ought to be. However, I was considerate enough not to give her too much pain.'

'You mean she did not even breathe a word?' Li asked.

'Oh, yes,' Liu scratched his head in recollection. 'She seemed to be so unaware of the whole process, that when I was inside her, she asked me to push in.'

'If she did not even know that you were already inside her, that part of her anatomy must have already been stretched by some other men,' Wang said firmly. 'How can you say she was a virgin when you had her?'

The three of them kept on arguing and eventually came to blows. Just then an old man walked by and asked for the reasons for their fight. After hearing their stories, the old man said philosophically, 'It makes no difference now. Even if your brides were virgins last night, they cannot be virgins today. After all, you do not sleep with your wives for a single night, or do you?'

THE DISPUTE OVER WHICH HALF

As regional prejudice has unavoidably played its part in the thinking of many Chinese, it is often asserted that the natives of Shansi province are very calculating with their money. A typical joke is about a rich Shansi merchant visiting a prostitute in Shanghai. Finding himself in Shanghai for the first time, he went to a prostitute with the intention of spending a whole night with her. But after he found out the price, he decided to have quick sex instead. The disgusted prostitute told him that it would cost him six dollars. The merchant shook his head and said, 'Too expensive. One can do a lot of things with six dollars. Would you consider accepting three dollars? That is, half the price?'

Upset by his meanness, the prostitute retorted, 'I will accept your half-price offer if you only put half of your thing in.'

'Done,' the Shansi merchant agreed immediately. He produced three silver dollars and put them carefully on the table.

Though this gesture took the prostitute by surprise, she had no alternative but to fulfil her part of the bargain. Elated, the merchant got on top of her and pushed his weapon into her completely.

'It was agreed that you only put half of your thing inside me,' she protested vehemently.

'Ah, when we discussed the price, we did not specify which half—lower half or upper half,' he said calmly.

Unable to refute his argument, the prostitute could only let him get away with his craftiness.

In the south-western province of Yunnan, one would often hear the joke about a fastidious magistrate and his wife. The magistrate, a man in his fifties, was very anxious to impress his young wife with his official position. He often went out of his way to reprimand his guards and servants to show off his authority. But in the back of his mind, he was constantly worried about his inability to satisfy his wife. Whenever he made love to her, the magistrate tried to time his endurance by listening to the sound of the footsteps of the night watchman. One night, however, he failed to hear the usual rounds made by the poor old soul.

Infuriated, he sent for the night watchman next morning and threatened to throw him in jail for his negligence of duty. The frightened man humbly but firmly told him that he had done his rounds as usual.

'But I did not hear you pass by my window even once,' the magistrate snapped. 'Can you tell me what I did last night?'

As the old man, through the gossip of other servants, knew about His Honour's secret anxiety, he tried to boost his male ego by giving a subtly worded account:

'Your Honour, when your humble servant passed by your window shortly after midnight, you were apparently busy hanging a scroll, for your honourable wife kept saying: "Higher, lower ... no, slightly higher.... Fine."

'Then, one hour later, when I came by for the second time, you and your wife were in the company of your brother-in-law, for, while Your Honour was panting, your honourable wife kept saying, "Brother, my dear brother!"

'At two a.m. I passed by your window again. It seemed you had just given your wife a shampoo. I heard her saying repeatedly, "Wipe the hair, wipe the hair." Your Honour, how could I have neglected my duty since I can tell of your activities in such detail?'

While listening to the night watchman's account, the magistrate figured out that he must have lasted at least two hours in his performance the previous night and was more than pleased. He tipped the night watchman handsomely and let him keep his job.

It seems that this joke must be a popular one, for many natives of Yunnan often refer to love-making as 'scroll hanging'.

TOO WINDY UNDER THE QUILT

With the peasants, one of the standard jokes is about a couple and their only child sharing one bed. In the old days, the Chinese peasants were so poor that they had to sleep with their child or children in the same bed. Under these circumstances, it was very difficult for the parents to make love without being detected by their grown-up children. As for Peasant Chang and his wife, the situation was even worse. Extreme poverty compelled them to share one quilt with their seven-year-old son. After months of frustration, Chang insisted one night that his wife should oblige him since the boy always slept soundly all night through. Having the urge herself, the wife agreed. They waited until the boy had fallen asleep. Then cautiously and lightly, they started to make love. But as it had been such a long time, they could hardly exert self-control and were getting more and more vigorous. When the love act was finally over, they could not find their boy, and a search was immediately started. Eventually, to their relief the boy was found sleeping soundly under the bed. They woke him up and asked for an explanation. Rubbing his eyes, the boy murmured, 'It was so windy under the quilt and in the bed, so I decided to sleep under the bed to stay away from the draught.'

Being non-religious as a whole, the Chinese also enjoy telling dirty jokes about Buddhist monks. A well-circulated joke successfully portrays the sexual frustrations of monks in a vivid manner.

In a Buddhist temple in Peking, the abbot was held in high esteem because of his strict observance of self-denial, self-examination and self-knowledge. One year, on the eve of the Buddha-bathing Festival, he summoned all the monks and warned them not to be tempted by the beautiful women pilgrims the following day. He ordered that all of them, himself included, should sit on their prayer mats with their legs folded in the Buddhist way. Then each of them would have a small drum placed over his legs while the women pilgrims poured into the hall of worship. Those who felt sexy at the sight of women would find that their members would rise up and knock against the strategically placed drums. Should this happen to anyone, he went on, a very severe punishment would be enforced. Naturally, all the monks had to obey his order.

Next day, as planned, the abbot and all the monks sat on their prayer mats with drums over their folded legs in the hall of worship. When the stream of women pilgrims filed in, every single monk yielded to the irresistible temptation. One after another, the small drum on the lap of each of them produced a bang, stifled and yet audible. But the drum on the abbot's lap did not produce any sound at all. After the women were gone, all the monks went up to the abbot to praise his ability to resist the temptation of sex. Speechless and pale, the revered abbot pointed at the drum on his lap. One monk ventured to move the drum away. Only now, everyone was shocked to see that there was a hole in it. Obviously, the abbot had felt so sexy that his erected member had penetrated the leather surface of his drum.

EGG IS HARDER THAN IRON ROD

About virility and endurance there are also plenty of jokes. A comparatively mild one is the story of three sisters getting together to have a frank discussion.

When the youngest of the three is about to get married, out of anxiety she begs her two elder married sisters to give her a premarital lecture. Close to each other as they are, the two elder ones are very willing to help her. They tell her about everything they experienced. Enlightened, the youngest sister begins to ask a few questions. Eventually, she asks her two married sisters to compare their husbands' members to something she knows so that she can have a better idea of what a penis looks like.

Thinking for a little while, the eldest sister says, 'His thing is like an iron rod, hard and enduring.'

'In that case, you must feel very contented each time.' The youngest sister cannot but express her admiration.

But unexpectedly, the second sister sneers contemptuously.

'Can there be anything harder than an iron rod?' the eldest sister asks aloud. 'Would you tell us what your husband's thing is like?'

'His is like an egg,' the second sister says calmly.

Upon hearing her words, both the eldest and the youngest sister laugh until their sides hurt.

'Listen, you two,'—the second sister shows no sign of perturbation —'I agree that an iron rod can be hard and stiff. But when you put it in a furnace, it melts immediately. While with an egg, it is just the opposite. When you put an egg in a saucepan to boil, the longer you boil it, the harder it becomes.'

Turning to her youngest sister, she continues, 'Now, can't you see that my egg is far superior to her iron rod?'

Speechless, the eldest sister has to admit defeat.

TWO CURRENT JOKES WITH POLITICAL FLAVOUR

In the early 1950s some sexual jokes began to be tainted with a political flavour. Shortly after the Russian leader Stalin's death, people in Shanghai, perhaps disgusted with the national mourning proclaimed by Chairman Mao, often whispered to one another about the effects of the mourning on the sex life of the Party cadres. One of the stories went like this:

A senior Party cadre happened to marry a woman activist on the eve of Stalin's death. After national mourning was proclaimed by the Central Committee, the wife refused to sleep with her husband because of her 'grief over the greatest loss suffered by the socialist world'. No matter how the husband reasoned with her, she simply turned a deaf ear. Racking his brains for several hours, the husband suddenly started accusing his wife of being a 'counter-revolutionary'. She flared up and challenged him to substantiate the charge. Calmly he told her: 'Since we are both Party members, our main concern is to carry on the people's revolution uninterruptedly. According to Chairman Mao, revolution must be carried on despite setbacks and disasters. Being revolutionaries, we make love for the sake of revolution. In other words, our love-making is a part of our revolutionary work. The fact that you have refused to cooperate with me shows that you have little regard for the course of revolution.'

'How about the death of Comrade Stalin?' the wife argued.

'It is because of his death that we should step up our revolutionary work in every field. Besides, his death means that we are now short of one comrade. To replace him, there is every reason for us to have intercourse as frequently as possible so that we may be able to bring into the socialist world a new comrade.'

Unwilling to be branded a 'counter-revolutionary', the wife agreed to fulfil her conjugal duty for the sake of the revolution.

Another popular joke is about how to apply Chairman Mao's thoughts to demolishing revisionism. Towards the end of 1957, the split between the Russian and Chinese Communists was already heralded among the rank and file in the Peking regime. But the Party secretary of a local branch in Manchuria paid no heed to this Party line. He had been living with a Russian woman technician for quite some time. His worried comrades found it their duty to give him a bit of 'gentle persuasion'. A meeting of criticism and self-criticism was organised with him as the target. In the meeting, his comrades concentrated their firepower on him for hours. At long last, it was his turn to criticise himself to show his repentance. But to everyone's surprise he claimed that he had only been following Chairman Mao's revolutionary theories faithfully. He stated: 'Chairman Mao has always enlightened us that we must attack the enemy at his weakest link, and Comrade Stalin has also said that no fortress can be taken without help from within. This is exactly what I have been doing. I know only too well that this Russian woman must be a revisionist. But to transform a revisionist into a true Maoist is a worthy task. Every night I never fail to read aloud to her some of Chairman Mao's precepts before making love to her. Since I can always satisfy her, this makes her realise the supremacy of Chairman Mao's thoughts. And I am convinced that she will turn against Khruschev and his like, provided she continues to sleep with me for a few more months.'

His comrades angrily denounced him for his way of distorting Chairman Mao's revolutionary theories. Tongue in cheek, he solemnly told them: 'Comrades, we must all strive to be good pupils of Chairman Mao. When Comrade Chiang Ching first went to Yenan, she was but a petit bourgeois actress. But our great helmsman cohabited with her despite her class background. And now, nobody can deny that she is a true Maoist. If Chairman Mao had never bothered to sleep with her, she might still remain a petit bourgeois.'

Having out-argued his comrades, this Party secretary carried on his affair with the Russian woman technician until she was recalled to Moscow.

TO WASH OR TO PRICK

For subtlety, the anecdote about the great 14th-century painter Ni Yun-lin is perhaps supreme. Ni Yun-lin had an obsession with cleanliness. One year, he went to Nanking as the guest of honour of his local admirers. After the elaborate banquet, the great artist was urged by his hosts to spend a night with Chao Mai-erh, the most famous prostitute of Nanking. Attracted by the beauty of Mai-erh, Ni graciously agreed.

After bathing herself in scented water, the famous prostitute went to bed with Ni. But she suddenly found the artist starting to sniff all over her naked body like a hunting dog. Then he asked her to take another bath. Though annoyed, she did as she was told. The artist sniffed again and made the same request. She suppressed her anger and took another bath. Still, Ni did not think she was clean enough, and the same process went on and on. When the famous prostitute eventually passed the sniffing test and the artist was ready to make love to her, it was already a new morning and she refused to do anything with him. After that this funny episode became a favourite topic of conversation among the artist's friends.

Though it is not usual for most Chinese to resort to practical jokes, the people of Hong Kong seem to enjoy them a lot. In the early 1950s, an enormous number of Chinese women in this British colony began to be anxious to have Westernised figures. To correct their natural deficiencies, some ingenious local businessmen rushed into the production of foam rubber brassières and hip-padding, which sold like hot cakes. Almost overnight, the streets in Hong Kong were flooded with Chinese women with big busts and swinging hips.

Naturally, this new miracle could hardly fool observant males, and the question of genuine or artificial breasts was often mentioned in their conversations. But the teddy boys went even further. Armed with pins and needles, they stuck them into the breasts or hips of passing women. Totally unaware of what had happened, many poor women unwittingly carried these trade marks around and so became a laughing stock.

THE LANGUAGE OF LOVE

Frankly speaking, these jokes would appear jejune if compared with the imagery that the Chinese literary language is capable of conveying. The literary heritage of 3,000 years has enriched the language to such an extent that metaphors, similes and classical allusions are extensively used by the literati in a most appropriate and expressive manner. The same is true of the language of love.

Take love-making for instance. It has a number of elegant and suggestion expressions. The most widely known one must be 'the clouds and the rain', but not many people can offhandedly tell the origin of this cliché. During the Period of the Warring States (481-221 B.C.), King Hsiang of Ch'u dreamed of making love to a beautiful goddess from Kaotang. But when he woke up and tried to find her, what he saw was the mountain peaks veiled in the clouds and washed by the rain. Since then, poets and scholars have used 'the clouds and the rain' to suggest love-making. Eventually, the expression became known to the ordinary people as well.

Another fairly popular expression for love-making is 'the phoenixes upside down'. It originates from the famous Yuan opera *The Story of the West Chamber* in which the playwright Wang Shih-fu used the expression to describe the love act between the young scholar and the debutante.

As Wang also used 'the dew drops into the blooming peony' to suggest the climax of love-making, the expression has since been adopted by better-educated Chinese.

The term 'fragrance-stealing' is often found in old Chinese novels as a subtle expression for having an affair. It dates back to the reign of Emperor Wu Ti in the Hsi Chin Dynasty in the 3rd century. At that time, one of the ministers, Chia Ch'ung, had a very attractive daughter, who had an affair with his handsome-looking clerk, Han Shou. The affair went on undetected for some time. One day, the emperor gave Chia Ch'ung some very fragrant incense as a special favour. To show her love for Han, his daughter took some of it to give her lover. When Chia smelled it on his clerk, he immediately realised what had happened and married his daughter to Han to cover up the whole thing. Thenceforth, 'fragrance-stealing' was included in the literary language.

If a man's wife is unfaithful to him, a subtle way to say it is 'his curtains are in disorder'. This expression was first used by a Han scholar called Chia Yi in one of his articles attacking the then high officials whose wives were notorious for their extra-marital affairs. According to the laws governing individual's dress in the Ming Dynasty, these men who worked in the prostitute houses were obliged to wear green turbans. As a result, a man with an unfaithful wife has since been widely referred to as a man 'wearing a green turban'. But a more popular title for him is 'turtle', for the Chinese believe that the female turtles are promiscuous by nature. This is also the reason why pimps are called 'turtle slaves'.

SAY IT WITH A FLOWER

Not surprisingly, Chinese poets like to compare women to flowers. But some flowers are more flattering than others. When a woman is likened to an orchid, it means that she has class and quality. A woman compared to a rose is one who is beautiful and yet not so accessible. A debutante is called a peony, which is the flower symbolising nobility and wealth. The winter plum blossom is the highest compliment for one to use in praising a chaste widow. Though the dahlia doesn't look very different from the peony, it can only be associated with a concubine. But any Chinese girl will be offended if she is compared to the peach blossom, which is the symbol of hard luck and easy virtue. Neither is the apricot blossom an appropriate expression of praise, for one of the T'ang poets described a woman with a seducing nature as 'a sprig of red apricot blossom climbing over the wall'. Any Chinese woman will be pleased to be likened to the lotus flower, which is the symbol of purity.

Flower, used generically, conveys a variety of meanings. When a woman fails to catch the eye of a man, it is suggestively said: 'The falling flower is willing but the flowing water is heartless.' To indicate a happy marriage, the expression is 'the perfect flower and the full moon'. If a woman is not that young, she is 'a flower in the late spring'. When a man and a girl are courting, they are 'by the flowers and in the moonlight'.

But of course, flower can also have a very different connotation. For instance, when a man goes to visit a prostitute, he is described as going 'to seek flowers and inquire about willows'. Hence, if a man suffers from venereal disease, he becomes a victim of the 'flowers-and-willow disease'. The fact that V.D. specialists in Hong Kong are called the 'yellow-and-green doctors' is because of association with the colours of flowers and the willow.

In the old days, both mandarin ducks and swallows were the birds of love in the Chinese eye. In wishing newly-weds good luck, they were often used as the subjects of paintings and the themes of poems. Similarly, fish in water were regarded as the symbol of a happy marriage. But when one speaks of a 'dew and water marriage', it is but a casual affair. Butterflies were also the symbols of lovers, though generally indicating a tragic romance. Behind this there is a sad folk story, known to practically every man and woman in the provinces of Chekiang and Kiangsu. It is said that a few centuries ago, a young girl, in the disguise of a man, went away from home to study under a famous scholar. There she met the young man of her heart. Without disclosing her identity, she hinted to him that he should call at 'his' home during the spring-break to be introduced to 'his' sister. But unfortunately, when she returned home before the youth, her father forced her to be betrothed to a wealthy young dandy. Now it was too late for the young man of her heart to do anything, although he had eventually recognised that she was a girl. He died of a broken heart and his parents buried him near where the wedding procession of the young girl was going to pass. On her wedding day, the reluctant young bride was carried in a red sedan chair to her groom's house. The moment her sedan chair reached the site of the young man's tomb, a thunderstorm started and the tomb opened. Without hesitation, the young girl alighted from her sedan chair and jumped into the tomb, which immediately closed again. The thunderstorm stopped and the sun shone gloriously. Since then, the story goes on, the souls of the young lovers have become a pair of huge butterflies, always seen circling gracefully over that tomb.

Obviously, this tragic story, whether true or not, must be regarded as the reflection of the yearning for free love by young people in those days.

LOVE NOT TO BE EXPRESSED IN WORDS

To the Chinese of past generations, however, love was essentially something to be cherished in the heart, not to be expressed in words. A young man and a young girl could be in love with each other for years, and yet neither of them would ever dream of saying 'I love you'. To them, to reveal one's feelings in such an outright manner meant lack of subtlety and inner depth. A wink, a smile, a sigh or a small gesture was always an adequate way of conveying one's love and affection.

When lovers were together, they would talk about the moonlight, the flowers and the stars, for this was the way for them to express their love for each other. Nor would a man praise a girl's beauty to her face. She should be able to judge his admiration by the way he looked at her or some casual words he used.

Thus it is that in Chinese classical poems the word 'love' can seldom be found. In the case of many poets, they would rather use expressions such as 'spring passion', 'spring musings', 'spring mood', 'everlasting longings' and 'mutual yearnings' instead.

Naturally, this kind of subtlety was characteristic of the upper and middle classes. As for cowherds and peasant girls, they could not have been half as subtle in expressing their emotions and passion. Nevertheless, the word 'love' would not come even from their lips. This may seem strange to many of us today, but it must be remembered that reticence and taciturnity are characteristic of the Chinese.

CHAPTER TWELVE

Sex and the Chinese Today

In the past quarter of a century, no other nation in the world has gone through more vicissitudes and upheavals than China. From 1949 onwards, political movements, thought-remoulding processes and social changes, constantly taking place on the Chinese mainland, have thrown the most populous nation into an artificial vacuum, completely isolated from the outside world. Under such conditions, the mode of life of more than 750 million people defies the most fertile imaginative power. Endeavours have been painstakingly made in the West to assess what has been going on behind the Bamboo Curtain, but conflicting reports and vague conclusions can hardly be claimed to have been helpful in presenting a clearer picture. However, amid the spate of ideological terms and political jargon used in analysis of Communist China, 'Puritanism' seems to have become a standard expression whenever the people's way of life comes into focus.

Actually, 'Puritanism', a term used by some China experts in the West, is totally unknown and unacceptable to the Chinese Communists in view of its religious and capitalist flavour. Nevertheless, it is obvious that the life of the ordinary people in China has been governed by a set of rules far more puritanical than any observed by the original Puritans themselves. This is what the Chinese Communists term 'political correctness' regarding one's private life, including sex and love.

THE 'GLASS OF WATER' PRINCIPLE

To understand the present Party line of exerting strict control over sexual relationships, it is necessary to go back to those days when Chairman Mao Tse-tung and his comrades were entrenched in the tiny mountainous village-town of Yenan in Shensi province and even earlier on. In those days, 'sexual liberation' was one of the incentives for Party members. The marriage system was denounced as a remnant of the 'poison of feudalism' and free love greatly encouraged. A man could go to bed with any woman who agreed to sleep with him, and the same was true for a woman. Casual sex of this kind was exceedingly popular, especially with the men. It was accepted by the Communists as 'a glass of water' principle—the implication being that having sex was just like having a glass of water.

The Communist leaders had to encourage promiscuity if they were to deal realistically with an existing situation. In the Party, there were about eight or nine men to a woman. If the man-woman relationship were to be channelled into marriage, the majority of the men would have been deprived of any sex life at all. Moreover, according to Mao's then theory, 'love is a petit bourgeois game which does not conform with materialism, while sex is as materialistic a need as food and water'. But what he did not frankly admit was that while the fate of the Party was in a very precarious state, emotional ties between individual members would unavoidably undermine the Party's interest.

Chairman Mao himself seems to have been a womaniser from the onset of his revolutionary career. Before he went to attend the First Normal School in Changsha, the provincial capital of Hunan, he was already married to a village girl at his father's behest. During the period when he and some schoolmates formed the New People's Study Society (1917-20), he still managed to chase after Tsai Ts'ang (now Vice-premier Li Fu-ch'un's wife) and one or two female members of the Society. Without success, he turned to court Yang Kai-hui, the petit bourgeois daughter of his teacher. After dancing close attendance on her for a couple of years, Mao married Yang in Changsha, though the village girl was still living under his parental roof. Then came the abortive 'Autumn Harvest Uprisings'. Leaving Yang and a couple of children behind, Mao fled to the Chingkang Mountain on the border of Hunan and Kiangsi. While Yang was detained by the Hunan authorities pending execution, he lost no time in marrying Ho Tzu-chen, a young girl in her teens, who was swept off her feet by Mao's revolutionary fervour. Despite the age difference, there was no question of their compatibility. Apart from bearing him two sons in succession, this third wife of Mao's fought beside him in many battles and saved his life on several occasions. She was also one of the very few women who went through the Long March (1934-35) with the defeated Red Army.

The outbreak of the Sino-Japanese War in 1937 caused the Nationalists and the Communists to form an uneasy alliance. The Red capital, Yenan, now openly became the Mecca for young leftists and revolutionary students from Peking, Shanghai and other big cities. Doubtless, the constant stream of young intellectuals pouring into Yenan strengthened the Communist Party—many of them are now the backbone of the second echelon in the Peking regime. But the immediate effect was that the sudden descent of sophisticated girl students on that mountain village visibly improved one acute situation: the imbalance of male and female population.

It was then that 'a glass of water' principle was abandoned. But since the number of girl students was still much smaller than that of sexually frustrated men cadres, the top-level comrades naturally took the first pick. Marshal Peng Teh-huai (the deposed Defence Minister) rushed into marrying a young history student called Pu An-hsiu from one of the Peking universities; Jao Su-shih (later to become the Chairman of the East China Military and Political Commission, imprisoned in 1954 under the charge of anti-Party activities) won as his wife Lu Tsui, praised as the Chinese Joan of Arc during the student movement in 1935. Marshal Lin Piao did not do too badly either; he picked a girl student called Lin Yu-ying. General Lo Jui-ching (the deposed Chief of Staff during the Cultural Revolution) lived together with Kung Teh-ming, a high school graduate from Shanghai. Lesser leaders got less attractive and less educated wives. Everyone seemed to be quite happy with this or that new find. But as 'husband' and 'wife' were considered to be too 'feudalistic', married couples were referred to as 'lovers'. Nor was a married woman supposed to use her husband's name.

THE MAO TSE-TUNG—CHIANG CHING ROMANCE

While Yenan was basking in the festive atmosphere of revolutionary weddings and childbirths, Chairman Mao appeared to be at a loose end. Ho Tzu-chen, his only surviving wife, had lost her looks considerably and though still in her late twenties, was not remotely comparable to those sophisticated girl students from Peking or Shanghai. A man with a pair of roving eyes like Mao just had to do something.

It was at this point that Chiang Ching, the present Madame Mao, came on the Yenan scene. A third-rate Shanghai film actress known under the pseudonym Lan Ping (Blue Apple), she was Li Yun-ho in real life. Having been the mistress of a university chancellor called Chao T'ai-mo, having married Chao's brother-in-law Huang Ching (alias Yu Chi-wei) and the Shanghai film critic T'ang Na (alias Ma Chi-liang) in succession, Chiang Ching arrived at the Mecca of Chinese revolution after she had been jilted by Tsang Min, a talented film director in Shanghai. She would not have been accepted by the Chinese Communists had she not been escorted by her re-enlisted husband, Huang Ching, a seasoned underground Party worker in a Peking university.

As she was not yet a Party member, Chiang Ching could only enrol at the Art College of Lu Hsun as a student. To the surprise of most senior Communists, Chairman Mao suddenly offered to give a course in Marxism at this college for fellow-travellers, despite his very heavy responsibilities in Party and military matters. In his eyes the third-rate film actress must have seemed a heavenly beauty, for it did not take the Chairman long to start an affair with Chiang Ching.

Mao would not have minded carrying on with her and Ho Tzu-chen at the same time, were it not for Chiang Ching's ultimatum. Ambitious and vain, she certainly did not fall in love with Mao, who was almost double her age. Her eyes were on his position as the Party Chairman. Declaring herself to be pregnant, she forced Mao to divorce Ho and formally marry her. No matter how the Chairman tried to explain to her the absurdity of marriage in name, she was adamant.

Helpless, Mao reported his decision to divorce Ho to the Central Committee—a compulsory step for every member on the committee to take concerning his private affairs. The opposition was unanimous. Headed by Liu Shao-chi, the committee members objected to Mao's unfair way of treating Ho Tzu-chen, who had done so much for the Party. They also dismissed Chiang Ching as a 'revolutionary opportunist' whose background was hardly proletarian. But Mao would not listen to sense. He even threatened to resign if his wish were not granted.

Consequently, the Central Committee gave in. Meanwhile, it was agreed that Mao must not divorce Ho, and that he could not start living with Chiang Ching openly until Ho and their two sons had arrived safely in Moscow. But the worst proviso in Chiang Ching's eyes was that she must not strive for 'political prominence' through her relationship with Chairman Mao. To be fair to Mao, it must be said he did honour his word until the outbreak of the Cultural Revolution in late 1966. It is equally interesting to know that many of the purged leaders in the past few years were those who had opposed Chairman Mao's decision to marry Chiang Ching.

As a matter of fact, Chairman Mao is certainly not the only one who has indulged himself in the habit of marrying young wives. Liu Shao-chi married his present wife Wang Kuang-mei in 1948 after a lightning romance. Before then, Wang worked as an interpreter with the Communist delegation to the Peking Military Executive Headquarters, a trilateral organisation responsible for supervising ceasefires between the Nationalists and the Communists during the period of General Marshall's mediation. A graduate of the Catholic University in Peking in the early 1940s, Wang Kuang-mei was definitely more sophisticated and better educated than Chiang Ching. It was about the same time that Marshal Lin Pao took his present wife, Yeh Ch'un, the daughter of his old comrade General Yeh T'ing. The present Foreign Minister Chen Yi was perhaps more discreet. He quietly married a young actress called Chang Ch'ien when he was the mayor of Shanghai, and his wife was deliberately kept out of the limelight for quite some years.

THE THREE TO ONE PERIOD AND THEN SCANDALS

It was not entirely without reason that these Chinese leaders seemed to be busy with changing wives once their Party gained control of the vast country. In spite of their staunch belief in Marxism, years of revolutionary struggle had deprived them of desires and comforts which few human beings can completely ignore. Their former wives might look all right in mountain caves or ancient villages during the period of civil war, but would be like fish out of water in the highly sophisticated atmosphere of Peking, Shanghai or Canton. Moreover, the ordinary concepts about divorce, marriage, bigamy and polygamy never really bothered them, so that during the long period of civil war it was not uncommon for a Party cadre to have three wives at the same time. He would keep one in the 'white' areas (Nationalist-controlled region), one in the Japanese-occupied areas and a third in the 'Liberated' areas. In those days, the expressions 'white wife', 'occupied wife' and 'liberated wife' were freely used by

Party members to one another, as if such a situation were the most natural thing under the sun. Now that the revolutionary victory had been achieved, this practice of taking a new wife without bothering to divorce the old one is, in fact, a much better arrangement than the former one of maintaining three wives simultaneously.

When the New Marriage Law was proclaimed in the early 1950s, it clearly stated that, if a man had married more than one wife before the law came into force, it did not constitute an offence of bigamy. Needless to say, those responsible for drafting this law were taking into account the far from simple marital relationships most comrades had enjoyed.

Though the aforesaid law did prove useful in stopping most Party members from further entanglements in marital affairs, the privileged few apparently carried on as in the past. One of the greatest of modern Chinese scandals happened during the Korean War. In 1952, a Chinese delegation was sent to Pyongyang to pay respect to the North Korean leader Kim Il Sung. But the deputy head of the delegation, Chin Shan, had other objectives. A veteran Party member and an actor by profession, he was high in Chairman Mao's favour. While in Pyongyang as a state guest, he slept with several Russian girls of the Soviet Red Banner Artistic Troupe which was in North Korea on a troop-comforting mission. Naturally he was warned by his comrades of this 'serious political error', but Chin Shan paid no heed. To make matters worse, he went on to have an affair with Kim Il Sung's personal secretary. This infuriated the North Korean prime minister, who protested to Peking. Chin was immediately sacked as the deputy head of the delegation and flown back to Peking for punishment. He ended up in a labour camp and nothing has been heard about his fate since.

The deposed Minister of Propaganda, T'ao Chu, was also known for his wanton life. When he was the First Secretary of the South China Bureau in Canton, T'ao had affairs with several leading actresses, according to the wall newspapers published by the Red Guards. He was also accused of picking pretty women comrades to work on his personal staff.

A scandal with plenty of comical touches is the one concerning Sa K'ung-liao, until recently Deputy Chairman of the National Minorities Commission. In the 1950s, he seduced the youngest daughter of Cheng Chen-tuo, the then Deputy Minister of Culture.

Already in his late 50s, Sa regarded himself as an ageless Romeo. Under the pretext of discussing literature and the Party line, he manoeuvred the teenage daughter of his old friend Cheng into bed. Despite the fact that he had a wife, who refused to divorce him, and the woman painter, Yu Feng, as his mistress, Sa went to see Cheng and asked for his permission to marry his daughter. Too shocked to say anything, Cheng frowned and asked him to leave. At that Sa suddenly went down on his knees, addressing his old friend as 'Daddy'. This was the last thing Cheng had expected. He, too, then knelt down and begged Sa to spare his daughter, who was really too young to know her own mind. Knowing his friend's inability to get out of awkward situations, Sa declared convincingly that Cheng's daughter was already pregnant and then rose and left. Two days later, he married the young girl, after obtaining the organisation's approval. Cheng was furious, but there was nothing he could do. The poor man could only ask his friends not to mention Sa's name in front of him. However, he was relieved of the dreaded ordeal of seeing his grand-child by Sa, for, in fact, his daughter was never pregnant.

THE CLEAN LIFE OF THE ORDINARY PEOPLE

In contrast, the ordinary people have been compelled to lead a clean personal life ever since 1949. Prostitutes were abolished in 1950; those who had musical talents were trained to be actresses of Peking Opera, while the rest were either sent to work in factories or on farms. In 1953, dance halls were ordered to close down and dancing girls forced to follow the footsteps of the prostitutes.

As for young students and workers, they are explicitly forbidden to fall in love, for no 'petit bourgeois sentimentalism' should be allowed to revive in a society in which 'politics takes command'. In any case, from a purely aesthetic point of view, drab boiler tunics of unisex design can hardly project the sex appeal of even the most voluptuous of bodies. Moreover, since girls have long ceased to wear make-up and have done away with all feminine touches, they certainly do not attract as much attention from the men as their counterparts elsewhere do. Then, too, incessant political discussions and the round-the-clock study of Chairman Mao's Little Red Book will sweep away whatever personal feelings anyone may have.

Nor is marriage supposed to be a personal matter. When a man and a woman decide to get married, both of them must submit several copies of written applications to their respective organisations and Party branches. They can be kept waiting for months before approval or disapproval will be given. In most cases, they will be sent for by their political commissars or Party branch secretaries to be enlightened about the need to submit 'individual interests to Party interests', which means that their marriage plans will have to be shelved. A man has very little hope of getting married under thirty, and a woman, twenty-five.

Pre-marital sex and casual affairs are both condemned as the 'remaining poison left behind by reactionary and capitalist society'. Adultery is regarded as a criminal offence because it damages the image of a 'socialist society'. When a man commits adultery with a married woman, the shadow of a labour-reform camp looms over him. In the 1950s, when a young Party cadre was caught sleeping with the wife of one of Chou En-lai's special assistants in a hotel room in Shanghai, he was sentenced by the Municipal Bureau of Public Security to serve fifteen years in a labour-reform camp.

Perhaps as a discreet way to exert birth control, husbands and wives are often sent to work in different towns. They may have the chance of meeting each other once or twice each year. The Chinese authorities have only been advocating birth control in the last few years, for 'population explosion' is still regarded as a 'reactionary theory' by Maoists.

But as far as the peasants are concerned, they seem to pay little or no heed to restrictions on marriage and birth control. Especially in the remote regions, peasants still believe that each man should have as many children as possible. Though Party cadres are instructed by their superiors to carry out 'gentle persuasion', they find themselves talking to stone walls. At present, it seems that the birth rate in the rural parts of China is still on the increase.

It has been possible, so far, to maintain the dual sex standard in Communist China chiefly through the Party control of mass media. The private life of the leader is guarded as a state secret. There is practically no way for people on the street to know what is happening behind the red walls of the people's Forbidden City in Peking. But for the exposures made by the Red Guard wall-posters during the recent Cultural Revolution, even the present sketchy information would not have come into the open.

THE BOOMING SEX TRADE IN HONG KONG

Lying just on the south tip of the Chinese mainland, Hong Kong is a totally different world. Though it is a place living on borrowed time, its four million Chinese inhabitants are making the best of it. The speedy industrial development and booming trade in this tiny British colony owe much to the tireless efforts made by ex-Shanghai business tycoons and industrialists, who were at one time aloofly dismissed as 'Shanghai refugees' by the local Chinese compradors and British taipans.

Apart from playing their roles in the current Hong Kong boom, these 'Shanghai refugees' have also brought with them a more sophisticated form of commercial sex. In the dance halls and cabarets, the Shanghai dialect is now as popular as the Cantonese.

An army of 'social flowers', film starlets and dancing girls from Shanghai have by now become the chief providers of sexual pleasure. They all have a price. Past masters at manipulating men, these women have been faring well in Hong Kong, especially during the economic boom. Knowing that most businessmen hate to become the topic of gossip columns of the local press, they always veil their associations with the type of customer in secrecy.

A certain starlet is one of the more resourceful gold-diggers. She used to be a regular customer of the Hong Kong-Macao ferry. Once or twice each week, she would take a day trip to Macao. It all looked very innocent. But in her first-class cabin, she had a different man each time. He had to pay 5,000 Hong Kong dollars (about U.S. $1,000) for this boating pleasure. As a result, in the course of a few years, this starlet has become one of the richest women in Hong Kong.

To most Chinese starlets in Hong Kong nothing is more profitable than spending a night with a young Chinese multi-millionaire from one of the South-East Asian countries. He is reputed to have an obsession about sleeping with 'film stars'. After a film actress has entertained him in bed for a single night, her reward is a cheque for 5,000 U.S. dollars plus a car of any make. The only embarrassing aspect for her is that this multi-millionaire, being exceedingly security-conscious, has to have his bodyguard at his elbow even when he is making love.

Meanwhile, the sex pedlars in Hong Kong are not slow to reap profits from the constant flow of tourists. Some shrewd businessmen have successfully combined tourism with camouflaged prostitution,

Such enterprises appear in the form of apparently harmless travel agencies. Through the aid of their old clients, these travel agencies have carefully compiled their own lists of potential customers. When someone in any part of the world shows interest in one of their tours, he will promptly receive a well-planned itinerary from the agency he has contacted. The moment his plane touches down at the Kai Tak Airport, an elegant Chinese girl will greet him by his first name outside the immigration counter. From that moment on, she will be his 'hostess' in every sense during his Hong Kong stay. First of all, she will drive him to their temporary 'home', which is often a well-furnished flat in one of the sought-after areas. A maidservant will respectfully addess him as 'master', waiting on him as if he were a lord.

By this time, he will feel completely at home. Taking a bath and changing into casual wear, he will find his Susie or Lucy already having his favourite drink mixed for him. Unless he prefers to dine out, his first meal will be a small banquet fastidiously prepared by the maidservant in the flat. Dined and wined, he and his 'hostess' can then appreciate the beauty of Hong Kong in a comfortable bed.

If he wants new suits made, a tailor will come to his place and take his measurements; and within twenty-four hours, the suits will be delivered. If he wants to do some shopping, his 'hostess' will take him around in her car. He will be taken to have seafood aboard the famous restaurant-boats in Aberdeen, to swim in Repulse Bay, to go racing in Happy Valley and to visit the leading night clubs.

It is not until the eve of departure that he will be presented with a bill, the amount of which will depend on the extent of his enjoyments. His 'hostess' will drive him to the airport to kiss him goodbye, like a wife. Doubtless, he will leave Hong Kong with a very deep impression.

THE NORMALCY AND SANITY OF THE MAJORITY

But naturally, sexual indulgences of such kinds are solely for those who can afford them. As for the majority of Hong Kong Chinese, they loathe sexual irregularities. To the older generation, pre-marital sex is still regarded as something against the traditional moral standard. They want their children to fall in love, get married and have babies in a manner acceptable and respectable. Though the younger generation may think differently, they mostly have to conform with the wishes of their elders, since family ties have by no means grown weaker in recent times. Indeed, it is because of the strength of these family ties that Chinese youths in Hong Kong have, as a whole, not yet drifted into permissive society like their contemporaries in the West.

Strangely enough though, the 'decadent influence of capitalist culture' seems to have led some of Chairman Mao's staunch loyalists astray. A prominent propagandist of the Peking regime is possibly the most welcome customer of many young waitresses in the leading Cantonese restaurants along Queen's Road Central. He has innumerable 'god-daughters' among these waitresses, and it is not infrequent to catch him pinching their bottoms in between serious discussion of Mao's thoughts or of the principles of International United Front work.

One of Chairman Mao's 'national capitalists' is believed to be an expert on food of aphrodisiac value. Before the Hong Kong riots in 1967, he often laid on dog-meat banquets in his huge mansion in Kowloon and all local Communist bigwigs were only too glad to be invited. On such occasions, the topics of their conversations could not possibly be pertinent to the people's cause.

In many ways, Hong Kong can be said to have become another Shanghai. While on the one hand there is the nouveau riche class, of conflicting political beliefs, indulging in material comforts and sexual pleasures, on the other hand there is the vast majority of honest, hard-working individuals who, through no fault of their own, have not been able to enjoy a more decent and secure life.

THE DILEMMA OF OVERSEAS CHINESE

With more than 750 million Chinese living under the people's democratic dictatorship on the Mainland, 13 million of them seeking comparative freedom in Taiwan and another 4 million struggling for identity in Hong Kong, the mode of life of more than 18 million Overseas Chinese scattered all over the world has necessarily become a matter of interest. Out of this number, more than 96 per cent have settled in Asian countries. In many South-East Asian countries, the Chinese settlers have made no little contribution to the national economy and social prosperity. They used to be able to preserve the customs and traditions which their forefathers brought with them many centuries ago. But in recent years, they have been encountering endless difficulties in maintaining their national identity in these countries, especially in Indonesia, Malaysia and the Philippines.

Though the Chinese started emigrating several hundred years ago, the emigrants in those days mainly consisted of labourers and small businessmen. But since 1949, the trend has completely changed. This is especially true in the case of the United States. It must be admitted that this new influx of Chinese, who have chosen to make America their permanent homeland, are probably now the core of Overseas Chinese communities. Among them, there are distinguished scholars, professors, scientists and business tycoons of international status. Unlike those old-fashioned Overseas Chinese, they are far better social mixers. They are not afraid of meeting the West, nor will they hesitate to present the East in its true colours.

But this does not mean that they do not have any problems. The main concern, however, is how to preserve some of the traditions and customs amid which they have been brought up and, more important still, hand them down to the next generation. It would be easier for them if they confined themselves to the vicinities of China Towns like their forerunners usually did. In those days, the Chinese in the United States always planned to return to their birth-places. It was then a common practice for young people of marriageable age to take a trip back to China to find a suitable partner. This might have been interpreted as a form of racial prejudice, but it was tradition and custom that guided them.

At present, things are completely different. The children of the new Chinese immigrants are more exposed to the culture and social influences of their adopted country than to those of their forefathers. The young generation, as a whole, do not have the chance of being brought up in a Chinese environment. Nor do they have the benefit of studying Chinese language and history in the proper way. In spite of their black hair and yellow skin, they think and reason more like Americans than Chinese.

To them, China is gradually becoming a geographical term. Since their roots are not in that vast country, Chinese traditions and customs cannot mean that much to them. As a result they tend to accept moral codes and social values inherent in American society. The same is true of their attitude towards sex and love. Unlike their fathers or grandfathers, they are more uninhibited about things such as virginity, pre-marital sex, marriage and divorce. It would not enter the minds of most of them that they should travel all the way back to the East to find a husband or a wife. Though no statistics are available, it is undeniable that the rate of mixed marriages has considerably risen among the Chinese younger generation in America.

Naturally, there are bound to be individuals who still want to marry from their own race. This seems to apply more to young students from Taiwan. In some cases, there is a dramatic or comic side to this desire. According to a recent issue of a Chinese publication in San Francisco, several Taiwan students have lost their potential brides because they failed to meet them at the airport. Due to the pressure of study or work, they sent their best friends to greet these girls from Taiwan on their behalf. But to their surprise, their friends never brought back the girls who had come out to marry them. A few days later, they found out that the girls had been married to their friends already. Now, it looks as if no Taiwan student in the United States would dare to ask any of his friends to meet his fiancée at the airport, for the risk is too big.

But, judging by the general tendency, there is a possibility that the younger generation of Chinese immigrants in America will eventually disassociate themselves from the traditions and customs which have meant so much to their elders. It would therefore be unreasonable to expect to find in them typical Chinese characteristics such as subtlety, reticence or a sense of proportion. They could become the first group of Chinese to blend in completely with their country of adoption.

As for the youths on the Chinese mainland, human nature may some day lead them to depart from the existing 'Puritanism' which has been imposed on their personal lives by the hierarchy in a most high-handed manner. But whether they will be able to resume or restore some of the traditional virtues and national traits is exceedingly doubtful. In the past years, history books have been rewritten, moral standards reset and freedom of expression suppressed. Between the China of today and of the historical past lies an unprecedented gap, which cannot possibly be closed.

The Chinese in Taiwan, Hong Kong and some South-East Asian countries may seem capable of upholding the torch of tradition to a certain extent. But, compared with the huge population on the Mainland, they are but of an insignificant minority, even if we do not take into account the geographical restrictions, political factors and social environments under which they have to live. Moreover, it must also be remembered that whatever they have brought out of China it is not the entity of Chinese culture and tradition. In this age, man may be able to walk on the moon, transplant hearts and harness natural forces. It is still unimaginable that culture and tradition can be uprooted from the earth of their growth and planted in another soil full of alien elements.

Select Bibliography

Shan Hai Chin (The Chinese Mythology)
Shih Chi, by Ssu-ma Ch'ien (Han historian)
Han Shu, by Pang Ku (Han historian)
T'ang Shu (The History of the T'ang Dynasty)
Sung Shih (The History of the Sung Dynasty)
Yuan Shih (The History of the Yuan Dynasty)
Ming Shih (The History of the Ming Dynasty)
T'ang Tai Ch'ung Shu (Collected works of the T'ang Dynasty)
Tai Ping Kuan Chi (Collected works by ancient Chinese authors)
The Erotic Adventures of Sui Yang-ti
The Sketch of the Maze Palace, by Han Wu (T'ang author)
Shih Shuo Hsin Yu, by Liu Yi-piao (Former Sung author)
Tzu Chung (The Ch'ing Anthology of Chinese Classic Poetry)
Cha Shih Mi Hsin (Secret Sketches of the Han Palace)
K'ung Ho Chien Mi Chi (Secret Sketches by the Supervisor of the
    Imperial Guard)
Su Nu Ching (The Manual of Lady Purity)
The Art of the Bedchamber, by a Han Taoist
Chin Ping Mei (18th Century edition)
Ching Yi Lu (Notes on Strange Things)
Pei Fu Lu (Notes on Brothels)
Fei-yen Wai Chuan (The Biography of Chao Fei-yen)
Wan Li Yeh Huo P'ien (Anecdotes of the Ming Dynasty)
Li Shih-shih Wai Chuan (The Biography of Li Shih-shih)
Hsuan Ho Yi Shih (Anecdotes of the Sung Dynasty)
Peng Ts'ao (The Manual of Chinese Medicinal Herbs), by Li Shih-
    chen (Ming physician)
Tzu Pu Yu, by Yuan Mei (18th-century author)
The Memoirs of the Master of Plum Blossoms, by Sung Feng-nien,
    1895

The Tales of the Ch'ing (Manchu) Palace, by Hsu Hsiao-t'ien, 1925
The Taoist Meditation, by Chiang Wei-chiao, 1928
Tai Chi Chuan (Shadow Boxing), by Chen Yen-lin, 1943
The Chinese Dynasty Chart, compiled by W. M. Hawley, 1953